THE FIRST
GERMAN THEATRE

THEATRE PRODUCTION STUDIES
General Editor: John Russell Brown

SHAKESPEARE'S THEATRE
Peter Thomson

VICTORIAN SPECTACULAR THEATRE 1850–1910
Michael R. Booth

THE REVOLUTION IN GERMAN THEATRE 1900–1933
Michael Patterson

RESTORATION THEATRE PRODUCTION
Jocelyn Powell

ENGLISH MEDIEVAL THEATRE 1400–1500
William Tydeman

THE ROYAL COURT THEATRE 1965–1972
Philip Roberts

JACOBEAN PRIVATE THEATRE
Keith Sturgess

THE FIRST GERMAN THEATRE

Schiller, Goethe, Kleist and
Büchner in Performance

Michael Patterson

ROUTLEDGE

London and New York

Ce

First published 1990
by Routledge
11 New Fetter Lane, London EC4P 4EE

Simultaneously published in the USA and Canada
by Routledge
a division of Routledge, Chapman and Hall, Inc.
29 West 35th Street, New York, NY 10001

Typeset by Columns of Reading
Printed in Great Britain by
T J Press (Padstow) Ltd, Padstow, Cornwall

British Library Cataloguing in Publication Data
Patterson, Michael
The first German theatre: Schiller, Goethe, Kleist and
Büchner in performance. – (Theatre production studies)
1. Germany. Theatre, history
I. Title   II. Series
792.0943
ISBN 0–415–03274–1

Library of Congress Cataloging in Publication Data
Patterson, Michael.
The first German theatre: Schiller, Goethe, Kleist and
Büchner in performance / Michael Patterson.
p.   cm. — (Theatre production studies)
Includes bibliographical references (p.   ).
1. Theatre—Germany—History—18th century.
2. German drama—18th century—History and criticism.
I. Title.   II. Series.
PN2652.P38   1990
792'.0943'09033—dc20   90–8277

ISBN 0–415–03274–1

To Jane

CONTENTS

List of illustrations   ix
Acknowledgements   xi
Preface   xiii

INTRODUCTION. GERMAN THEATRE IN THE
EIGHTEENTH CENTURY   1

1 SCHILLER AT MANNHEIM: *THE ROBBERS*   21
  Acting style at Mannheim   33
  The première of The Robbers   37
  Iffland's performance of Franz Moor   46
  Conclusion: some ideas of Schiller on the theatre   50

2 GOETHE AT WEIMAR: *IPHIGENIA ON TAURIS*   53
  Misconceptions   53
  Goethe as theatre director   56
  Iphigenia on Tauris *in performance*   84
  The amateur staging of Iphigenia on Tauris   87
  Professional productions of Iphigenia on Tauris   92
  The dramatic structure of Iphigenia on Tauris   98
  Verse structure   100
  Actual stage directions   104
  Implied stage directions   105
  Conclusion   108

3 FROM THE EIGHTEENTH INTO THE
  NINETEENTH CENTURY   111
  Ludwig Tieck   116

4 KLEIST IN PERFORMANCE: *THE PRINCE
  OF HOMBURG*   123
  The early stage history of The Prince of Homburg   123

The Prince of Homburg *as a piece for the theatre*   129

5 BÜCHNER IN PERFORMANCE: *WOYZECK*   140
  The text of Woyzeck   144
  The structure   148
  The characters   149
  The setting   152
  The language   153
  Conclusion   156

CONCLUSION   158
*Appendix 1 Theatre Rules for the Mannheim National
  Theatre (1780)*   161
*Appendix 2 Instructions regarding committee
  meetings (1782)*   165
Chronology 1767–1837   167
Notes   185
Bibliography   193
Sources of illustrations   197
Index   198

ILLUSTRATIONS

FIGURES

1 Cross-section of the Mannheim National Theatre.   28
2 Ground-plan of the Mannheim National Theatre.   29
3 The town of Weimar (XVIII is the theatre, V the   62
  palace).
4 Ground-plan of the Weimar Court Theatre. Note   64
  the sliders and traps on the stage.
5 Cross-section of the Weimar Court Theatre.   65
6 Reconstruction of the interior of the Weimar Court   66
  Theatre by Alfred Pretzsch.

PLATES

A view from the wings

1 The director reprimands an actor in *Minna von*   10
  Barnhelm for improvising (Reichardt's *Theater-Kalender*,
  1794). Note the sliding wing-flats and candles.

The Robbers at Mannheim

2 Picture-gallery scene. Wing-flats.   24
3 Picture-gallery scene. Perspective backdrop.   25

The Robbers at Weimar

4 Costume designs (l. to r.) Karl Moor, Amalia,   32
  Old Moor, Franz Moor, Hermann.
5 Karl Moor: 'That is my father's voice.' (IV, 5).   33

ILLUSTRATIONS

Iffland as Franz Moor

6 'Is there anyone who sits in Judgment above the   49
   stars?' (V, 1).

The Weimar Court Theatre

7 The theatre after its renovation by Thouret in 1798.   61
8 The auditorium after the rebuilding in 1825.   68

The theatre at Lauchstädt

9 The auditorium in 1908.   70
10 View of stage from the balcony.   71

Weimar actors

11 Karoline Jagemann.   73
12 Corona Schröter.   86
13 Corona Schröter as Iphigenia, Goethe as Orestes   89
   (1779).
14 Sketch of the 1802 production with Friederike   91
   Vohs as Iphigenia.
15 Friedrich Haide.   93
16 Amalie Wolff.   95
17 Karl Ludwig Oels.   97
18 Pius Alexander Wolff.   99

Ludwig Tieck

19 Tieck's production of *A Midsummer Night's Dream*.   120

Heinrich von Kleist

20 The set for the Berlin production of *Das Kätchen*   125
   von Heilbronn.

ACKNOWLEDGEMENTS

Grateful acknowledgment is due to the following for permission to reproduce illustrations: Goethe-Museum, Düsseldorf (Plates 5 and 18); Goethe-Nationalmuseum, Weimar (Plate 17); Landesbibliothek, Weimar (Plate 16); Otto Müller Verlag, Salzburg (Plates 19 and 20); Nationale Forschungs- und Gedenkstätten der klassischen deutschen Literatur in Weimar (Figure 6); Tempelhof Verlag, Berlin (Plates 4 and 8).

My thanks are also due to John Russell Brown for his patience, encouragement and consistently sound advice.

PREFACE

When I studied German drama at university in the sixties, not once was I invited to consider any play as a text for performance. The works for the stage of Schiller, Goethe, Kleist and Büchner were discussed solely as literary texts without any acknowledgment that most of them had been written with a particular kind of theatre in mind and for a particular type of audience. I passed my examinations without the knowledge that Goethe had spent twenty-six years as Director of the Court Theatre at Weimar, producing plays and training actors, or that Schiller, after being writer in residence at the National Theatre in Mannheim, had worked in the theatre with Goethe in Weimar. More importantly, I read these plays from the great age of German drama without any sense of how they would work on stage before a living audience.

For a great age it undoubtedly was. Suffering from its political divisions and the unfortunate historical habit of serving as the battleground of Europe, Germany was very late in enjoying a flowering of its national theatre. England and Spain had already established a vigorous theatre tradition in the sixteenth century, and France followed in the seventeenth. But in Germany the eighteenth century began without any native theatrical tradition. There were wandering players performing coarse farces and crude enactments of historical events; on the other hand, there was the amateur theatre of the Jesuit schools, usually performed in Latin. That the century ended in Germany with some of the finest writing for the theatre in Europe, is remarkable.

Fortunately, the narrow vision of drama as literary text no longer prevails. In this respect, John Russell Brown's

Shakespeare's Plays in Performance, treading in the footsteps of Granville Barker, has been decisively influential. For German theatre, apart from much excellent work in German, there has been the invaluable work of Marvin Carlson (*Goethe and the Weimar Theatre* and *The German Stage in the Nineteenth Century*) and of John Prudhoe (*The Theatre of Goethe and Schiller*). There has predictably been far less written about the theatrical aspects of Kleist and Büchner, since neither author had any success on the commercial stages of the early nineteenth century.

This book is the first attempt in the English language to trace the remarkable growth of German theatre from its unpromising situation in the first half of the eighteenth century to its recognized position in the cultural life of the nation in the 1800s. We shall see the efforts to found a German National Theatre, the newfound seriousness of the theatre work at Mannheim and Weimar, and the development in prestige of the acting profession. By 1800 German theatre was no longer a side-show at a fairground or a way of exercising pupils in rhetoric; it was a major cultural force in the nation, a forum for political debate, and a rallying-point for those speaking the same tongue to join in nationhood.

This is the story of the first *German* theatre.

INTRODUCTION

German theatre in the eighteenth century

The miserable state of German theatre until the final third of the eighteenth century was the result of several factors. Since Germany was divided into 360 states, each with its own laws, currency, measurements and its almost invariably despotic regime, there was no Paris or London to provide a cultural capital for the German-speaking peoples, nor any substantial cultured bourgeoisie to provide a dependable theatre audience. Even at the courts where cultured entertainment was promoted, taste and manners were copied from the French and Italians. This showed itself above all in the low regard in which the German language was held: university lectures were given in Latin, Germany's leading philosopher, Leibniz, wrote all his later works in French, and even the national hero Frederick the Great considered German as suitable only for speaking to one's horse.

While the German courts could enjoy quite sophisticated musical entertainment, the scope for plays, especially in German, was severely limited. This was reflected in the buildings available for performance. By the mid-eighteenth century many courts boasted magnificent well-equipped opera houses, in which Italian operas were performed for the courtiers (on the whole, bourgeois audiences were excluded – a source of grievance, since it was they who paid the taxes to finance these lavish spectacles). On the other hand, plays had to be performed in makeshift theatres, often no more than a shed or the back-room of a tavern. If a luxury like heating was available, this was usually proudly announced on the playbill as a special attraction.

Because of the lack of a regular theatre-going public, it was not possible to perform in one venue for any length of time, and so most theatre companies in the eighteenth century consisted of travelling players, who were treated by the authorities in the same way as jugglers, mountebanks, beggars and other vagrants. Acting troupes were also constantly under attack from the clergy – hardly surprising when in a Catholic city like Vienna the Papal Index itself was banned, since the mere titles of censored books might prove too salacious. On the other hand, Puritan elements condemned the theatre for its sacrilegious representations, arguing, for example that to imitate thunder was to challenge God's power. One piece, which was eventually banned by the church and is here described by the actor Ekhof, was typical of theatrical performance in the early eighteenth century:[1]

> Troupes of travelling players, who speed through the whole of Germany from one fair to another, amuse the mob with common farces. . . . One comedy, performed everywhere with the greatest frequency was called *Adam and Eve or the Fall of the First Beings*. It has not yet been completely banned, and I recall seeing it performed in Strasbourg. Eve was a fat woman whose body was covered in canvas painted in unconvincing flesh-colours and who had a little belt of fig-leaves stuck to her skin. Poor Adam looked just as ridiculous, but God the Father wore an old dressing gown and had a huge wig and a long white beard. The devils were played by clowns. . . . Otherwise everything was hideous: a poor wooden booth served as a theatre; the decorations were pathetic; the actors, clothed in rags and second-hand wigs looked like coachmen disguised as heroes; in a word, the comedy was a success only with the rabble.

The poor theatre facilities and the need to travel in search of an audience meant that scenery had to be very rudimentary and adaptable to different spaces. Indeed, most plays performed had a single setting, thus supporting out of economic necessity rather than from aesthetic conviction one of the central tenets of French neo-classicism, the Unity of Place. In the case of plays requiring a change of set, this was usually effected by the use of a mid-curtain, often crudely painted, before which a scene could be played while a new backdrop and possibly furniture were set up behind. In this way it was possible, for example, to move from an interior to a woodland scene and on to a new interior with only very brief breaks in the performance.

This fluency of performance remained a characteristic of German theatre throughout the century, typified by the insistence of Iffland, later to become Germany's major theatre director, that his actors should be allowed no more than five minutes for costume changes. This practice was later to be justified by the high-flown term *liaison des scènes*,[2] and would lead to the curiously 'Brechtian' device of changing sets in full view of the audience, sometimes even while actors continued to play the scene in the foreground. No doubt the need to play scenes as continuously as possible was for the wandering players a question of holding the attention of the spectators, especially where other attractions might draw them away from the play if intervals lasted for more than a few minutes. However, it also points to a certain level of theatrical sophistication in audiences of the day, in that they were prepared to disregard the comings and goings of stage-hands just as a Japanese audience will discount the presence of the black-robed assistants in Noh theatre.

Strangely though, given the audience's willingness to create settings in their imagination, there seems to have been no attempt to return to the use of the bare stage of the Elizabethans. The short-lived but influential Johann Elias Schlegel (1718–1749) had argued that there was no point in attempting to create realistic scenery on stage, since it was impossible to construct real houses – just as it was pointless to seek realism in dialogue when one could not reproduce the authentic speech of servants. This approach could theoretically have led to considering the abandonment of scenery altogether, but this development was to await Tieck in the nineteenth century. Perhaps the tawdry surroundings in which most plays had to be performed made audiences demand some token décor, and, of course, a visual signifier of the place of action was usually necessary, since few plays contained, as Shakespeare's do, indications of setting in the dialogue. Thus, even among the poorly equipped migrant troupes a backdrop was *de rigueur*. If it was the backdrop of an interior, furniture would be painted on to it, unless the furniture had to fulfil a

3

function in the scene. Exterior scenes were hardly differentiated; even for permanent theatres later in the century Stieglitz, a writer on theatre architecture, recommended that a woodland setting could double as a garden.[3] Whatever refinements were later introduced in terms of wing flats and perspective scenery, the basic approach was to remain unchanged from the days of the wandering players: a perfunctory set which could lay no claim to realism, a curious conjunction of two-dimensional painting and three-dimensional objects and actors.

While buildings and scenery left much to be desired, the wandering troupes paid considerably more attention to the quality of their wardrobe. Costumes are more easily transported and maintained than scenery, and the actor's vanity makes the question of costume a matter of far greater significance than what he or she acts in front of. Statistics are not available for the early 1700s, but by 1790 Schröder's wardrobe cost over 60,000 Marks, whereas he spent only 20,000 on sets and music, and in 1811 his expenditure on costumes rose to 22,598 Marks, while that on sets stood at 3,020 Marks. The standard costume for all plays for at least the first half of the century was based on the court dress of Versailles: heavily embroidered rococo dresses, high wigs and hats for women, and knee breeches, silk jackets and wigs for men. Again, while some gesture was later made towards authenticity, the practice of performing in costumes that hardly differentiated between Ancient Romans and eighteenth-century courtiers called on considerable imaginative participation by the audience.

The most important development in theatre technique that accompanied the move into purpose-built theatres later in the century was therefore not so much in the externals of set or costume but in acting style. Since the wandering players had to command the attention of frequently rowdy audiences, performances were unsubtle, loud and declamatory, and frequently resorted to improvisation to cover lapses of memory or to evoke an easy response from the playgoers. However elevated the theme of the play, injections of comedy were essential to keep the spectators happy, and virtually every production had to be enlivened with the presence of the stock clown, the Hanswurst.

Indeed, one of the most significant moments in the history of the German theatre was the symbolic banning of the Hanswurst from the stage by Karoline Neuber's troupe in Leipzig in October 1737. In fact, the Hanswurst figure was far too robust an individual to accept banishment, and of course he survived for many decades after.

One reason for the longevity of the Hanswurst and for associated knockabout comedy was the special financial rewards actors were given for slapstick. Thus in Vienna there was a table of approved remuneration as follows:

For each flying through the air	1 fl.
For each jump into water	1 fl.
For each jump over a wall or from a rock	1 fl.
For each disguise	1 fl.
For receiving blows	34 kr.
For receiving a box on the ear	34 kr.
For receiving a kick of the foot	34 kr.
For each bruise	34 kr.
For having water poured over you	34 kr.
For each fencer in a duel	34 kr.[4]

Nevertheless, Karoline Neuber's banishment of the Hanswurst was one of the many important attempts to raise German theatre from a crude form of popular entertainment to the level of an acknowledged art-form. If we may speak of the birth of German theatre, then Karoline Neuber was the midwife.

Born in 1697, Karoline Neuber was to demonstrate one advantage of the socially unacceptable nature of her profession: it allowed her as a woman a far more significant role than would have been possible in the patriarchal structures of conventional society. From her acquaintance with the theatre in Strasbourg, she introduced discipline in speaking and gesture on the French model. Unfortunately this frequently involved meaningless posturing, like placing all one's weight on one foot while the toes of the other foot barely touched the ground or using curved gestures with the arms (portebras). However, the seriousness of her approach attracted the attention of the academic and critic, Johann Christoph Gottsched, and in 1727 he invited her to assist in the reform of the theatre. Lacking any substantial national tradition, they both turned to the French for their inspiration, Gottsched committing the absurdity of translating the tragedies of Corneille and Racine into German alexandrines. While rhyming hexameter couplets based on the syllabic structure of French prosody create a strikingly elegant medium for French tragedy, in German verse, which is based like English on stresses, alexandrines come across as excruciatingly plodding doggerel. Furthermore, the neo-classical unities of place, time and action added theatrical constraints to performance, which rendered Karoline Neuber's work even more lifeless. This obsession with structure was taken to such an extent that in the case of the three-act piece *Fausse Agnès* by Destouches, which was translated by Gottsched's wife, the cast had to leave the stage on the pretext of first taking coffee and later a meal in order to create the 'necessary' five acts.

While Karoline Neuber achieved the distinction of twice performing at a court theatre (in 1734 and 1735), her well-intentioned efforts predictably met with little public acclaim, and there was not as yet an established body of intellectuals who might have recognized the value of her innovations. Her personal career went into decline. Her troupe's visit to the Russian court proved a financial catastrophe, and in 1740 she quarrelled with Gottsched and broke off relations with him. She died in 1760 near Dresden, alone and in poverty. It is a sign of the low regard in which her profession was held that her coffin was not allowed to pass through the church gate into the graveyard but had to be lowered over the wall.

Perhaps Karoline Neuber's greatest contribution to eighteenth-century German theatre lay not so much in what she achieved herself but in the possibilities she opened up for those who were to follow. Notable amongst these was Johann Friedrich Schönemann, who had worked with Neuber for ten years before founding his own troupe in 1740. Schönemann's acting style appears characteristic of the first half of the eighteenth century. He played Corneille's Essex 'with a rigid expression and with his eyes always closed . . . (in those days this was supposed to indicate nobility!)'.[5] In 1750 the Duke of Mecklenburg in Schwerin offered Schönemann patronage, requiring him to spend eight months a year at Schwerin, but allowing him four months to tour, a period which the troupe usually spent in Hamburg. This kind of arrangement, which both afforded a theatre company financial security and yet permitted the actors some freedom of movement and exposure to a wider public, became common practice in the second half of the century.

In his turn, Schönemann spawned a number of major talents, Konrad Ekhof (1720–1778) and Konrad Ackermann (1712–1771) being the most prominent among them. Even amongst his contemporaries Ekhof was named 'the father of German acting', and Lessing, the major playwright before Goethe and Schiller, had nothing but praise for him: 'in even the smallest [role] he is acknowledged to be the foremost actor, and one regrets only that one cannot see him play all the other parts.'[6] It was Ekhof who initiated a much more natural style of playing, which was to become the hall-mark of the National Theatre at Mannheim. No doubt his acting style would appear to us outrageously formal and mannered. Certainly, the anecdote told by an English visitor, to whom Ekhof performed the alphabet, making him at turns weep, laugh and be terrified, suggests a highly technical actor. But in the context of the hollow declamation of his own age, he had begun to develop a quality of performance which corresponded much more closely with real human behaviour as the audience apprehended it. While still with Schönemann, Ekhof founded an academy of actors in Schwerin in 1753, *Die Academie der Schönemannschen Gesellschaft*, which introduced the innovation that plays should be read and discussed by the actors prior to performance. Before this actors were never called upon to consider a play in its entirety; they merely learnt their own roles, their cues and their entrances and exits. Now at last an attempt was made to consider interpretation and to establish a 'grammar of acting'.

Ekhof worked at the Court Theatre in Weimar from 1771 until 1774, before moving to the Court Theatre of Gotha. Here he had Iffland, Beck and Beil as pupils, who were later to form the core of the Mannheim company. At Gotha, beside the development towards more natural acting, Ekhof insisted on more realistic staging, using economical settings and dressing his actors more appropriately – no more peasants in satin and wigs.

With Konrad Ackermann, Schönemann's other distinguished successor, we come to another major if short-lived episode in the development of German theatre, the founding of the first National Theatre. Ackermann had already been at the forefront of theatre building: his construction of a theatre in Königsberg in 1753 was the first purpose-built playhouse of the century. In 1742 Schönemann had just failed to erect a theatre in Berlin because of the King of Prussia's lack of interest, and Franz Schuch had had to abandon his plans in Frankfurt because of the opposition of the clergy. When Ackermann was forced to flee from Königsberg before the advancing Russians in 1764, he built a new theatre the following year in the Gänsemarkt in Hamburg. This was to be the base of the first National Theatre.

At first it might seem strange that a nation split into 360 independent states should even consider a centralized concept like a National Theatre. In many ways there was no reality underpinning the term 'German'. The Holy Roman Empire continued to exist in name only: by 1772 the disastrously underfunded Imperial Court, the *Reichskammergericht*, had 61,233 cases awaiting trial, and the Emperor existed without revenues, army or state church. However, the one thing that did unite the German peoples, despite the multiplicity of states within which they lived, was their language. We have already seen that generally German was sneered at by courtiers and intellectuals alike, but this attitude was gradually changing. Already, despite his slavish imitation of the French, Gottsched had helped to promote a sense of German identity, significantly entitling his major theoretical work *Versuch einer kritischen Dichtkunst vor die Deutschen* (*Essay at a Critical Art of Poetry for the Germans*, 1730). But a much more significant contribution to a sense of nationhood was made in 1757 by the Prussian defeat of French forces at the Battle of Rossbach during the Seven Years' War (1756–1763). It gave a huge fillip to national pride for German-speaking troops to have routed the 'perfumed Frenchies', and Germans would now look more and more towards the kingdom of Prussia as the focus of their nation, and indeed, in the next century, Prussia was to be the agent of German unification – to the exclusion of the formerly much more powerful Empire of Austria.

In Lessing's comedy set in the aftermath of the Seven Years' War, *Minna von Barnhelm* (1767), there is a scene between a precious Frenchman and the leading male character, the Prussian officer Major von Tellheim. Here, significantly, it is the Frenchman's attempts to speak German that are ridiculed, and when in desperation he appeals to von Tellheim to speak French, the latter replies, 'Sir, I would seek to speak it in France. But why here?'.

German language then was coming to be acknowledged not only as an acceptable medium for intellectual and literary discourse but also as the rallying-point for the German 'nation'. It was in fact the only objective source of cultural identity, and there was, outside the theatre, no national forum where German was spoken – no national parliament, no central court, no Académie Française. The role assumed by the stage in becoming the promoter and guardian of the German language is now enshrined in the phrase *Bühnensprache* ('stage-language'), the approximate equivalent of the English 'Queen's English' or 'Oxford English' (indicators of the influence of Court and University respectively on the English language). Moreover, the rising class of the bourgeoisie also had no public forum in which they might effect social change or influence the course of political life. Once more, the theatre could be looked to as the one place where moral and social issues might be debated in public – a view of the stage exemplified by Schiller's essay of 1784, 'Die Schaubühne als eine moralische Anstalt betrachtet' ('The theatre considered as a moral institution'), and also witnessed to in the title of a recent book on the theatre of the period: *The Moral Burgher's Night-School.*[7]

A National Theatre was therefore thought of not merely as a means of raising the quality of German theatre but also as a way of promoting German identity and values. Almost a century after the founding of the Comédie Française in 1680 – and two centuries before the building of the British National Theatre – attempts were made to establish a similar institution on German soil. In 1764 there were efforts made to this end, improbably in the tiny town of Hildburghausen and also in Vienna with talk of a 'Nationalbühne'. But it was in the bourgeois citadel of Hamburg, a free city with a busy port and a thrusting merchant-class, that the first German National Theatre came into being. It opened on 22 April 1767 in the theatre that Ackermann had built two years previously. Although it was founded on the principle, parallel with the operation of court theatres, that it should receive subsidies to protect it from commercial pressure, there remained too little

Plate 1 The director reprimands an actor in *Minna von Barnhelm* for improvising (Reichardt's *Theater-Kalender*, 1794). Note the sliding wing-flats and candles.

public support to maintain it, and within two years it was already forced to close.

Brief though this episode was, it had established the principle of a publicly funded theatre, and during its short life had attracted to it the most important German theatre theoretician of the eighteenth century – Gotthold Ephraim Lessing. There are three aspects to Lessing's work which represent a major contribution to the development of German theatre.

First, he helped to strengthen the German sense of national identity. We have already mentioned his play *Minna von Barnhelm*, which, although a comedy, treats quite seriously of issues immediately relevant to the audience of the day, above all the question of reconciliation between two of the hostile nations in the Seven Years' War, Prussia and Saxony, represented by the two main characters, Tellheim and Minna herself. Goethe, who had been an enthusiastic member of the audience when the play was performed in Leipzig, described it in his novel *Dichtung und Wahrheit* as 'the first theatre production taken from serious life with specifically contemporary content'.[8] Prior to this, the theatre had drawn its themes mainly from classical, mythical and grand historical subjects, while a German setting was generally thought suitable only to generate broad humour. After the success of *Minna von Barnhelm* and of Johann Elias Schlegel's piece about a German folk-hero *Hermann* (1766), many plays with German characters and German settings were written, most notably Goethe's piece set in the German Middle Ages, *Götz von Berlichingen* (1774). Of this trend Wieland wrote approvingly:[9]

> German history, German heroes, a German setting, German characters, morals and customs were something quite new on German stages. Now what can be more natural than that German audiences derived the greatest enjoyment from at last finding themselves transported as though by a magic wand to their own fatherland, to familiar cities and places, amongst their own countrymen, to their own history and constitution, in short amongst beings with whom they felt at home and whose characteristics they recognized as being more or less typical of our nation?

The second major contribution of Lessing was to develop the existing tradition of bourgeois drama, which was associated with Diderot and Nivelle de la Chaussée in France. Already Gellert had written a number of 'lachrymose comedies' (*weinerliche Lustspiele* on the model of the *comédies larmoyantes*), but now Lessing explored the potential of this existing tradition in a more serious manner in his two 'bourgeois tragedies' *Miss Sara Sampson* and *Emilia Galotti*. *Miss Sara Sampson* is a play which now appears stilted and unlikely to generate emotion, but an eye-witness of the première on 10 July 1755 in Frankfurt an der Oder reported: 'The audience listened for three-and-a-half hours, as motionless as statues, and in tears.'[10] Once again a strong feeling of empathy, now from the standpoint of class rather than from national identity, revealed the newfound relevance of theatre to the lives of a large and increasingly prosperous element of German society.

Lessing's third major contribution to German theatre was his part in the discovery of Shakespeare. Already in 1759 (in his *17. Literaturbrief (Seventeenth Letter on Literature)* he had castigated Gottsched for his misguided efforts to remodel German theatre according to French neo-classical principles and pointed writers instead towards the inspiration of Shakespeare. The English writer, Lessing argued, was in every respect more suited to the German temperament than were Corneille and Racine. This recommendation had a decisive effect on two aspects of German playwriting. First, it led to the adoption of blank verse as the preferred medium for serious drama, and in fact Lessing's own *Nathan der Weise* was the first major German play to be written in blank verse. Secondly, it encouraged writers to discard the constraints of the neo-classical rules and to risk the portrayal of wider historical themes, using a multiplicity of settings and a wide range of characters. As the young Goethe enthused in the speech he gave on Shakespeare's name-day (*Zum Schäkespears Tag*, 1771):[11]

> I did not doubt for a moment that I would renounce conventional theatre. The unity of place seemed so frighteningly confining, the unities of action and time such tiresome fetters of our imagination. I leapt into the free air and felt for the first time that I had hands and feet.

Although never himself practically involved with the work of theatre, Lessing had always had close associations with stage companies. His early satirical comedy, *Der junge Gelehrte (The Young Scholar)* was performed by Neuber in 1748, and his *Miss Sara Sampson* by Schönemann in 1755. His appointment to the National Theatre in Hamburg was as 'theatre poet', an ill-defined post, in which he operated as a kind of resident critic, a useful function undertaken in German theatres today by the so-called *Dramaturg*. In his time at Hamburg Lessing reported on the productions at the National Theatre and reflected generally on the nature of theatre. The product of these deliberations was the *Hamburgische Dramaturgie (Hamburg Dramaturgy)*, arguably the most important discussion of theatre in the German language until the writings of Brecht. Indeed, one of Brecht's central concepts of *Gestus* ('gest') was a term employed by Lessing in the *Hamburgische Dramaturgie*, and, despite the characteristically eighteenth-century language, one may recognize in Lessing's pronouncement about the need to give visual expression to abstract ideas the seeds of Brecht's own more socially oriented theories:[12]

there is one kind of significant gesture [or 'gest'] which the actor should observe before all others, and with which he cannot otherwise instil light and life into a moral statement. In a word, this is the individualizing gesture. Morality makes a general statement, drawn from the special circumstances of the person who acts. In its generality this statement becomes to some extent divorced from the action; it seems like a digression whose relevance to the present is not perceived by the less attentive or less intelligent members of the audience. If there is therefore a means of making this relevance concrete, of restoring visual clarity to the symbolic nature of morality, and if this means should lie in certain gestures, then the actor should not neglect their usefulness.

Despite the interest of this passage, in which Lessing helped to develop an awareness of the importance of the visual elements of performance, and so took an early step towards the semiotics of today, he writes regrettably little about actual acting technique. As J.G. Robertson observes: 'No aspect of the

Hamburgische Dramaturgie falls more disappointingly short of expectations than that which is concerned with the actor's art.'[13] This was perhaps understandable, given the sensitivities of the actors with whom Lessing was obliged to work, but it does mean that we can deduce little about acting style from Lessing's critical writings.

Nevertheless, Lessing stands as the most important figure in German theatre prior to Schiller and Goethe. His work in Hamburg was the major contribution of the period to establishing theatre not only as a respectable form of entertainment but also as a moral force in society. His appointment as *Dramaturg*, no doubt resulting from the dependence of eighteenth-century German theatre on translations and adaptations, would have a decisive influence on the growth of German theatre as a serious aspect of culture (in contrast, for example, to the tendency in Anglo-Saxon nations to regard theatre as 'show-business'). Of the many on whom a paternity order might be served, Lessing can lay greatest claim to being the father of German theatre.

When Ackermann died in 1771, two years after the failure of the Hamburg National Theatre enterprise, his troupe was taken over by Friedrich Ludwig Schröder (1744–1816), his stepson. Schröder developed further the naturalistic trend initiated by Ekhof. Heinz Kindermann described this as follows:[14]

> Ekhof's 'naturalness' seemed pronouncedly stylized when compared with the veristic performance style of Schröder which sought a direct imitation of life. This style, with the help of which Schröder from his Hamburg base established the world of Shakespeare and of the dramas of the *Sturm und Drang*, relates to Ekhof's as radical naturalism does to stylized realism. Ekhof sought 'naturalness', Schröder sought 'nature'; Ekhof demanded 'verisimilitude', Schröder demanded 'truth' at any price. Both pursued closeness to life, but with totally different means: Schröder attempted to reproduce naked reality on stage with the use of every possible detail. Ekhof by contrast was more selective, leaving aside the merely accidental and emphasizing only the most significant even in what was necessary.

After playing for a year in Hamburg, Schröder toured to Berlin, Vienna, Munich, and Mannheim, and in 1774 he performed Goethe's *Clavigo* and *Götz von Berlichingen*. He was notable for being the first director to give fees to playwrights, a further sign of the convergence of the theatre with literature. He was also responsible for some of the most important early productions of Shakespeare in Germany. His *Hamlet*, with Franz Brockmann in the title-role, proved so popular that it was played every fifth day. Despite a supposed enthusiasm for Shakespeare amongst the public, it was in fact very difficult to perform his plays as they stood with any degree of success. It is told how Schröder's production of *Othello* in Hamburg in 1776 caused members of the audience to faint and to give birth prematurely, and the play had to be rewritten to provide a happy ending, in which Othello and Desdemona lived on as a contented married couple.

By the final third of the eighteenth century, then, German theatre had undergone a radical change. In place of the wandering players there were a number of distinguished theatre companies, based on their own theatres at courts or in the towns. Reichardt's *Theater-Kalender* for 1774 lists fourteen theatre companies. There were six more the following year, and by the 1790s there were well over thirty. Actors were now no longer social outcasts: after his success as Hamlet, Brockmann received the kind of public adulation we would now associate with a pop star, with his image being reproduced on tobacco tins and playing cards.

Admittedly, the financial rewards for actors were still pitiful. When Ekhof performed with Schönemann, he received 1 Taler, 16 Groschen a week (just about enough to buy a pair of shoes, as we learn from an entry by Schönemann in his accounts). Even as Director of the Gotha Court Theatre, Ekhof's annual salary never exceeded 600 Talers plus 30 cubic metres of firewood. The actor Genast reports that in Weimar he managed to get by with 1½ Talers a week for modest board and lodging, so Ekhof's salary of some 12 Talers a week does not seem too miserly. However, it pales into insignificance when compared with the generous remuneration heaped on performers of the Italian opera (for example, in 1748 the stage-designer Ferdinando Galli-Bibiena received an annual salary of 2266 Talers).

15

The repertoire of German theatres had also undergone a transformation. In place of the crude *Haupt- und Staatsaktionen* of the wandering players and the mainly French repertoire of those troupes with more serious pretensions, there was now a much wider variety of pieces performed. Between 1754 and 1771 Ackermann's troupe gave the following number of performances by major playwrights: Voltaire (95), C.F. Weisse (69), Destouches (69), Molière (63), Goldoni (50), Lessing (45), Krüger (38), Brandes (28). As will be seen, French writers still dominated the repertoire, and English authors were infrequently performed by any companies; only Colman, Thomson, Lillo and Moore were occasionally produced, and Goldsmith and Sheridan became known towards the end of the century, but Shakespeare's plays had to wait for Schröder in the 70s, and even then these were usually adaptations by Weisse.

Even at the National Theatre in Hamburg commercial success remained the determinant in the choice of plays.[15] Two-thirds of the plays performed from 1767 to 1769 were comedies. Despite Lessing's admonitions, even here French plays tended to predominate, Molière, Marivaux, Destouches, La Chaussée, Voltaire, Beaumarchais and Diderot all being represented. Only one Corneille was performed and no Racine. Significantly, the principal German piece in imitation of French classical tragedy, Gottsched's *Der sterbende Cato* (*The Dying Cato*, 1731) was not mounted. German authors, however, were at last being produced more and more. Apart from Lessing, whose *Minna von Barnhelm* was performed sixteen times, works by the following were seen by the Hamburg public: Schlegel, Cronegk, Brawe, Weisse, Sturz, Brandes, Löwen, Schiebeler, and Pastor Schlosser.

As we shall see, even at Weimar, where Goethe made the most strenuous attempts to educate the taste of his audience, light comedies remained the most common fare. Even Schröder, who adventurously encouraged the young writers of the *Sturm und Drang* ('Storm and Stress') and, as we have seen, produced Shakespeare for the first time, felt unable to give a place in his repertoire to as revolutionary a piece as Schiller's *Die Räuber* (*The Robbers*, 1781). Indeed, in Vienna Schiller's plays were banned altogether (it was not until 1850 that *Die Räuber* had become respectable enough to be performed at the Burgtheater).

So, although a vast improvement had taken place in German

theatre in the course of the eighteenth century, many undesirable aspects persisted. On the credit side, the theatre had found a thoughtful and critical audience. From the 1750s theatre critics made their first appearance and soon, as with Lessing at Hamburg, the post of *Dramaturg* was created, which gave to major theatre companies a well-read individual who would advise on the repertoire without having any personal interest in grasping a leading role for himself. The starting-time of performances was moved from four in the afternoon to seven or eight o'clock in the evening. This was partly due to improvements in theatre lighting, but was more an indicator of the establishment of theatre as an element of bourgeois social life instead of its former role as a sideshow in the market place.

On the debit side, the German theatre had lost much of the vigour and popular base of the wandering players without as yet replacing this loss with the excellence of the serious drama that was to emerge with Schiller, Goethe, Kleist and Büchner. In the first three-quarters of the eighteenth century, the only German playwright of any quality was Lessing, and of his works few, with the exception of *Minna von Barnhelm*, are still performed today.

Although a more cultured bourgeoisie was now showing an interest in the theatre, the emphasis remained, as we have seen, on fairly mindless entertainment. Where more demanding material was offered, it usually had to be tailored to make it more attractive: hence the happy endings of Shakespearean tragedies or the typical playbill, advertising *Romeo and Juliet – or the Surprising Outcome in the Graveyard*.[16]

While actors too had developed a more serious approach to their craft, the recommended practice of Ekhof that a play should be read and discussed before rehearsal remained very much the exception. Even at the prestigious Royal Theatre in Berlin the attitude to rehearsal was very casual:[17]

> It seems that Herr Koch does not believe in rehearsals. One cannot otherwise conceive how such ridiculous errors could occur in entrances and exits. The actor says: I see him coming, and turns towards the left side of the stage to face the approaching character, whereupon the latter enters from the right.

This failure to work on the entirety of the play was due in part to the fear of piracy of scripts, so that it was anyway safer to allow actors to have access only to their own roles with their cues rather than to give them copies of the entire play which might have been stolen by or peddled to rival companies. It was also due to the increasing pressure to offer a constantly changing repertoire. While the theatre was primarily a mobile one, travelling from place to place in search of its audiences, there was not much need to alter the programme in the course of a season. But once a company was settled in a town or at a court, they had to provide constantly varied entertainment for the limited audience of the locality. Even though it was not uncommon for audiences to return to sit through the same production several times over, few plays were performed more than two or three times, and five performances of the same piece would constitute a major success. Pressure simply to get a piece on the boards was therefore so great that careful preparation was a largely unattainable luxury. While at the court of Queen Mathilda of Denmark in Celle, Schröder was called upon to produce ten grand buffo operas in eight weeks, and even in the more leisurely atmosphere of the Weimar Court Theatre a programme was mounted that would be beyond the reach of the best subsidized of German theatres today. Understandably then, rehearsals were still generally very casual affairs. The *Einsager* (prompter), whose function extended well beyond his indispensable duty of prompting during performance, organizing rehearsals, trimming the candles in the interval and generally operating as stage-manager,[18] would distribute roles and perhaps suggest entrances and exits, but that would be all. With luck, lines would be learnt, but even this was not always certain. Herdt, working in Berlin with Iffland, walked on to stage at the beginning of Schiller's *Jungfrau von Orleans (Maid of Orleans)* and had to leave again immediately, because the prompter was not in his box and Herdt could not recall his opening line.

A not untypical case of a provincial theatre is reflected in the report on the playhouse at Brünn (now Brno in Czechoslovakia), which flattered itself with the designation, Brünner National-Theater:[19]

> The Manager and Director, Karl Wothe, has the rare talent of being able to distribute roles without knowing

the content of the play. Whether this distribution is suitable or not is a matter of indifference to him, so long as he imagines he has fulfilled his duty as Director. Partly from laziness, partly for political reasons he never comes to rehearsals. He considers that actors know their craft, and anyway he is utterly redundant.

Predictably, actors, being unable to depend on careful preparation or directorial advice, relied on their own virtuosity. This was the beginning of the star system, and from 1777, when Bock left Gotha on an individual tour, it was common practice for the most successful to be invited to give guest-performances away from their own company. Such performances were then often slavishly copied by the host company. Even at Mannheim, after Schröder had played there in 1780, the director Dalberg insisted that three of his actors should exactly imitate Schröder's performances. In these circumstances, any notion of operating as an ensemble was very rare, and one of the most important improvements in theatre work at the end of the century was the creation of an ensemble spirit, as at Weimar. Generally, when an actor was speaking on stage, other actors stood around waiting for their cue, at best exuding an impression of utter boredom, at worst flirting with the audience. By contrast, Ekhof and Dorothea and Konrad Ackermann were all praised for their silent acting. If actors could upstage others by extravagant entrances or exits, by commanding a strong central position on stage, or by indulging in some irrelevant business, then they would do so. It is in the light of such practices that we shall have to view Goethe's apparently tiresomely prescriptive 'Rules for actors'.[20]

Technical aspects of theatre had improved considerably from the early years of the century. More care was taken with scenery, as we shall see in the examples of Mannheim and Weimar, and the stages were better lit. While in 1740 Schönemann had spent only one Taler on candles for an evening performance, 180 Talers a night was the norm later in the century, and it is recorded that the Berlin opera spent 2,771 Reichstaler in one evening on candles. Costumes were also less uniformly based on a corrupt version of the court-dress of Versailles. Eventually, three types of costume predominated: first, an all-purpose 'Ancient' costume, which did not differentiate between Greece or Rome. Already in 1744 in her production of Gottsched's *Dying Cato* Karoline Neuber had attempted to introduce togas, but was met with ridicule. The breakthrough came in 1775, when Charlotte Brandes wore a flowing white dress for her role as Ariadne at the Court Theatre of Gotha. Second, there was an all-purpose 'Oriental' costume, particularly favoured for pieces like Voltaire's *Semiramis*. Finally, there was the contemporary bourgeois costume of breeches, jacket and pig-tail for men and full embroidered dresses for the women. With the rise in popularity of the so-called *Ritterdramen* (medieval pieces such as Goethe's *Götz*), historical costume and armour were added to the list.

Since actors were required to provide their own costumes, there was often little coherence in style, and the need to outdo each other led to absurdities like servants being better dressed than their mistresses and war-weary soldiers appearing in immaculate uniform. As a critic wrote in 1788:[21]

> There is nothing more gaudy and tasteless than the costumes on most German stages – especially in plays from the Middle Ages. Usually we are presented with a pattern book of all ages and peoples: English hats with German armour, modern shoes with antique hose, French hairstyles with Spanish court-dress. Instead of a simple, light dress, clinging to her natural shape, a Greek maiden wears a garish mixture of French and idealized costume, and German knights go to battle without helmets or armlets.

The signs did not look particularly auspicious for the creation of the first German theatre. Much had improved, but the platform for new works of serious literary merit was still badly wormed. It was above all the second great National Theatre at Mannheim and the Court Theatre at Weimar that provided the opportunity for the two outstanding playwrights, Schiller and Goethe, to develop their talents.

1

SCHILLER AT MANNHEIM
The Robbers

In Mannheim I lost nearly all my enthusiasm for drama.
Now it is beginning to revive in me once more, but I still
have a horror of the terrible mistreatment of plays on our
stages. I yearn impatiently for the theatre where I can
give rein to my imagination and do not see the free flight
of my feelings so astonishingly inhibited. I am now well
aware of the limits which wooden walls and all the
necessary circumstances of theatre practice impose on the
writer, but there are even more narrow limits, drawn by
those with small minds and limited talents, but which are
leapt over by the genius of the great actor.[1]

Schiller's relationship with the Mannheim National Theatre
was not always an easy one, but without the support he found
there, his career as a playwright would undoubtedly have
taken much longer to develop. It was Mannheim that was
courageous enough to stage Schiller's first play, *Die Räuber (The
Robbers)*, written while he was still at school. It was also at
Mannheim that, despite the open disapproval of his writing by
his ruler, the neighbouring Duke of Württemberg, Schiller was
appointed writer in residence at the theatre from 1783 to 1785,
and both his next two plays *Die Verschwörung des Fiesko zu
Genua (The Conspiracy of Fiesco in Genoa)* and *Kabale und Liebe
(Intrigue and Love)* were premièred there.

The *Hof- und Nationaltheater* (Court and National Theatre) of
Mannheim was created by the Duke Karl Theodor as a
consolation to the town when he decided to move his court to
Munich in 1777 after the death of Prince Maximilian III of
Bavaria. The following year Freiherr von Dalberg was appointed

Manager of the new National Theatre and succeeded in attracting Iffland, Beck, Boeck and Seyler to Mannheim in 1779. From the start Dalberg insisted on holding regular meetings of the company to discuss the repertoire and general questions about theatre. The deliberations of these *Ausschüsse* (committees) were precisely minuted, checked by the participants and eventually published. In this way Dalberg established a completely different attitude to theatre work from that which was possible in the slapdash routine of most other companies (see Appendices I and II). As writer in residence Schiller was obliged to attend the meetings of the *Ausschuss* from October 1783 to May 1784 and had to read three plays and present his comments on them to his fellow members. The payroll for the new company affords interesting insights into their levels of remuneration and distribution of roles:[2]

Mme Seyler	Queens and lead-roles in tragedies	1000 Fl.
Mme Brandes	Romantic heroine in tragedy and comedy, also light roles	1200 Fl.
Mme Toscani	Tender roles and second romantic heroine	1200 Fl.
Mme Kummerfeld	Soubrette and comic roles	600 Fl.
Mme Wallenstein	Character and naive roles	500 Fl.
Mlle Brandes	Lead-roles in operas, small roles in comedy	300 Fl.
Mme Poeschel	Supporting roles in operettas and small walk-on parts in comedies	400 Fl.
Herr Boeck	Heroes and romantic leads in tragedies and comedies	1400 Fl.
Herr Beck	Young and light roles	500 Fl.
Herr Iffland	Comic old men, character roles, also Jews	700 Fl.
Herr Beil	Comic servants, peasants and light roles	600 Fl.
Herr Meyer	*Raisonneurs* and sophisticated roles	800 Fl.
Herr Backhaus	Low-comic roles	300 Fl.

Herr Zuccarini	Officers and sophisticated roles	600 Fl.
Herr Brandes	Bombastic roles	900 Fl.
Herr Herter	Old officers, also second *raisonneurs*	300 Fl.
Herr Haferung Herr Trinkle Herr Toscani	Small walk-on parts and stop-gaps	1206 Fl.

This list is revealing in several respects. First, it will be noticed how couples and even families performed together (Mme Seyler was the wife of the Director). Given that actors were still regarded as social outcasts, intermarriage was quite common, and offspring would often continue in the theatre tradition of their parents. Second, it is clear that remuneration was dependent above all on public acclaim; thus the more glamorous younger roles earned more than the older serious ones (this having nothing to do with the actual age of the actor – Boeck, the romantic lead, being thirty-six in 1779 and Iffland, portrayer of old men, only twenty).

Most importantly, though, this document shows the well-established practice of the *Rollenfach* (stock-roles). Given the commercial pressures on most theatre companies, this was a necessary evil, just as it was to be in the nineteenth century in the British and American stock-companies. While the custom of casting according to type was obviously expedient, it also meant that actors were seldom challenged by a role and so fell easily into repetitive mannerisms and stereotyped characterization. At least at Mannheim nineteen actors, many of them contracted for two years, were engaged, compared with the average company size of twelve to fourteen. (Under Goethe at Weimar, for example, the company averaged fifteen, and it was only towards the turn of the century, especially with the need to cast for Shakespeare and for the *Ritterdramen* such as *Götz von Berlichingen*, that acting troupes increased in size to between twenty-five and thirty.) The somewhat larger company at Mannheim allowed the distribution of roles to be a little more flexible than was possible elsewhere at the time, and with the more complex writing of Schiller and Goethe it soon became impossible to cast so obviously according to type (significantly, it was Iffland who was cast as the young villain,

Plate 2 Picture-gallery scene. Wing-flats.

Plate 3 Picture-gallery scene. Perspective backdrop.

Franz Moor, in the première of *The Robbers*). It was Goethe at Weimar who eventually managed to grow beyond the *Rollenfach* system almost entirely.

One important innovation that Dalberg strove for was an undermining of the star system and the establishment of a true ensemble feeling in the Mannheim company by requiring all actors to take walk-on parts when necessary. That this was not always successful is revealed by one of the Mannheim 'protocols':[3]

> It is shameful how often smaller roles, which certainly contribute as much as bigger roles to the perfecting and fleshing out of the whole, are assiduously spoilt by certain actors and are made a mockery of; [. . .] Herr Iffland performed in such a way that it was impossible to understand or comprehend the nature of the part – just like someone who at every moment wishes to imply: 'Dear audience, pity me that I have to play a minor role.'

It seems though that Iffland's conceit was not typical and that the Mannheim company became renowned for their ensemble spirit, actors often gathering in the wings to approve the performance of a fellow-actor.

The theatre at Mannheim[4] had been converted from a former hospital. The stage area was generous (16 metres wide by 16 metres deep), with a one metre rake from rear to front, but since there was no forestage, all action had to take place behind the proscenium arch. This caused the acoustics to be poor and may account, in part at least, for the common complaint about naturalistic mumbling by the Mannheim actors. In common with most permanent theatres of the day, scenery was created by the use of a backdrop, with seven wing-pieces either side of the stage, usually mounted on sliders to allow more rapid set changes (see Plates 1 and 3 and Figures 1 and 2). Sometimes the stage would be foreshortened by lowering the backdrop halfway or more downstage, as we shall see in *The Robbers* or as indicated by a stage direction such as that at the start of Act 2, Scene 6 of Schiller's *Die Jungfrau von Orleans (The Maid of Orleans*, 1801): 'The back-drop opens. The English camp is revealed in flames.'

The wing-pieces would be painted in perspective, so that images on the downstage flats would relate to normal human height, while the flats behind would be painted on a correspondingly smaller scale until one reached the backdrop, which, in the case of a forest or a mountain landscape, for example, might have trees or peaks less than two metres high. Even in interiors, doors might be painted on to the backcloth that were only two-thirds or even half the height of the actor. In Plate 3 the door at the rear cannot be more than a metre and a half high and is probably lower still. Clearly, entrances were impossible from the back, and it looked grotesque if an actor ventured too far upstage, dwarfing the tree, door or mantelpiece. Even towards the end of the nineteenth century German directors were wrestling with this problem, especially as better lit stages encouraged actors to retreat from the footlights. Saxe-Meiningen, in his production of Schiller's *William Tell*, even used bearded children working in the background to help out the illusion of perspective, but this was hardly a satisfactory solution.

Actors made entrances into interiors simply by stepping between flats, often beside a wing-piece with a door painted on it. This frequently led to absurdities, as reported by Hagen in 1773: 'Often the actors exit by the windows and re-enter through a mirror. They charge through the walls with aplomb, even though the room has several doors.'[5] Where it was essential to have a practical door, these would be set between the flats, usually between the second and third wing-piece, but this would often spoil the illusion of perspective. Despite proposals for improvements in this system, it dominated German theatre practice for about a century and a half. One suggestion was to set the wing-pieces diagonally, since this would have covered the wing-space better, thus concealing actors waiting for their entrances, who were all too frequently visible to the audience sitting at the sides of the auditorium. But this again would have spoiled the perspective and would have made it difficult to line up the flats neatly with the borders. It would also have obscured the light from candles or lamps set behind the flats. The box-set was introduced to Germany from France by Schröder as early as 1790 (it did not come to England until at least 1832). While it was obviously much more convincing for interior scenes, it once again created problems of lighting, and was so cumbersome to change that it was suitable only for pieces with a single setting. Besides, the

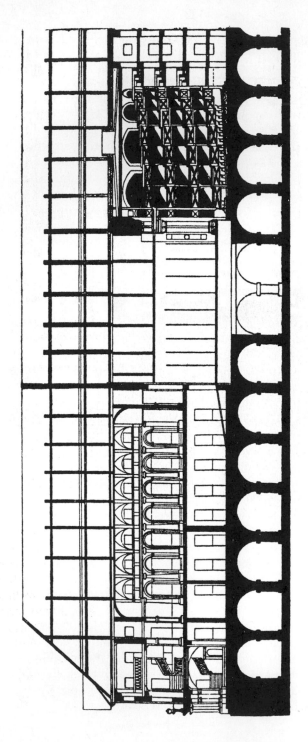

Figure 1   Cross-section of the Mannheim National Theatre.

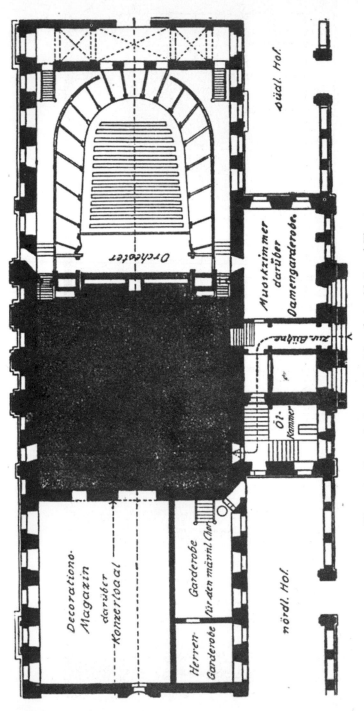

Figure 2 Ground-plan of the Mannheim National Theatre.

open wings had certain obvious advantages, as Brandes recorded in his autobiography:[6]

> The Queen began to express her anger . . . with as much composure as possible, when a hand suddenly appeared from the wings and started to deal her a few sharp blows to the head . . . , accompanied loudly by the words: 'Give it a bit of fire, you bitch!' The hand disappeared, and the Queen, electrified by this encouragement, began from that moment on to immerse herself in her role.

Lighting at this time was usually by means of candles of wax or tallow (see Plate 1). These smoked, sputtered, smelled, spread soot and dripped wax on actors and costumes, and had to be trimmed between acts. The small auditorium (20 metres by 16 metres) at Mannheim was dimly lit with a single chandelier with eight candles. The stage was also lit with a chandelier, but this would have had to be hung so high to clear the borders that it would not afford much illumination. In addition, lighting was from below or from the side, from footlights or from behind wing-pieces, with a method of winching up the lights once they were lit. Since it is quite rare in nature for a face to be lit like this (from the reflection off snow, or from the sunset, for example), theatre lighting at this time was very unnatural; the light from footlights was also not very flattering.

The tenacity in European theatre of perspective scenery and of footlights is surprising.[7] To this day, footlights will still be found in many school and village halls (often still referred to as 'floats' to recall the time when candles were floated in water for safety), despite the fact that electric lamps provide much more natural light from above than from below. It is worth considering why. In such proscenium arch staging the front curtain opens to reveal a three-dimensional picture, magically lit. It is a world unto itself, enclosed within the strict lines of perspective. Into this world step the magical beings, the actors, who will exist only for as long as they are seen on stage. They will then step out of this world when their parts are complete, to vanish from sight once more. This instant transition from not-being to being can only be accomplished when one can pass unimpeded into the side of the picture. In a box-set with a real door, the actor has to open the door and swing it open before the entrance can be made. There is a process of gradual revelation through a real door in place of the instant and magical arrival of the player on to the scene. In the same way the footlights provide a barrier between actor and audience, and effectively prevent the performer from seeing the audience, thus creating the 'dark hole' of the auditorium, so approved of by Stanislavsky.

In approaching Schiller's *The Robbers*, Dalberg was concerned not only to make the piece theatrically viable but also to avoid any political controversy that the piece might attract. For both these reasons he decided to remove the action from the contemporary setting demanded by Schiller, whose opening stage direction stipulates: 'The setting for this story is Germany, the time about the middle of the eighteenth century.' Instead he insisted on removing it to a medieval setting, to the period of the Emperor Maximilian. There were certain obvious practical advantages: this period was popular with audiences, and the costumes were to hand (see Plate 4). It would also dissuade the authorities from seeing Karl Moor's condemnation of his age as an overt attack on existing institutions. Indeed, when the play was staged in contemporary costume in Leipzig in September 1782, it was banned after the second performance.

Dalberg also had a more serious theatrical reason for his decision, which he defended eloquently, when the *Ausschuss* of 17 November 1781 protested against the use of 'old German costumes':[8]

> *The Robbers* can, according to all notions of what is theatrically effective, be performed only with idealistic veneer and costumes of the past. For where is the least degree of probability that in our present political circumstances and state constitutions such events could occur? This piece in modern dress becomes a mere story and untrue.

Thus the prompt-book lists stylized costumes in brightly coloured satin and velvet with 'half-armour' for the leading robbers. The actress playing Amalia provided her own embroidered skirt and top and, as custom at Mannheim dictated for all actresses except those playing peasants, would have had to wear gloves throughout. Certainly the costumes

Plate 4   Costume designs. From left to right: Karl Moor, Amalia, Old Moor, Franz Moor, Hermann.

Plate 5 Karl Moor: 'That is my father's voice.' (IV, 5).

would not have been historically accurate, nor was there great consistency in the stage properties used; for example, the robbers were armed with anachronistic flintlocks.

ACTING STYLE AT MANNHEIM

Much more significant than the details of costumes and props – and a major contribution by the Mannheim National Theatre to the development of theatre in Germany – was Dalberg's theoretical exploration of acting style. In 1782, the year of the première of *The Robbers*, Dalberg posed a question to the *Ausschuss*: 'What is meant by "natural", and what limitations should be imposed on this in theatrical performance?'.[9] As we shall see in Iffland's reply, the eighteenth-century German conception of 'nature' did not refer merely to a reality to be imitated but had qualitative implications of a perfect creation to be represented as finely as possible.

The director Meyer began his reply by defining 'naturalness' as an exact recreation of reality. In order to achieve this, an actor had to have knowledge of every passion 'in all their different degrees, circumstances and relationships', for 'anything that goes by the name of passion must be discovered by the actor within himself, if his expression is to be natural'. With this Meyer established the basis of Mannheim 'naturalism' as being rooted in the experience of the actor.

Meyer went on, however, to insist on acting technique as a necessary component of natural performance:

> It is therefore impossible without artistic study to achieve the correct presentation of a character's passion, and natural anger, love, terror, etc. can appear most unnatural with regard to what is 'natural' in the theatre, if they are nothing more, nothing less than the actor's own feelings without their being suited to the character portrayed. It may be natural, but it is not the naturalness of the matter in hand and is therefore unnatural.

He summarized the two main demands on the actor as follows:

> 1. The actor must know himself exactly, that is to say, he must know to what extent this or that outburst can remain natural and apply this to the character he is portraying. 2. His expression must be clear and precise for the furthest member of the audience without seeming a caricature to the nearest one.

Another director, Rennschüb, argued along very similar lines, recommending also authenticity of feeling tempered by conscious aesthetic control:

> Only the actor who feels his role will deceive the audience into believing that they are watching scenes of real life. [. . .] If he also possesses propriety and is in control of his body, then this natural action which is wholly appropriate to the plot will acquire the quality of portraiture.

Here we encounter the characteristically eighteenth-century influence of painting on the theatre. The curious European phenomenon of the proscenium-arch or 'peep-show' stage impelled scene-painters and actors into regarding the theatre as a series of moving tableaux. In his essay *Laokoon* Lessing had already spoken of drama as a 'speaking painting' and argued in his *Hamburgische Dramaturgie*: 'As visible painting the highest law [of the theatre] must be that of beauty; but as painting in transition it need not always lend to its groupings that harmony which makes old works of art so impressive.'[10] It would be in Goethe's work at Weimar that the attempt to emulate the quality of the pictorial arts would be most assiduously pursued.

Clearly, it was very difficult to invite actors to live out their emotions on stage and at the same time to offer aesthetically pleasing images to the audience. So Rennschüb was forced to admit that each actor adopted the style that met with greatest public approval:

> Each of our good actors has his own favourite method with which he will perform his roles; and if through this presentation he receives applause and is clapped, then he has achieved his goal and is happy. He will then always defend his performance style as being the correct one and therefore the most natural.

He went on to express the hope that more uniformity might be achieved in acting style, which would be 'of great use for the German theatre'.

The actor Johann David Beil referred to great actors of the past in his attempt to describe what is natural in the theatre, making especial mention of Ekhof and Schröder. The talent of these great men, he argued, rested on their ability to use their art to *appear* to be natural: 'the theatre can only present reality transformed ("verwandelte Natur"), and . . . an actor may never be the passion or mood itself but can only embody the pure art of imitation.'

Iffland gave the lengthiest answer to Dalberg's question. He began by considering what was implied by the word 'natural', and interpreted the word in idealistic terms: 'The word nature is an image, the greatest, the boldest that has ever been ventured – the image of God's creation! . . . . Nature and perfection are therefore synonymous.'

Moving on from these philosophical considerations, Iffland also referred to the art of painting in his search for a definition of the art of acting: 'The theatre is a painting of man, of his passions and actions. By presenting man in the role he performs, the actor brings the painting to life.' Iffland argued that in this act of creation inspiration was essential, and that this inspiration would come about only if the actor made himself or herself a worthy channel for this inspiration. In this way Iffland attempted to overcome the dichotomy between nature and art established by the other respondents. He seemed to imply not so much that the actor's technique was required to harness his or her natural impulses, but that artistic training was a prerequisite for the emergence of the 'natural'. As he elsewhere asserted: 'The best means of portraying a noble figure is to be one oneself.'[11]

He concluded by pointing out that, where true inspiration was lacking, technique would at least maintain a certain quality in the performance:

> The actor will fulfil his obligation if he employs the gift or art of speaking. I believe that one should encourage good or moderate actors in the art of speaking. On off days or when unwell, at least they can fall back on good vocal delivery.

This may seem odd advice from an actor, about whom Schiller's only complaint was that he swallowed his words and rushed his speeches.[12] However, this is not only sound practical advice but also provided the basis for the development of good speech in the theatre, paving the way for Goethe's work at Weimar and the eventual establishment of *Bühnensprache* as the norm of spoken German.

At the next sitting of the *Ausschuss* Dalberg summarized the views of his respondents and drew conclusions, perhaps predictably emphasizing the need for discipline in his troupe. He insisted, for example, that each actor should be familiar with the whole play, so that each role could be seen in relationship with all the others. He insisted too on the importance of remembering entrances, lines, moves and exits, in order to give the actor freedom to be natural:

> The most natural actor is therefore the actor who, after thorough exploration of every detail of both his own role and that of the play itself, and after the precise correction of each passage in rehearsal, surrenders himself in the actual performance to his own feelings and to the mood and inspiration of the moment.

It is first of all remarkable that the German theatre was here already pondering the art of acting, a profession which had until a few years previously at best been regarded as a craft and at worst was thought of as being on a par with jugglers and mountebanks. Moreover, if one sets aside the eighteenth-century terminology and reads 'emotions' for 'passions', we encounter here a very modern view of the art of acting. The insistence that actors should have experienced for themselves the emotions they portray predates Stanislavsky's notion of 'emotion memory' by well over a century, and like the so-called 'first director', Dalberg and his associates wrestled with the problem of relating internalized emotion to the needs of external theatrical presentation.

It must be admitted that, under the pressures that existed at Mannheim, with the constant need to produce new work and the resultant perfunctory rehearsals, there was little hope that an ideal relationship between authentic feeling and clear, disciplined expression could be discovered. The mediocre continued to rely on stock emotional gestures; the younger and more talented members of the group subscribed to the *Sturm und Drang* cult of genius, surrendering themselves to their emotions but lacking vocal discipline and any concern with the play as a whole. It seems that only rarely, as in the case of Iffland, whose performance as Franz Moor will be examined below, some synthesis between emotional effusion and aesthetic control was achieved. But at least Mannheim had placed the issue on the agenda, and had decisively affirmed that an accurate imitation of reality was to be striven for, and so laid the foundations of naturalism in the German theatre. It was left to Goethe at Weimar to produce the kind of training and order that would be the foundation of a more poetic if less popular form of theatre.

THE PREMIÈRE OF *THE ROBBERS*

The première of *The Robbers* took place on 13 January 1782 – on a Sunday evening, the evening usually reserved for the more popular genre of comedy. It began at five o'clock and did not end until a quarter past nine. Many members of the audience, some of whom had come from towns as far afield as Frankfurt, Mainz and Darmstadt, occupied their seats from one o'clock onwards to make certain of not missing a piece that, since its anonymous publication the previous summer, had already gained considerable notoriety. That they were not disappointed in their expectations is revealed by an eye-witness account of the performance:[13]

The theatre resembled a madhouse: rolling eyes, clenched fists, stamping feet, hoarse shouts in the auditorium! Complete strangers embraced each other in tears, women staggered almost fainting towards the exits. It was a general dissolution as in the time of Chaos, from whose mists a new creation springs forth!

Despite this colossal excitement most critics adopted a negative attitude towards the play: 'After a few more five-hour-long performances the stalls will exact justice on this work of larceny and murder and will banish it for all eternity!'[14] One of the sternest critics of the piece was a certain 'N', writing in the *Wirtembergisches Repertorium der Literatur*, who transpired to be none other than Schiller himself:[15]

The day before yesterday Herr Schiller's *The Robbers* was at last performed. . . . The author has admittedly rewritten it for the stage, but how? Certainly only for those who are enthused by Dalberg's industrious spirit: for everyone else, at least those I know, it remains an untidy piece. It was impossible to keep to five acts. The curtain fell twice between scenes, so that the stage-hands and actors had time for changes, entr'actes were performed, and so seven acts emerged.

Clearly Schiller was somewhat irked by the technical problems that the staging of his piece caused and above all by the changes introduced by Dalberg (the first production of *The Robbers* as written by Schiller did not take place until 10 November 1861). The many set changes, together with the entr'actes including music specially composed by Danzy, slowed the performance considerably and diffused the dramatic tension, on which the success of the piece must depend.

Schiller wrote *The Robbers* in 1779–80 while still at school, and it bears many of the hallmarks not only of Schiller's own adolescence but also of its theatrical period, the so-called *Sturm und Drang*. Written heavily under the influence of Shakespeare, *The Robbers*, which in the stage manuscript has the alternative title *The Lost Son* (*Der verlorene Sohn*) boasts an untidy, rambling, melodramatic plot. It contains forged letters, disguised messengers, with two sons – one noble, one villainous – and an old father who, like Gloucester in *King Lear*, is deceived into believing that his good son has betrayed him and that his evil son loves him. It is a piece full of powerful rhetoric and philosophical utterances, its extreme emotionalism sometimes slithering into banality.

An unsympathetic summary of the plot is provided by Bertolt Brecht who had seen the play performed at a Trade Union gathering in 1920:[16]

> This work of Schiller's youth shows in wild and unsubtle scenes the moving story of [Karl], a youth of promise, who suffers because of the criminal machinations of his own brother Franz, an evil villain. Franz blackens him in the estimation of his old father, and, in wild defiance, Karl rejects the path of conventional morality to go to the Bohemian Woods as the head of a band of robbers. Here he performs good deeds before returning home to find his father starving in a tower (after his noble beloved and fiancée, Amalia, has not even been able to recognize him). He frees his father and has bloody vengeance carried out on his brother – after which he gives himself up to the police.

The following table indicates how, according to the promptbook, Dalberg attempted to overcome the problem of presenting the many different settings of the piece:[17]

Published text		Stage version	
I.1.	Hall in Moor's castle	I.1.	Hall in Moor's house
I.2.	Inn on Saxon border	I.2.	Inn. Tap-room with doors
I.3.	Moor's castle (Amalie's room}		
II.1.	Franz's room	II.1.	As I.1.
II.2.	Old Moor's bedroom		
II.3.	The Bohemian Woods	II.2.	The Bohemian Woods
III.1.	Garden	III.1.	Garden
III.2.	By the River Danube	III.2.	By the River Danube
IV.1.	Countryside near Moor's castle}		

IV.2.	Gallery in the castle	IV.1.	Gallery in Moor's castle
IV.3.	Another room in the castle		
IV.4.	Garden	IV.2.	Garden
IV.5.	Nearby wood	V.	Wood
V.1.	View of many rooms	VI.	Room in Moor's house
V.2.	As IV.5.	VII.	As V.

The play would have opened with the full stage used. This was the so-called 'Porcelain Room', decorated as it was with porcelain ornaments painted on to the wing-flats and back-drop. The setting would suggest opulence and yet, given the fragility of porcelain, might indicate the frail state of the old Count Moor. The only piece of furniture was 'a rich armchair' into which Moor soon sinks, a crumpled figure dwarfed by the perspective depth of the vast hall, on hearing Franz read a letter containing false news of Karl's debauchery. As the curtain opens, Moor and his corrupt son, Franz, are discovered in conversation, reinforcing for the audience the illusion of observing a real encounter. There is no breach with realism: no opening monologue or asides to reveal to the audience the deceit of Franz, as one finds, say, with the similar treachery of Edmund in *King Lear*. Given Franz's deformed appearance ('the most repulsive of all human types thrown into one heap') we may conclude that we are not in the presence of the hero of the piece, but there is no ostensible reason why we should not accept the truthfulness of his assertions until he is alone on stage. Suddenly the mood of the scene is shattered: after his father's tearful exit, Franz bursts into scornful laughter and launches into a long and violent monologue, revealing his deceit and carefully removing the accusing letter which has, needless to say, been penned by himself.

The second scene, set in an inn in Saxony, was in the Mannheim stage version 'a tap-room with doors; two tables, six chairs, six glasses, and two bottles of wine'. This would have been achieved by bringing on the necessary furniture and props, changing the sliders and by lowering a backdrop halfway down the stage, thus creating an enclosed space which contrasted well with the opulence of the first scene. Instead of the orgy that the audience might be expecting after the descriptions of Karl in the first scene, we discover him quietly seated with a single companion, 'engrossed in a book'. Admittedly, the book is soon laid aside so that he can fulminate against the flaccid age in which he lives, an age devoid of heroes. The scene becomes more and more animated as further companions arrive, one of them bearing the false news from Franz Moor that Karl has been entirely rejected by his father. After a lot of shaking of hands, clapping of backs and further emotional displays by Karl ('foaming and stamping on the ground') the friends somewhat improbably resolve to form a robber band with Karl as their leader.

Once again, with a powerful sense of theatrical contrast, the next scene – after the first interval – returns to the peace and space of Moor's castle. Schiller's original scenes occupy three different locations in the castle: the room of Amalia, Karl's fiancée; Franz's room; and the bedroom where Count Moor lies dying. Each of these settings provides a special focus: Amalia's space is penetrated by the unwelcome presence of Franz; Franz has his own space in which to plot against his brother; and, predictably, the dying Moor is seen in his own chamber. In the rewritten stage version Dalberg had, for the sake of theatrical convenience, set all these three scenes in the neutral space of the 'Porcelain Room' of the first scene. There is an obvious loss here, and there is also the problem of having to manoeuvre the dying Moor on to the stage, presumably helped on by a servant. The only possible gain, apart from the obvious benefit of flow of performance, is that there is some increase in tension by seeing Franz's scheming take place in such a public space.

The truth is, however, that Schiller had not taken proper account of the contingencies of the theatre practice of the day. It is interesting to observe how, after working at Mannheim, he learnt to write in a manner more suited to the practical needs of the contemporary stage. *The Robbers* contains fifteen scenes and demands thirteen different settings, five of them exterior scenes. But his next play, *Die Verschwörung des Fiesko zu Genua* (*The Conspiracy of Fiesco in Genoa*, 1782), is divided into seventy-four French scenes but requires no more than nine different settings, all of them interiors except for a street and a courtyard and one short scene set in a 'Terrible wilderness'. His 'bourgeois tragedy', *Kabale und Liebe* (*Intrigue and Love*) of the following year contains thirty-seven French scenes but is played in only four different settings, all of them interior. Even on the broader canvas of his later historical tragedies Schiller learnt the need for discipline in the demands he made on the theatre. Thus in *Mary Stuart* (1800) each of the first three acts has its own setting, while the two final acts change location only once each.

Returning to *The Robbers*, the scene of the dying Moor is significant in that it contains music. Schiller's sense of theatricality often encouraged him to introduce music into his pieces. Only his more austere historical pieces (like *Mary Stuart*) and his choral tragedy *Die Braut von Messina (The Bride of Messina*, 1803) contain no music. In the present case it is Amalia who sings to the dying Moor while she accompanies herself on the clavier. Since there is no reference in the prompt-book to a clavier (which would have anyway been unsuitable for the Mannheim medieval setting) or to any other instrument on stage, we may assume that in fact at Mannheim Amalia was accompanied from the orchestra pit.

The stage was now transformed – no doubt after a lengthy wait – to the first exterior scene, the Bohemian Woods, which would have been a stock woodland setting of the Mannheim Theatre, with a grassy tussock downstage to provide an opportunity for a robber like Spiegelberg to sit. Schiller's stage directions provide for Karl Moor to enter on horseback, again reflecting a lack of concern with practicalities. The act ended with a flourish, the robber band proclaiming its defiance to all authority and running off with swords drawn to the sound of horns.

After the second interval the curtain revealed Amalia in the 'Satyr Garden', singing to the lute, possibly mimed on a dummy instrument, but almost certainly played by a member of the orchestra. It is likely that the garden was also created by using a backdrop halfway downstage, and possibly still retaining on each side the two front sliders from the wood scene, so as to expedite the next change to the scene 'By the Danube'. Certainly these 'wood' sliders were used for the Danube setting, an asymmetrical design with rocks projecting from the wing-pieces on stage right.

Once again the first three scenes of Schiller's fourth act were confined in Mannheim to the one setting, the picture gallery of Moor's castle (see Plates 2 and 3), but the loss of the different settings is here not so significant. In this protracted seventh scene of the Mannheim production Schiller added an encounter between Franz and the retainer Hermann, which revealed that the old Count was not in fact dead but imprisoned in a nearby tower. Clearly Dalberg had felt that the late revelation of Old Moor in the tower was melodramatic and unprepared for, and that Hermann's behaviour would be hard to explain without Franz's exhortations to secrecy, accompanied by appropriate threats.

The following scene is described in the prompt-book as 'Garden: flower-garden with five wing-pieces; at first wing-piece stage-right a bower with grassy bank'. This would appear then to be a different setting from the former 'Satyr Garden', although no doubt the same wing-pieces were used, and the 'grassy bank' was doubtless that used in the Danube scene. What is certain is that again the full depth of the stage was not used, since the prompt-book specifies the use of only five of the usual seven wing-pieces. Interestingly too there is no mention of the lute required by Schiller's stage direction, which provides for a desperate exit by Karl, who having taken Amalia's lute and sung two lines of her song, then 'flings the lute away and runs off'.

The Mannheim fifth act opened with music of a rather different nature: the robbers, camped in the open, sing a rowdy song about their exploits. It is a woodland scene with the ruined tower in which, it transpires, the old Count Moor is incarcerated, and no doubt it used the same wing-pieces as the earlier Bohemian Woods scene. A major difference here was a backdrop suggesting a night sky, and during the scene 'it gets gradually darker', a busy time for the stage-hands dousing the candles behind the wing-flats or reversing their reflectors to give the impression of twilight. Despite the play's notoriety, this is in fact the first scene in which there is a killing on stage, when the loyal robber Schweizer stabs the treacherous Spiegelberg. It is not clear how realistic such onstage killings would have been, but it is unlikely that much stage-blood was used, given the stiff reprimand that Dalberg had given to Boeck:[18]

A belly soaked in blood – I cannot imagine a more revolting image in the theatre. A good actor like you,

Herr Boeck, should never resort to such gimmicks to gain a cheap effect on the audience. For what effect can it have other than disgust and revulsion?

After this violent action Karl sits among the sleeping robbers and sings, and as midnight strikes in the distance, contemplates suicide. He is then disturbed by the arrival of the loyal servant Hermann who has come to bring food to the nearly demented old Count Moor in his tower. After a pathetic reconciliation between father and son, Karl resolves to wreak vengeance on his brother, and once again the robbers storm off.

This leads into the technically most difficult scene of the production, the sixth act at Mannheim, in which the robber band attack Moor's castle and set it on fire. Schiller's stage directions read in part: 'Tumult on the streets. Screams – crashes. . . . Stones and firebrands fly in. Panes of glass shatter. The castle burns. . . . The fire gets out of control.' Apart from a good range of off-stage sounds, the violence of the attack was suggested visually by using black wing-pieces with flames painted on to them. Initially, the stage was lit centrally by a candelabra and by the lamp carried by the servant Daniel. This subdued central lighting would have allowed the audience to discount the dark wing-flats, whose fire motif could then be brought into prominence by being illuminated more and more strongly as the scene progressed. It is unlikely that the shattering of windows was represented other than by sound, and it is hard to see how the flying firebrands noted in the prompt-book could have been used with any degree of safety. Possibly alert stage-hands dressed as servants were charged with the task of extinguishing them as soon as they landed on stage.

In Schiller's original text the scene ends with two more violent deaths: Franz strangles himself with the cord from his hat, and the robber Schweizer, cheated of his chance to capture the abominable Franz, improbably shoots himself. No doubt in response to Dalberg's desire to avoid the excessively melodramatic and in order to throw the death of Amalia into greater prominence, Schiller rewrote this episode to allow Schweizer to capture Franz and bring him to Karl in the next scene.

This final scene returns to the setting of Act 4 Scene 5 (the fifth act at Mannheim). The prompt-book indicates that there was no lighting at all at the sides of the stage. Some illumination would have come from the footlights, which were lowered during the scene, giving a suitably eerie effect to this emotionally charged dénouement. But the main lighting effect came from the moon, described by Schiller himself as follows: 'The moon moved slowly across the backdrop in a way that I have never seen in the theatre, and in accordance with its motion spread a natural and fearful light across the land-scape.'[19] Karl Moor, now identified in the text solely as Robber Moor, feels himself too contaminated by his crimes to reveal his identity to his father and is seen in poses of pain, passivity and self-doubt (cf. the stylized image of this in Plate 5). The mood suddenly changes with Karl's joy at the arrival in chains of Franz, who is flung into the tower where his father has been incarcerated (the prompt-book very thoughtfully has a reminder to place a sack of straw on the steps to break his fall). The mood then changes again as rapidly with the arrival of the deranged Amalia, who has been captured by other members of the robber-band. After the predictable death of the old Count Moor there follows the most shocking piece of action in the piece, the murder of Amalia by Karl. This must have been the kind of moment that sent the audience reeling to the doors. After this terrible emotional climax the ending of the play is curiously muted. Instead of the melodramatic suicide that one might have predicted, Karl exits quietly in search of a poor man who will benefit from the reward offered for the robber captain's arrest.

Clearly this production, which required twenty stage-hands in place of the usual dozen to effect its ten set changes, alter the lighting levels and produce off-stage sound, was an adventurous one in terms of the theatre practice of the day, and it was a particular honour for the young Schiller that Dalberg was prepared to invest so much time and effort on an untried play. The première must have made a theatrical impact with its multiple settings, often skilfully contrasted, its onstage violence and its exciting sixth act of the storming and burning of the castle. But this alone would hardly have sufficed to cause such an overwhelming reaction in the audience, one which makes the première of The Robbers one of the more memorable first nights in the history of theatre. 'The theatre resembled a madhouse' not because of the undoubted staging skills of Dalberg and his production team, but because of the alliance of Schiller's violent language with an acting style that, in the place of the rhetorical and bombastic style of the eighteenth century, revealed naked emotion in the actor's performance.

IFFLAND'S PERFORMANCE OF FRANZ MOOR

If this first explosion of Schiller's genius is to continue to have its volcanic effect in the German theatre, then let us seek to do it justice and not encourage actors to perform parts of it against the intentions of the author. . . . The violence and bigness, with which Schiller's play throws us into wonderment, are only bearable when the characters remain in balance.[20]

Goethe

Mannheim was to prove a valuable training ground not only for Schiller but for a young actor who was to become the star of the German stage, August Wilhelm Iffland. He had begun his career at the Court Theatre of Gotha in 1777 at the age of eighteen and transferred to Mannheim two years later. Entrusted with the role of Franz Moor, he seems to have discovered a means of presenting convincingly the power and emotional excess of the Mannheim style. Schiller himself was suitably impressed with the young man's contribution:[21]

Herr Iffland who played Franz . . . pleased me best of all. I confess that I had considered this role an impossibility, since it is not really suited for the stage, and I have never been so pleasantly proved wrong. In the final scenes Iffland showed himself a master. I can still hear him in his expressive pose, in an attitude of defiance against the loud affirmation of nature, uttering his evil 'No!' and then, as though touched by an invisible hand, collapse in a faint [V,1]. . . . You should have seen him praying on his knees, as the rooms of the castle burned all round him – If only Herr Iffland would not swallow his words and get carried away by his own declamation.

Indeed, it was Iffland's skill in performance that established the role of Franz Moor as one of the most sought-after in the German theatre, ousting Karl, the actual hero of the piece, as the dominant figure.

Iffland continued to play the role for many years after, 'modifying it to fit in with his personality' (Goethe), [22] and learning to temper the violence of the role with theatrical discipline. On seeing his guest-performance at Weimar in 1796 a critic commented on Iffland's ability to combine 'psychological and dramatic truth': 'In him the highest art becomes in every way living nature. . . . Everyone listened to him with fresh enjoyment and honoured an artist who always remains faithful to nature without ever losing sight of himself or his art.'[23] Attending the same performance was the critic Carl August Böttiger. Although, as Johann Manso observed, it was impossible to set down in writing the quality of Iffland's performance ('For anyone who has seen Iffland, [Böttiger's] book must seem like the worst kind of empty waffle'[24]), and although fourteen years separate Iffland's creation of the role from his guest-performance in Weimar, Böttiger's account still remains the best evidence of the great actor's talent:[25]

The true artist . . . rejects the help of caricature when he can succeed through inner strength. For this reason Iffland had thoughtfully refrained from making himself uglier with costume or make-up. Other actors illustrate the words of the author: 'Why did Nature force me to bear this burden of ugliness?', by squinting or by appearing in a Judas costume with red hair and bushy eyebrows. The author himself implies that Franz Moor should be deformed by a hunchback. . . . But Iffland decided he could dispense completely with this superfluous sign of his ugliness.

The main characteristic of this monster is cowardly cunning. So his initial coldness is very fitting for his deceptive manner, and would seem out of place only if Iffland had not at several points allowed the passion to shine through that boils and rages within.

I wish to refer to the monologue at the beginning of the second act, where he appraises the Furies of the soul with which he intends to torture his father to death. Anyone who failed to recognize inner truth in this speech must consider twisted facial expressions and convulsively deformed gesturing to be the true expression of passion, and believe unnatural roaring or groaning to be the height of declamatory style. As though in a portrait, truthful down to its finest shading, we saw the terror in the violent twitching of his hands and in the thrown back posture of his body. . . . How fearful and yet how revealing of the unfathomable evil of this villain was the winsome smile with which he consecrates the beneficent Graces, past and future, to become the executioners and helpmates of his plan, and how convincingly he delivers the demonic shout of joy: 'Triumph! Triumph! The plan is forged!', as the monster leaves the stage. A lesser actor might have felt the need to bellow this song of triumph and would have been all the more assured of applause, since the average audience responds with wilder or more restrained applause in direct proportion to a greater or lesser shattering of their ear-drums. But a cunning, deceitful villain never jubilates so loudly; for even the walls have ears. Iffland delivered this ending with firm self-assurance without any trace of screaming ecstasy.

A moment in Iffland's performance that I found just as distinguished and true came during the report which the disguised Hermann gives to Old Moor about the death of his beloved Karl. Franz leans on the back of the chair on which his old father sits and, with murderous gestures and a wild glint in his eyes, secretly enjoys the misery which his charade has cast over his father and Amalia. Then he waits with head thrust forward and bulging eyes to have the sensuous thrill of catching on Amalia's face every trace of the pain that is tearing the grieving fiancée apart. . . . Even the coldest member of the audience must have felt an involuntary shock of horror.

I have very little to say about the scene in which Franz is beset with despair and plagued by . . . conscience before he is captured by the robbers.

The author, whose imagination is so full of misty figures and gigantic shapes, added several lines after the words: 'Is there anyone who sits in Judgment above the stars? No! No!'. But this is pure nonsense if the actor has done justice to what has gone before. Iffland omitted

Plate 6 Iffland as Franz Moor: 'Is there anyone who sits in Judgment above the stars?' (V,1).

everything up to the words: 'And yet . . . if there were someone?' But what devastating truth lay in what remained! His face was tilted upwards, his expression at first ardent, then staring, his body stretching upwards in a motionlessly rooted pose, his right hand reaching out in an attitude of defiance, his left pressed against his breast as though for protection [cf. Plate 6]. He cried out: 'Is there anyone who sits in Judgment above the stars?', then paused. A soft, fearful, terror-struck 'No!' A further pause. The feared thunderbolt does not strike him. So the blasphemous atheist becomes bolder. 'No!', he roars viciously for a second time, clenching his fist against heaven and audibly stamping his foot. Now he has destroyed the Being above the stars. But then he is suddenly seized by Hell itself. His hair stands on end, he stumbles forward on to his knees. A pause of total annihilation. A flash of lightning passes through the darkened soul, and the Divine Judge appears to him with his scales hung in the firmament. 'And yet . . . if there were someone!', he murmurs, the sound rattling up from the depths of his breast. 'If you were to be called to account! This very night!' What the most fiery imagination of the reader . . . only dimly sensed, was embodied by Iffland's acting in vivid performance.

What we see here in Iffland's performance is the fusion of emotional intensity with complex thinking, such as had been sought by the respondents to Dalberg's question about 'naturalness in acting', and it is just such a fusion that lies at the centre of Schiller's thinking about the nature of theatre itself.

CONCLUSION: SOME IDEAS OF SCHILLER ON THE THEATRE

On 26 June 1784 Schiller read a paper to the *Deutsche Gesellschaft* in Mannheim, which he later published under the title 'Die Schaubühne als eine moralische Anstalt betrachtet' ('The theatre regarded as a moral institution'). His main thesis is that the theatre fulfils a special function in society by uniquely combining the aesthetic pleasures of the senses with the moral concerns of reason: 'the stage . . . offers an endless vista to the spirit in its thirst for activity, gives nourishment without excess to the soul of all, and combines the education of the intellect and of the heart with the noblest entertainment.'[26] The theatre does not merely state moral truths; it embodies them and makes them a subject for our active contemplation:[27]

> The theatre is the communal channel through which the light of wisdom pours down from the better, thinking part of the populace to spread in gentler rays through the whole state. More correct ideas, purer principles, nobler feelings flow from here through the veins of the people.

Setting aside the painful elitism, we see Schiller here following in Lessing's footsteps in according to the hitherto spurned art of the theatre a high moral function, and asserting, in an even more polemic statement than anything in Lessing, that the theatre might be the source of Germany's nationhood: 'If we lived to have a national theatre, then we should also become one nation'.[28] After Bismarck and Hitler we can only smile at such naivety, but it stands as a testimony to the changed status of the theatre in Germany by the end of the eighteenth century.

Unfortunately, it became only too clear to Schiller that, apart from the satirical comedies of writers like Molière, the theatre does not contain clear moral statements. Indeed, in tragedies such as *Richard III* and *Macbeth* we are invited to empathize and even admire heroes who fly in the face of morality. In a later essay, 'Über das Pathetische' ('On the representation of suffering', 1793), Schiller acknowledges this problem:[29]

> Let us take the example of the self-immolation of Peregrinus Proteus at Olympia. Judged morally, I cannot applaud this action, since I recognize that it is motivated by an impulse which rejects the *duty* of self-preservation. Judged aesthetically, I am pleased by this action and I am pleased by it because it witnesses to a strength of will which is able to resist the strongest of all instincts, the *instinct* of self-preservation.

Thus our enjoyment of the a-moral tragic hero results from our affirmation of the freedom of the human spirit: the hero demonstrates the autonomy of the human will, and while this may not serve a moral purpose, in a deeper sense it is morally purposive, because the energy displayed by the tragic figure reveals to us the ability to resist the purely physical side of our being.

Now Iffland's acting contained within it something of this duality of experience and also strove to achieve some sort of a synthesis. On the one hand he sought to reproduce the intensity and energy of extreme emotions and, on the other, he tried to represent these in a reflective manner. What is striking is that in Schiller's theoretical writings on drama he reflects elements of theatre practice that he encountered as a young man in Mannheim. It would be overstated to suggest that Schiller's aesthetic theories derived from his acquaintance with practical theatre work, but he must certainly have been influenced by it – proof again that the performance aspect of the works of a major writer such as Schiller is of decisive importance.

2

GOETHE AT WEIMAR

Iphigenia on Tauris

It is a ridiculous prejudice, cried [Wilhelm], for people to decry the [acting] profession, when they have so much cause to respect them. If preachers are justifiably accounted the most honourable members of a state for proclaiming the word of God, then one can surely regard actors as honourable too; for they communicate the voice of nature to our hearts, they dare to plunge into the unyielding bosom of humankind with changing moods of joy, seriousness and pain, so as to purify sentiments that we only dimly feel and so as to call forth divine echoes of our love and devotion for one another. What place is more free from boredom than the theatre? Where else are people brought closer in brotherhood than when they hang on the appearance and words of an individual and are lifted up together to a higher plane? What are statues and paintings compared with the living flesh of my flesh, compared with this *alter ego*, which suffers and is joyful and directly touches every nerve within me?[1]

MISCONCEPTIONS

After the exciting theatrical breakthrough of the *Sturm und Drang*, Goethe's work in Weimar is bound to look like a theatrical cul-de-sac. Instead of anticipating the developments of the nineteenth century, his search for a style that would lift 'mankind . . . in brotherhood . . . to a higher plane' seems all too clearly to be a throwback to French neo-classicism.

This impression is not aided by the distorted descriptions of Goethe as Director of the Court Theatre at Weimar: one hears how he conducted rehearsals with a baton, insisting that the actors follow his beat while speaking verse; how he drew squares on the stage like a chessboard, requiring actors to move from square to square as the 'Master' dictated; or how he strait-jacketed his actors by making them follow a series of 'Rules', which ranged from the emptily formal to the patently absurd.

It all fits in neatly with the stereotype of Germany's greatest genius, who did not have the decency to die while still a young and passionate man, but who went on to become not only the acknowledged grand old man of German literature, but also an accomplished bureaucrat, a Privy Councillor at a rural court. Where his work in the theatre is taken into account, it would seem that this could hardly be much more than an extension of his official duties and must therefore have been handled with all the authoritarian pomposity and official dryness one might expect in such a situation. This kind of response to Goethe reminds one of a teacher grudgingly awarding the top grade to the brightest child in the class, while secretly finding the little bookworm a bit of a bore.

Whether motivated by envy or by genuine apprehension about the effect Goethe was having on the theatre of his day, such myths about his manner of working gained currency in his own lifetime. It is told how Eduard Genast, one of Goethe's most loyal actors, was greeted by the actor Ferdinand Esslair, with the words: 'Well, and is Herr von Goethe still playing chess with his actors?'.[2] Later, on the occasion of the Weimar Court Theatre's visit to Halle in 1808, a scurrilous pamphlet entitled 'The seed sown by Goethe'[3] was published by an actor called Karl Reinhold, who had reason enough to dislike the Weimar troupe, as he had been placed under house arrest by Goethe for boxing a fellow actor on the ears and who had been finally dismissed from Weimar for incompetence. The pamphlet contained a quite inaccurate summary of Goethe's 'Rules for actors', including, for example, the 'rule' that all tragic actors should have something of the cannibal in their facial expression. It also, somewhat more fairly and wittily, attacked the elevated style of the Weimar actors:[4]

A small movement of the facial muscles, as in children who are forced to drink rhubarb-juice, is just about permitted. For the rest total stillness is required, especially since the Greeks take their poison the way our ladies eat ice-cream.

After Reinhold there were others who were only too happy to trample on Goethe's grave. In his Naturalist play *Die Ratten* (*The Rats*, 1911) Gerhart Hauptmann devotes a scene to a parody of Goethe's supposed style of theatrical instruction: the director Hassenreuter requires his pupils to stand in predetermined chalk squares and beats out the metre with a letter-opener. One of the pupils, Spitta, speaks out against the dead formalism of this method and condemns Goethe's 'Rules for actors' as 'nothing but mummified nonsense'.[5]

More recently, in the recent BBC Television series *All the World's a Stage*, Ronald Harwood repeated the allegation that Goethe 'divided the stage into numbered squares, and he simply told the actors which square to go to, like wooden chess-men'.[6]

If the image of the elderly bureaucrat with baton and chalk directing the Court Theatre according to inflexible rules and the demands of neo-classical good taste is a distortion, wherein lies the truth? Goethe's actual contribution to the creation of a German theatre was fourfold.

First, in place of the haphazard process by which a text found its way, more or less recognizably, on to the stage, Goethe introduced to the German theatre commitment, discipline and seriousness. Individual flair, which had characterized most German acting in the latter half of the eighteenth century, gave way under Goethe to a much greater concern with the production itself and to a sense of responsibility towards the ensemble.

Though not particularly enthusiastic about the Weimar Court Theatre, Madame de Staël found herself able to comment favourably on the discipline of the company:[7]

> In Vienna the prompter gives almost all the actors every word of their role in advance, and I have seen him follow Othello from one wing to the other in order to feed him the lines he has to speak at the back of the stage where he kills Desdemona. The theatre at Weimar is infinitely better organized in every respect. The prince who rules there, a man of intellect and an enlightened connoisseur

of the arts, understands how to harmonize good taste and elegance with the boldness that allows new experiments.

Second, Goethe made it possible for verse drama to be performed on the German stage with intelligence and sensitivity. Outside Weimar Schiller's verse dramas often had to be 'translated' into prose before the actors could cope with them (as in Schröder's première of *Don Carlos* in Hamburg in 1787). The ability to speak verse well not only transcended regional speech differences – an essential prerequisite to the establishment of a national theatre – but also made it possible to perform the greatest tragedies in the German language, not only those of Goethe and Schiller themselves, but eventually also of Kleist, Grillparzer, Hebbel and the translations of Shakespeare by Tieck and Schlegel.

Third, while Goethe's major concern was with speech in the theatre, he was also very aware of visual effect on stage, achieved not so much through the use of conventional spectacle as by a painter's eye for careful composition. His avoidance of the commonplace and ugly, and his aesthetic awareness of theatrical groupings and movement were important forerunners of the Meiningen style which was to transform European theatre a century later.

Fourth, while it is undeniable that Goethe's own major works for the stage lack Schiller's more obvious theatricality, they are for that very reason particularly rewarding to analyse as pieces for performance. By distilling his yearnings, passion and anger in the strict form and rarefied atmosphere of *Torquato Tasso* and *Iphigenia on Tauris*, the young Goethe created a tension between content and form, which, as we shall see, yielded interesting theatrical results.

GOETHE AS THEATRE DIRECTOR[8]

Just think that the boring period of French taste had only just ended, that Shakespeare still seemed fresh, that Mozart's operas were new works and that Schiller's plays appeared here year after year directed by the author himself . . . . I can't deny, it was really something.[9]

Weimar would seem an unlikely place for the establishment of a cultural centre, one that would one day give its name to the first national democracy in Germany, the Weimar Republic. The capital ('not so much a small town as a large chateau', as Madame de Staël remarked) had at the end of the eighteenth century a population of some 7,000, and was a stable and in some ways idyllic little society.[10] Although there were, predictably, large differences between rich and poor, there was little extreme poverty (according to the 1786 census there were 102 paupers living off alms in Weimar itself – an insignificant number for those days). Like many similar small states in Germany, the Duchy with its population of under 100,000, was ruled over by a benevolent despot, in this case a young Duke by the name of Carl August.

It was he who invited Goethe to come to Weimar in 1775. Goethe was then twenty-six, while Carl August had only just attained his majority at the age of eighteen. At first the two men indulged in a series of wild escapades, and there were understandable murmurings about Goethe's appointment as Privy Councillor the following year. He however proved himself to be a conscientious servant of the state, and when eventually an official was sought to take over the running of the Court Theatre, Goethe's combination of creativity and administrative experience made him the ideal candidate.

There had been a long theatrical tradition in Weimar. Operas had been performed at the court from the end of the seventeenth century. Then, in 1756, a company of court actors was formed under Doebbelin, but it had to be disbanded two years later on the death of Duke Ernst August, Carl August's father. Ten years later, in 1768, at the instigation of the Dowager Duchess Anna Amalia, a new troupe was formed, this time under the direction of Heinrich Koch. When in 1771 Koch went to Berlin, he was replaced by the Seyler–Ekhof company who continued to perform much-loved short plays with music ('Singspiele') and also introduced the court and its bourgeois guests to more substantial fare, including plays by Lessing, Molière, Marivaux and Goldoni.

On 6 May 1774 the castle, and with it the theatre it contained, was burnt down. The Duchess escaped the flames in her nightdress, an excusable breach of court protocol, and Ekhof and Seyler were forced to seek employment elsewhere, which they found at the neighbouring court of Gotha.

Therefore, when Goethe arrived in Weimar on 7 November 1775, there was a theatrical tradition at the court but no theatre to pursue it in. The previous month a temporary stage had been constructed, which could be assembled in the ballroom of the master of the hunt, Anton Hauptmann, whenever the court wished to indulge its propensity for amateur theatricals. Predictably for someone who had been stage-struck since playing with a toy theatre as a child, Goethe could not restrain himself from participating in these enterprises, and took leading roles in plays such as Cumberland's *The West Indian* (1776, and again in 1778 with Ekhof) and his own *Geschwister* (*Brother and Sister*, 1776) and *Die Mitschuldigen* (*The Accomplices*, 1777). Although the performances were prepared with some care and, especially in the case of the musical offerings, a lot of time and money was invested, no really substantial work was produced until the performance of Goethe's own *Iphigenia on Tauris* in 1779.

Early in 1780 a new theatre with a permanent stage was built in the Redoutenhaus (or Stronghold) opposite the palace; this was to be the home of the Court Theatre until its destruction by fire in 1825. Despite the improved facilities of the new performance space, interest in the amateur theatre dwindled. This was due in part to the sudden death of the court carpenter, Mieding, recorded in a famous poem by Goethe. Mieding had constructed the stage, sets and special effects for most of the productions. But the major reason for the decline in enthusiasm was the increasing pressure of governmental duties on Goethe. A few more amateur productions were mounted, including a successful outdoor presentation of Goethe's *Die Fischerin* (*The Fisher-Maiden*) in July 1782, but the time had come to hand the theatre back to a professional company.

Unfortunately, good troupes were not so easily found as they had been a decade or two previously, and the forty-strong company that arrived at the end of 1783 was to prove a disappointment. The one merit that Joseph Bellomo's performers had was the range of their repertoire: in addition to the inevitable musical pieces, they offered the new bourgeois drama and *Ritterdramen*, Goethe's *Clavigo* and *Egmont*, Lessing's *Minna von Barnhelm* and *Emilia Galotti*, Schiller's *Robbers*, and the first productions of Shakespeare in Weimar

(*Hamlet, King Lear, Macbeth, A Midsummer Night's Dream, The Merchant of Venice, Julius Caesar* and *Othello* – all in various palatable adaptations). Given this range of work and the number of performances, seldom of the same piece twice (643 in their seven years at Weimar), it is small wonder that the quality left much to be desired. The news that Bellomo had accepted a new engagement in Graz in 1791 was therefore received with some relief in court circles.

After some fruitless attempts to replace Bellomo's company, it was decided to appoint Goethe as Theatre Director (*Intendant*), a post which he held, often unwillingly, until 1817. The task was never an easy one. First, there were the considerable pressures on his time from all his other activities. By now Goethe was, in addition to being Privy Councillor, the Director of the War Commission and of the Commission of Roads and Canals and the President of the Bureau of Finance. Meanwhile, he was not only engaged in a considerable amount of creative writing, but had also begun his researches into optics, geology, botany and comparative anatomy. Second, Goethe found himself having to maintain a balancing act between the demands of court taste, the need to make the theatre pay its way, and, not least, the responsibility of his own artistic judgement. It was the kind of problem that he dramatized in *Torquato Tasso*, his play about the court poet of Ferrara, and especially in his Prologue to *Faust*, in which the Theatre-Manager and the Poet argue about their differing views of theatre:[11]

> THEATRE-MANAGER
> Let's give the public what it wants,
> Since they're an easy-going lot.
> The stage is set, the curtain's hung,
> A party's what they hope they've got.
> They're out there with expectant eyes,
> Patiently waiting for some surprise . . .
> They are not used to what is best,
> But they have read so many texts.
> How can we make things fresh and new,
> And entertain with meaning too?
> Of course I like to see the crowds
> Thronging their way through narrow gate,

Or queuing up before it's four
To buy a ticket ere too late.
To get a seat they'd break a head
Like starving men with hunks of bread . . .
POET
Oh speak not of uncultured hordes
Whose very sight destroys our soul . . .
No, lead me rather to heavenly realms
For there alone a poet's whole . . .
External glitter'll never weather,
But truthfulness will live for ever.

Goethe's first task, then, was to satisfy the courtiers, one of
whom he had himself become, thanks to his unsought-after
ennoblement to 'von Goethe' in 1782. As in Bellomo's day,
performances were given three times a week, usually in the
late afternoon, throughout the winter months in Weimar and
less regularly in the summer resort of Lauchstädt. The theatre
received a court subsidy (initially of 1,098 Talers), in return for
which courtiers and their servants would be granted free
admission. Needless to say, court protocol was observed here
as carefully as anywhere in the Duchy: applause had to be
'orderly' (only *The Robbers* proved an exception, since the
courtiers did not attend, and the largely student audience
could give free rein to their enthusiasm). If the Duke were
present, the audience had to wait for him to clap before they
were permitted to contribute their own applause. Laughter,
too, was subject to ducal approval. The story is told of one
ageing lady of the court who awoke from her post-prandial
doze to hear the Duke chuckling over some remark that had
been whispered to him. Eager to show willing, she burst into
appreciative laughter and clapping, only to discover that the
object of her attention was a bemused stage-hand involved in
changing the set. On one occasion, when the audience was
moved to hilarity by Schlegel's heavy-handed adaptation of
Euripides' *Ion*, Goethe leapt to his feet, banged his stick and
commanded the audience not to laugh. Even more draconian
were the measures taken against a court official who hissed at
the première of Kleist's *Der zerbrochene Krug (The Broken Jug)* in
1808: he was immediately placed under house arrest for his ill-
mannered behaviour.

Plate 7   The theatre after its renovation by Thouret in 1798.

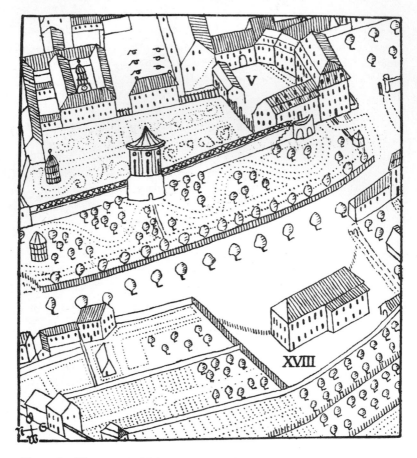

Figure 3   The town of Weimar (XVIII is the theatre, V is the palace).

It is clear that in such a context a certain decorum had to be preserved on the stage as well as in the auditorium. In both respects Versailles still set the tone. So it is little wonder that *Othello*, for example, was performed with a happy ending (8 June 1805), and it is clear that, inasmuch as *Iphigenia* was intended for a Weimar audience, it had to avoid a violent outcome. Indeed, at one time Goethe sought to introduce a men-only evening once a week, so that he might at last present plays with erotic or violent incidents without causing offence.

Since the Weimar theatre could accommodate some 500 to 800 (the exact capacity is difficult to establish, as there was standing room and bench seating), the court itself could hardly fill the theatre three times a week. It was the rule, therefore, to admit a paying public, which consisted in part of the local bourgeoisie and foreign visitors and also, especially on Saturday nights, of students from the neighbouring university of Jena. Apart from the occasionally disruptive behaviour of the students, one of whose preferred pastimes was to throw cherry stones at the actors, the audience at Weimar was genteel and peculiarly consistent, given that virtually every educated citizen must have been a theatre-goer. With such a predictable and homogeneous public, Goethe could embark on a process of long-term education towards higher theatrical standards.

The theatre which Goethe inherited was within easy walking distance of the main court buildings (see Figure 3). In 1798 he arranged for the architect Thouret to renovate extensively the Redoutenhaus theatre of 1780. The 'new' theatre was a long, elegant structure, some 50 metres long, with three separate entrances in its facade: for the actors, for the bourgeoisie and for the nobility (see Plate 7). The 1798 reconstruction reduced the depth of the stage by over 2½ metres, but created a much better designed and more congenial auditorium (see Figures 4 and 5). Goethe described it as follows:[12]

> The design is tasteful; serious without being heavy, pompous or pretentious. Above arches painted like granite, which form an ellipse to enclose the stalls, can be seen a circle of doric columns, in front of and beneath which seats for the public are provided behind a bronze balustrade. The columns themselves give the impression of ancient yellow marble, the capitals are bronze, and the cornice above is in a kind of grey-green marble. Directly above the columns are arranged different masks, which portray stock characters according to ancient models, ranging from tragic dignity to comic distortion. Above and somewhat set back from this cornice is a gallery.

No pictorial record of the auditorium now exists, but one may gain some impression of its intimacy from the 1908 photograph of the sister-theatre in Lauchstädt (Plate 9), although here there was no gallery. A reconstruction by Alfred Pretzsch is seen in Figure 6. From this one may observe the distinctly hierarchical nature of the seating. The cheapest seats, those in the gallery,

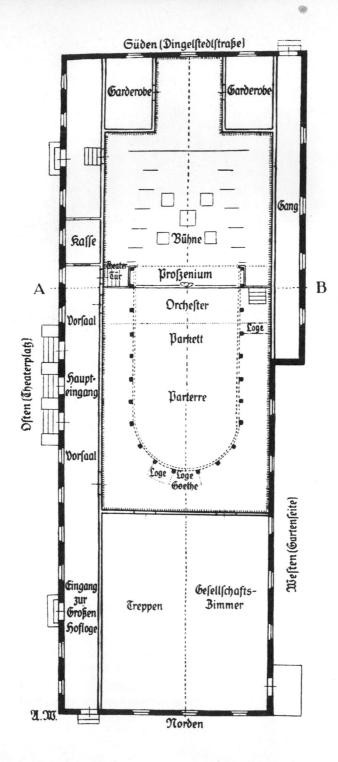

Süden (Dingelftedlftraße)

Garderobe   Garderobe

Gang

Kaffe

Bühne

Theater-
Tür

Proßzenium

A - B

Orchefter

Vorfaal

Loge

Parkett

Haupt-
eingang

Parterre

Vorfaal

Loge   Loge
Goethe

Offen (Theaterplaß)

Weften (Gartenfeite)

Eingang
zur
Großen
Hofloge

Treppen

Gefellfchafts-
zimmer

A.W.

Norden

Figure 4 Ground-plan of the Weimar Court Theatre. Note the sliders and traps on the stage.

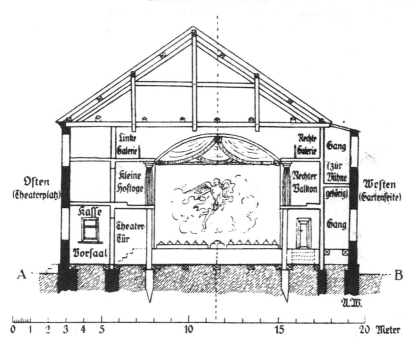

Figure 5 Cross-section of the Weimar Court Theatre.

cost three groschen and would have been occupied by the
students and poorer bourgeoisie, sometimes even by peasants.
The stalls with their benches covered in red cloth cost eight
groschen and were filled with the more prosperous bourgeoisie.
It was here that the more serious theatre-goer would sit, away
from both the rowdiness of the gallery and the formality of the
court. At the back and sides of the stalls there was also
standing-room underneath the arches, when the theatre was
especially full. The balcony was the level on which the Duke
and his court sat, and only the most wealthy would occupy the
boxes to left and right of the court, at twelve groschen a head.
Because the division between boxes was no higher than the
balustrade, they afforded no privacy, and the sight-lines were
appalling; no matter, so long as one could be seen alongside
the court. The Duke himself, predictably, had the one good
seat in the house, from which the perspective scenery would
look moderately convincing and from which one was not
obliged to look into the wings. Beside him in his box would sit

Figure 6 Reconstruction of the interior of the Weimar Court Theatre

his closest associates, including the *Herr Intendant*, Goethe himself. An impression of how imposing the ducal box must have seemed can be gained from the photograph of the Weimar Court Theatre after its rebuilding in 1825 (Plate 8). The stage was a reasonable size for a court theatre of the day, measuring 11.6 metres wide by 9.2 metres deep, with the proscenium opening just over 7 metres wide by 6.5 high. The stage, which was gently raked, was shut off at the back by a backcloth 7.9 metres by 5.9 metres, which, owing to the lack of flying space, had to be taken up on to a roller. Down either side of the stage were five sliders, into which wing-pieces on trucks could be winched to effect a change of scene. As can be seen from Weichberger's ground-plan (Figure 4), there were also five generous-sized traps in the stage. The 1908 photograph of the Lauchstädt Theatre (Plate 10) shows the kind of view of the Weimar stage that would be enjoyed by someone seated on the balcony to the left of the ducal box. The front-curtain at Weimar was painted by the architect Thouret and represented the Muse of Poetry holding in each hand the masks of Comedy and Tragedy (see Figure 5).

Lighting in the auditorium was achieved primarily by a large central chandelier, which of course remained lit throughout the performance but could be drawn up into the dome to lower the intensity of light. The sources of illumination on stage were standard: a row of footlights together with sets of lights fixed behind the wing-pieces. An innovation in the 1798 theatre was the replacement of the smoky and dim tallow-candles with so-called Argand lamps. These lamps, which had been invented by Argand fifteen years previously, introduced the basic principle of the paraffin lamp, in which the glass chimney allows the smoke to be burnt by the flames. They were not only much cleaner but also brighter than candles. Writing in 1810, Langhans claimed that with these lamps even the largest stages could be 'agreeably illuminated right to the centre'.[13] Since the stage at Weimar was only a little more than half the width of the largest stage in Germany, the Argand lamps must have made the stage seem brilliantly lit for the period.

If there was little about the theatre's architecture and equipment that was distinguished, there was initially even less to make it remarkable with regard to its repertoire. When Goethe re-opened the theatre on 7 May 1791 after the

Plate 8   The auditorium after the rebuilding in 1825.

departure of Bellomo, it was with a performance of a popular melodrama, Iffland's *Die Jäger (The Huntsmen)*. This was to set the tone for much of the programme of the subsequent years. In fact, in the twenty-six years of his directorship, the Court Theatre produced 601 different pieces, of which no less than a fifth were by Iffland or Kotzebue. They could be categorized as follows: 249 comedies, 123 'Schauspiele' (serious plays with a happy outcome), 104 operas, 31 'Singspiele', 17 farces, and only 77 tragedies. Indeed, it was really only after the première of Schiller's *Wallensteins Lager (Wallenstein's Camp)*, with which the new theatre opened on 12 October 1798, that Weimar began to develop a repertoire somewhat more adventurous than that to be found in any other German theatre of the day. In a letter to Georg Sartorius, Professor of Politics in Göttingen, on 4 February 1811 Goethe tried to justify the undemanding nature of much of his repertoire:[14]

> In the theatre everything . . . depends on a fresh and immediate effect. People do not want to reflect, think or make an effort; they want to respond and enjoy themselves. That is why lesser pieces are often more successful than better ones – and quite rightly too.

From this it is clear that Goethe thought in terms of the literary worth of his programme ('lesser', 'better'), as opposed to what was actually successful in the theatre. And success of course meant what was well received by the Weimar audience. By this token he could also utter the absurd assertion that Shakespeare 'does not write for the theatre, he never considered the stage, it was too confining for his great genius'.[15] Indeed, the theatre that Goethe knew was not one that Shakespeare wrote for, and no doubt Goethe considered his own plays in some respects almost too good for the stage. Certainly, he showed great reticence about performing his own works, only grudgingly and after some delay allowing his *Iphigenia* and *Tasso* to be produced. Until its Weimar première in 1829, from which Goethe was significantly absent, *Faust Part One* had been given only a private reading by Goethe; and of the 2,618 performances of the theatre under his directorship, only 185, or 7 per cent, were of his own plays. Clearly, however, he hoped – and his successful introduction of Schiller's tragedies helped to prove it – that he would be able to educate the public to

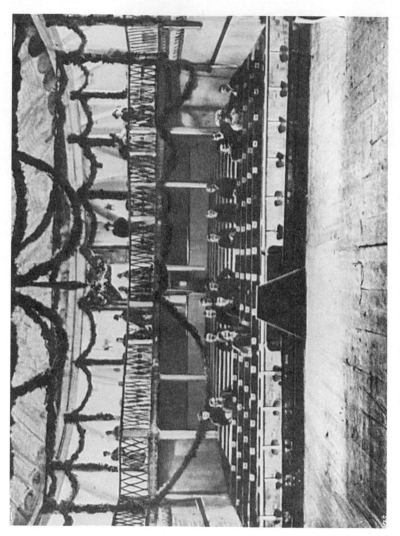

Plate 9 The auditorium at Lauchstädt in 1908.

Plate 10 View of the stage at Lauchstädt from the balcony.

appreciate more demanding works on stage: 'Our theatre is still in a state of becoming.'[16]

Goethe's major contribution to the development of the German theatre lay less in the externals of theatre design and choice of play than in his new approach to working with actors. When Bellomo left, Goethe engaged nine of Bellomo's former troupe and gathered other actors together from theatres as far apart as Hanover and Prague, until his new ensemble totalled eleven men, nine women and five children, none of them with a particularly strong reputation.

The leading Weimar actors received eight to nine Talers a week, a not ungenerous provision, since according to Genast[17] he paid only one and a half Talers a week for lodging, breakfast, lunch and services. As Privy Councillor Goethe himself had received an initial salary of only fifteen Talers a week. By 1820 their position had improved even further: five of the actors were receiving as much as or more than the Privy

Councillors, the Mayor or the Duke's personal surgeon.[18]

One of the actors, Franz Joseph Fischer, was appointed *Regisseur*, a post similar to that of stage-manager in the British theatre of the period, i.e. the person responsible for the organization and supervision of rehearsals, including entrances and exits and basic moves. Later the *Regisseur* was replaced by a rotating system, whereby actors would take it in turns on a weekly basis to conduct rehearsals (*Wöchner*). After 1793 the company was slimmed down to an average of fifteen (ten men and five women), and the quality began steadily to improve.

As it transpired, the most unfortunate company decision Goethe made was the engagement of Karoline Jagemann (see Plate 11). She was the daughter of the court librarian who had begun a successful acting career under Iffland in Mannheim and made her stage début in Weimar on 18 February 1797. Both beautiful and talented, she not only captivated the audience but also won the heart of the Duke. She became his mistress and was eventually ennobled as Frau von Heygendorf. It was not an easy situation for Goethe, especially as she repeatedly used her influence in intrigues against him. Finally, it was her insistence that a French poodle should perform on the Weimar stage that contributed to Goethe's decision to retire from the theatre in 1817.[19] Goethe was, however, fair in his assessment of Karoline Jagemann's abilities. To Eckermann he said:[20]

> I may have had some influence on her, but she was never really one of my pupils. It was as though she was born for the stage and was in every way as confident and assured, as adept and as perfect as a duck in water. She had no need of my instruction, she instinctively did the right thing, perhaps without knowing it herself.

But if the wilful and talented Jagemann exploited her position as the prima donna, most of the Weimar actors benefited greatly from belonging to a coherent ensemble under the firm direction of an efficient administrator and a creative artist. Two factors were particularly helpful. First, the Weimar Court Theatre had abandoned *Rollenfächer*, the type-casting of actors. While certain actors were naturally better suited to certain parts, Goethe made a habit of extending an actor's range by casting her or him against type:[21]

Plate 11 Karoline Jagemann.

If [an actor] seemed to me to have a rather too fiery nature, I cast him in phlegmatic roles; if he seemed too quiet and slow I gave him fiery, lively characters, so that he would learn to deny himself and enter into the spirit of a stranger.

73

Second, Goethe fostered an ensemble spirit in the company. Kotzebue, who was otherwise grudging in his respect for Goethe, wrote: 'Here it is not a matter of everyone for himself and God for us all; here everyone stands first for the company and last for himself; here no-one pushes himself forward to shine on his own.'[22] One way of maintaining this ensemble feeling was through Goethe's insistence that all actors had to take a walk-on part if the show demanded it. As he once said, anticipating Stanislavsky's oft-quoted remark that 'there are no small parts, only small actors': 'There are really no such things as minor roles; they are all essential elements in the whole.'[23] Indeed, in 1796, the leading actor Anton Genast had to be reprimanded for refusing to accept a walk-on part, and Paragraph 3 of the 'Theatre Regulations', drawn up in 1808, read: 'Anyone who refuses to play an extra on the pretext of an undocumented illness or with the excuse that he or she already has a role in that play or opera shall pay one taler.'[24]

Such disciplining of actors was not exceptional for the period but seemed to have been enforced with particular rigour in Weimar. The restrictions on actors extended even to their private lives. When Johann Friedrich Wilhelm Deny, who played Arcas in the 1802 production of *Iphigenia*, sought permission to marry in 1809, the request was initially refused by Goethe on the grounds that married actors made extra financial demands on the theatre and – in a disconcerting blend of prurience and high moral tone – warned against the tarnished image of an actor known to be no longer a virgin:[25]

> The audience seeks not only moral and aesthetic enjoyment but also sensual pleasure. An untouched maiden or a pure youth in suitable roles arouse quite different emotions, and one's heart and mind respond to their performance quite differently from that of persons about whom the opposite is known.

In fact, by insisting on the very need to preserve the moral conduct of the actors, the Duke obliged Goethe to agree to the marriage. After seeking certain assurances, for example that Deny's wife would not seek to act in the company, Goethe finally consented.

Other matters of discipline were more obviously pertinent to the actual work of the theatre. Various regulations and admonitions were issued to the effect that actors should learn their lines before going on stage, and that they should not invent new lines when they got there, whether for comic effect or to bridge the gaps in their memory. At a time when any given actor might well be rehearsing three new roles a week, such reminders were unfortunately necessary. Kleist relates an anecdote about the theatre management in Königsberg which had issued strict warnings against the actor Unzelmann's tendency to improvise. On one occasion he was on stage with a horse, which defecated loudly in the middle of a scene. 'Unzelmann interrupted his speech, turned abruptly to the horse and said: "Hasn't the Director warned you not to improvise?"'.[26]

Rehearsals were now also to be taken seriously. The young Gotthardi attended rehearsals at Weimar and was impressed by the discipline and concentration of the actors. At most theatres of the day the actors wore their outer garments during rehearsal and fiddled with canes and parasols: 'They all imagined they had done enough if they reeled off their lines in a monotone like a schoolboy reciting his homework.'[27] By contrast, the Weimar actors disencumbered themselves of their street paraphernalia, were not permitted to wander aimlessly about the stage and in fact worked on the text 'as though they were in front of an audience'.[28]

Rehearsals normally began in Goethe's own accommodation with a read-through. Anton Genast described the formality of such occasions in his diary.[29] Goethe would sit at the head of the table and begin proceedings by rapping with his key. At this stage no roles were allocated, and the whole play was read aloud by the actors in turn, with Goethe controlling the change of reader and pace of delivery with the tapping of his key. Dull as this procedure may seem, it did acquaint the cast with the play as a whole, so that before actors began to think in terms of their individual parts, they were forced to consider the overall structure of the piece – precisely the recommendation that Brecht was to make to his actors about a century and a half later. The second read-through was with allocated roles but still concentrated on the basic rhythm of the play. At the third read-through the parts were read in character with corrections and recommendations by the director:[30]

In the read-throughs actors learn to avoid exaggeration and errors in their roles. . . . Read-throughs are indispensable for most actors, so that they can work through the spirit of their parts and hear the soul speaking instead of just lines memorized by rote; . . . faults can be noted and the inartistic eradicated.

After the actors had been given time to learn their parts, there would follow a blocking rehearsal, when entrances, exits, basic moves and groupings would be agreed. There would then be one or two further rehearsals on stage and a final dress rehearsal, when the actors would normally for the first time work on the set and in costume. Most plays, therefore, reached performance with less than twenty hours of rehearsal time, but this might still be regarded as a generous allocation for the period. It was also common practice for further individual rehearsals to be arranged for actors having difficulties with their roles. Moreover, for more important plays, such as Schiller's tragedies, weeks and even months were devoted to group discussion of the piece before rehearsals began – the kind of luxury possible only in the subsidized world of the court theatre. The most notable instance of this was the eight years' preparation that preceded the production of Calderon's *The Constant Prince* in 1811.

Goethe's work with actors ranged from the totally practical to the application of a sophisticated aesthetic. Under the former heading was his insistence on clear audibility. This was sometimes a matter of correcting lazy habits and merely required a reprimand from Goethe, as in his admonition to Friedrich Haide, who played the Duke of Orange in Goethe's *Egmont*: 'I really would like to hear what I wrote thirty years ago!'.[31] As a last resort, actual dismissal had to be threatened, as in the case of Graff, who was later to play Thoas in *Iphigenia on Tauris* and who was once rebuked by Goethe with the observation that 'all important and passionate speeches . . . had remained totally unintelligible'.[32] This concern with proper vocal projection forms the starting-point of Goethe's 'Rules for actors', the first two sections dealing exclusively with this aspect of the performer's craft.

The contentious and often misrepresented ninety-one 'Rules for actors'[33] resulted from the actor Unzelmann's encouraging

Goethe to set up an acting school for his performers. In an attempt to establish certain 'Euclidean elements' of acting, especially for work on a production of *Julius Caesar*, Goethe compiled a set of 'rules' which he dictated in 1803 to Pius Alexander Wolff and Karl Grüner, and which were eventually published by Eckermann in 1824.[34]

The first two rules concern the elimination of dialect characteristics, and the following fifteen deal with accurate pronunciation. In Goethe's insistence on a clear, dialect-free use of language, one can see the beginnings of *Bühnensprache* (stage-language) which to this day characterizes the delivery of the German actor.

A further section considers appropriateness of dress. Since, as in other theatres, costuming was left almost entirely to the individual actor who had to provide his or her own costume, there were, even in terms of contemporary expectations, gross improbabilities in appearance. Thus it was not uncommon for a simple shepherdess to make her entrance in full court finery with a large hat tilted fashionably well down on the left side of her head, thereby not only stretching the audience's credibility about her rustic origins but also effectively blocking her face from view whenever she looked to the right.[35]

Another of the Weimar theatre papers deals with a trivial point but is symptomatic of Goethe's whole understanding of the stage. In a memorandum dated 9 December 1796 he protested that one of the actors in a comic operetta had smoked a pipe on stage: 'Landau should not actually smoke tobacco. I wish actors would convince themselves that certain kinds of reality are offensive in the theatre.'[36]

This was not merely a question of good taste; it was much more a matter of the intrusion of 'reality' into the 'truth' of the theatre, as in Chekhov's famous complaint about Stanislavsky's naturalistic sound-effects that they were like sticking a real nose through a portrait. The relationship between the real world and its representation in art was a matter of fundamental importance to German writers of the eighteenth century, steeped as they were in a tradition of idealistic philosophy. For Goethe, straightforward imitation could never be enough: he believed, like Plato, that since the so-called 'real' world was anyway only a pale reflection of the true reality beyond (what Kant was to call the *Ding an sich*), it was pointless and misleading for art to attempt to represent what was itself only a representation. It was the function of art to reveal the *Urbild*, the essential image lying beneath surface reality. So: no pipe-smoke.

In an article written in 1798 for his own periodical, *Propyläen*, Goethe confronted the relationship between what he here called 'verisimilitude' and 'truth'. The article purports to be a discussion between a member of the audience, who complains about a performance he has attended in which there were painted human figures on stage, and an apologist for the theatre, who defends this element of the design. The theatre-goer insists that everything he sees in the theatre should seem real:[37]

> If this were not what I expect, why does the set-painter go to so much trouble to draw every line exactly according to the rules of perspective and to paint every object as perfectly as possible? Why do research into costume? Why spend so much money striving after accuracy to transport me to the correct period? Why lavish the highest praise on the actor who expresses emotions most truthfully, who in speech, posture and gestures most closely approaches the truth, who deceives me so well that I imagine I am no longer seeing an imitation but the thing itself?

But the apologist counters by reference to opera:

> But when the good people up there greet each other and pay their compliments in song, when they sing aloud the contents of love-letters which they receive, when they give voice in song to their love, their hatred and to all their passions, when they sing fighting and sing dying, can you claim that the whole performance or even a part of it seems true, that it even has the semblance of truth?

The spectator concedes:

> If the opera is good, it does indeed create its own world in which everything proceeds according to certain laws, a world which must be judged by its own laws and which must be responded to according to its own characteristics.
> APOLOGIST. Does it not follow therefore that truth in art

and truth in nature are totally different, and that the artist should never strive to give his creation the appearance of reality? . . .

SPECTATOR. Then be so good as to explain why a perfect work of art appears to me as real?

APOLOGIST. Because it is in harmony with your higher being, because it is above nature [*übernatürlich*] but not outside nature [*außernatürlich*]. A perfect work of art is a work of the human spirit, and in this sense is also a work of nature. But by bringing together disparate objects in harmony and by embracing even the meanest object in its full significance and dignity, it stands above nature. . . . The true lover of art sees not only the truth of what is imitated but also the excellence of the selection, the brilliance of the composition and recognizes that the little world of art stands above the real world of nature.

The argument is well summed up in Goethe's observation to Eckermann about Claude Lorrain's paintings: 'The pictures possess great truth but not a trace of reality.'[38]

This aesthetic had its parallels with the contemporaneous *beau idéal* school of painting in England, which numbered Barry, Opie, Fuseli and, above all, Sir Joshua Reynolds, amongst its exponents. In his third 'Discourse on art' of 1770 Reynolds argued that it was the wish of the 'genuine painter' that 'instead of endeavouring to amuse mankind with the neatness of his imitations, he must endeavour to improve them with the grandeur of his ideas'. He should look beyond 'accidental deficiencies, excrescences, and deformities of things' and portray an 'abstract idea of their forms more perfect than any original'. 'This idea of the perfect state of nature, which the Artist calls the Ideal Beauty, is the great leading principle, by which works of genius are conducted.'[39]

It was this concept of Ideal Beauty that influenced John Philip Kemble in his approach to acting, and the same thinking characterized Goethe's attitude to theatre: 'First and foremost the actor must consider that he should not only imitate nature but should also present it in an idealized form, that in his performance he should unite the true with the beautiful.'[40] So reads Rule 35, and when Goethe uncharacteristically went backstage to compliment his actors on their performances in

Zacharias Werner's *Der vierundzwanzigste Februar (The Twenty-fourth of February)*, he enthused: 'Now we have arrived at the point I wanted you to reach; nature and art are wholly united.'[41]

It seems unlikely that there was any direct influence from either Kemble or the *beau idéal* movement. Goethe was certainly familiar with Fuseli's work (he had planned to write an article on him for his *Propyläen*), but the Swiss-born Fuseli impressed Goethe more with the wildness of his subjects and his exaggerated style than with any notion of elevated beauty.[42]

A more certain influence from the pictorial arts was that of William Hogarth, whose *Analysis of Beauty*, first published in 1753, had been translated into German and was known to Goethe. In this treatise, 'written with a view of fixing the fluctuating ideas of taste',[43] Hogarth attempts to define beauty, referring to concepts like fitness, variety, symmetry, simplicity, intricacy, proportion, etc. Most interesting for our purposes is the section on 'action', where he laments the lack of a systematic approach to action (and therefore to acting): 'Action is a sort of language which perhaps one time or other, may come to be taught by a kind of grammar-rules; but, at present, is only got by rote and imitation.'[44] For the individual actor Hogarth recommends 'daily practising movements with the hands and arms, as also with such other parts of the body as are capable of them. [This] will in a short time render the whole person graceful and easy at pleasure.'[45]

Interestingly, in considering the staging of scenes, Hogarth urges the pursuit of beauty and truthfulness independent of the immediate meaning of the text:[46]

> The actions of every scene ought to be as much as possible a compleat composition of well varied movements, considered as such abstractly, and apart from what may be merely relative to the sense of the words. Action consider'd with regard to assisting the authors [sic] meaning, by enforcing the sentiments or raising the passions, must be left entirely to the judgment of the performer. . . . What I would have understood by action, abstractedly and apart from its giving force to the meaning of words, may be better conceived by supposing a foreigner, who is a thorough master of all the effects of

action, at one of our theatres, but quite ignorant of the language of the play; it is evident his sentiments under such limitations, would chiefly arise from what he might distinguish by the lines of the movements belonging to each character.

These remarks not only anticipate Brecht's insistence on the importance of 'gest' and the semiotician's awareness of the significance of action on stage, but also suggested to Goethe a fundamental approach to the theatre.

In order to pursue truth rather than reality and beauty rather than literal meaning in the theatre, Goethe paid attention not only to precise and elegant verse-speaking but also to every element of the stage-picture. He was very aware of creating attractive groupings on stage:[47]

He always found it very disturbing if two actors or even three or four actors stood close together on one or other side of the stage or in front of the prompter's box, when the action did not require it. To avoid these empty spaces on stage he exactly determined the positions of the actors.

He recommended to actors that they might think of the stage as a chess-board and memorize their moves in terms of stepping from one square to another. To undisciplined actors outside Weimar this must have seemed like playing chess with the cast, but in fact the proposal was no more than a precise way of giving standard instructions by a director to an actor. What is more important is the way Goethe conceived of the stage as a picture, a word he frequently used when referring to positions on stage.[48] In accordance with Hogarth's advice, it was more important for actors to fill the space pleasingly (and one must remember that the stage was normally lit with one general wash) than for them to stand in realistic proximity to one another. For the same reason Goethe recommended that an actor who is being addressed should always take a step downstage of a speaking actor, so that the latter is turned more towards the audience – 'a rule', commented Anton Genast, 'which of course should be observed by every sensible actor who is more concerned with the whole than with his or her own ego.'[49]

The same concern with visual beauty extended to the actor's

use of gesture. In what to us seems pedantic obsession with detail, Goethe described ideal hand positions (see Plate 13):[50]

> Rule 48. The two middle fingers should always remain together, the thumb, index and little finger remain somewhat bent. In this way the hand is held in the proper position and can carry out all movements in their correct form.

Again, such a recommendation has to be considered in the context of the period, when actors were liable to fiddle with fans, handkerchiefs or other accessories, or gesture with heavy, ill-considered movements. Here, as with all his 'rules', Rule 90 has to be remembered: 'One should make all these technical and grammatical precepts one's own and keep on practising them until they become second nature. All stiffness must vanish, and the rule must become merely the hidden basis of living action.'[51] In order to achieve this quality of living action based on a firm discipline, actors had to begin by denying their own individuality. Wilhelm Meister, in Goethe's novel, learned from his mentor Serlo that someone who merely plays himself is not an actor; and in his essay, 'Weimarisches Hoftheater' ('Weimar Court Theatre') of 1802, Goethe enunciated one of the 'major principles' of his theatre: 'The actor must deny his personality and learn to transform it sufficiently to enable him in certain roles totally to conceal his individuality.'[52] The same point was made by Goethe when he remarked to Eckermann that the actor's craft 'demands a constant denial of the self and a constant self-surrender and existence in the mask of a stranger.'[53]

In his insistence that actors must suppress their individuality, Goethe turned his back decisively on the prevailing theatrical style of the day, which – whether in the so-called 'naturalist' school exemplified by Schröder in Hamburg or by the more extrovert actors at Mannheim – emphasized the individuality of the actor. By doing this he seemed to threaten what to many, both then and now, is the life-blood of the theatre – the unique personality of the actor.

But this denial of the self was a positive and not a negative process: as the seventy-seventh rule for actors states: 'It is . . . absolutely necessary that the actor be totally free of all habits, so that in performance there can be a complete assumption of the role and so that the actor's mind remains preoccupied solely with the assumed figure.'[54] This opening up of the self to total concentration on the theatrical task in hand is not so very far removed from the *via negativa* of Grotowski in our own time. Like Goethe before him, the Polish director begins with dismantling habits of thought and behaviour by subjecting the performer to a rigorous discipline. Clearly his work is much more intimate and personally challenging than anything Goethe might have undertaken, but the fundamental attitude is similar.

Goethe's ideas on theatre, though born of a coherent aesthetic, were not just philosophical abstractions; his concerns were altogether more immediate, namely with his own audience. Writing to Schiller about a performance he had seen in Leipzig in 1800, he complained:[55]

> It cannot go on like this: naturalism and sloppy, unconsidered behaviour in general and particular. Not a trace of grace or decorum. A lady from Vienna said very pertinently: the actors did not behave at all as though the audience were present. In the recitation and declamation of most of them there was no indication of any desire to be understood. There was no end of turning of backs or of speaking upstage.

Many of Goethe's rules were commonsense advice to respect the audience: the need for clear diction, the slightly upstage position of the speaking actor, the avoidance as far as possible of turning one's back on the audience. The attitude was quite simply stated in Rule 38: 'The actor must always consider that he is there for the sake of the audience.'[56]

By serving his audience in this way Goethe helped to preserve and promote a theatrical strain that was essential to the healthy development of German theatre. Without his contribution the pursuit of aural and visual beauty on stage might have been confined almost exclusively to opera and the dance. Spoken theatre might, for much longer at least, have failed to move beyond chivalric romances, domestic pieces and trivial comedies. Goethe's elevated style was a response to and a preparation for native German tragedy and for the establishment of Shakespeare as the best-loved playwright of Germany.

Goethe was no arrogant autocrat; his theatrical activity

proceeded instead from a deep sense of humility, of responsibility towards the needs of serious theatre. 'The artist belongs to the work, and not the work to the artist',[57] he once remarked to Riemer, and this was nowhere more true than in the theatre. Both director and actor were to subjugate their own creative imaginations to the needs of the play. His *Iphigenia on Tauris* provides a fine example of this process at work.

IPHIGENIA ON TAURIS IN PERFORMANCE

The play is not without difficulties. It is rich in inner life, but poor in external action. It is a matter of projecting this inner life outwards. It is full of effective elements which derive from the many different horrors that underlie the action. The printed word is of course only a pale reflection of the living inspiration I felt at the time of composition. But the actor must take us back to this first enthusiasm which fired the writer about his subject. We want to see powerful Greeks and heroes, the fresh sea-breezes blowing towards them, who, though frightened and haunted by all kinds of evil, give strong utterance to the promptings of their hearts. But we do not want actors with feeble emotions who recite their roles off the top of their heads, least of all actors who cannot even remember their lines. I must admit I have never succeeded in seeing a perfect production of *Iphigenia*.[58]

At first sight *Iphigenia on Tauris* would seem a singularly inappropriate work to demonstrate Goethe's understanding of theatre. A neo-classical piece with a cast of five, a single setting, no violent on-stage action, and written in iambic pentameters, it has understandably been perennially regarded as a piece of literature rather than as a text for performance. Nearly all critical discussions of the piece have disregarded the performance dimension of the work, despite Goethe's long involvement with theatre practice and despite his warning, uttered to Eckermann: 'A play on paper is nothing at all.'[59] Goethe firmly believed that a play, like a symphony, must be performed in order that its quality might emerge fully. The discussion that follows will therefore refrain from retreading the steps of a century and a half of critics, who have analysed thoroughly the dramatic structure, characterization, poetry and thought of *Iphigenia*, and will instead examine what is arguably Goethe's finest piece of dramatic writing as a piece for the stage. On the whole, the approach will be that of Hogarth's 'foreigner, who is . . . quite ignorant of the language of the play' and who is therefore forced to concentrate on visual and auditory signals which are largely independent of the meaning of the words.

The first version of the play, in prose, was written in six weeks (14 February to 28 March 1779), while Goethe was touring the country to conscript soldiers. Goethe had found the raw material for the piece in Euripides: the story of Orestes, who, pursued by the Furies for murdering his mother, seeks redemption by following Apollo's command that he should steal the statue of Artemis (or Diana) from the barbaric island of Tauris. On Tauris he encounters his long-lost sister, Iphigenia, now priestess of Diana, who is required to preside over the sacrifice of any Greek landing on Taurian shores. Fortunately, she recognizes her brother and, in Euripides' version, collaborates with Orestes in his theft of the statue of the goddess. Thanks to Athene's intervention they are able to sail back to Greece with the statue, and so lift the curse from the House of Tantalus.

Clearly, Goethe was dissatisfied with the original. In Euripides the central conflict is an external one: apart from some gentlemanly debate between Orestes and Pylades about who should undergo the sacrifice, the only conflict is between the barbaric Taurian custom of human sacrifice and, for the Greek audience, the legitimate desire of the three noble Greeks to escape with the statue by any means possible. Tricking a barbarian king was not a particularly edifying theme for a man of Goethe's sensibilities. In his version, therefore, the Taurian king Thoas becomes as noble and as central a figure as the Greeks. Having responded to Iphigenia's pleas to suspend the practice of human sacrifice, he threatens to reinstate it only in order to compel Iphigenia to accept his offer of marriage. The central conflict of Goethe's version is within Iphigenia herself: she is faced with the choice of participating in her brother's plan and so deceiving her erstwhile benefactor, Thoas, or of abandoning her brother to his fate and so destroying any hope of future redemption. Placing her faith in reason and human-

Plate 12   Corona Schröter.

ity, she finally resolves to reveal the truth to Thoas. There is
not even any need to steal the statue, since Orestes now
reinterprets Apollo's command to restore 'the sister' to Greece
as referring to Orestes' sister, Iphigenia. This interpretation is
more acceptable in German, since possessive pronouns are less
common than in English. It does not sound odd to speak of
'the sister', whereas English would prefer 'his' or 'your' sister,
which would of course remove the ambiguity of Apollo's

command. By this not wholly fortunate device, Goethe allows truth to triumph, replacing the mechanical return of an 'exiled' statue and the intervention of a goddess with the inner renewal of the restoration of humanity.

It is an undeniably Utopian resolution, one that Goethe himself admitted was 'devilishly humane'. Given that Thoas is prepared to use the threat of reintroducing human sacrifice to force Iphigenia to accept an unwanted marriage, there is no strong reason to suppose that he will respond so generously to her confession that she and Orestes had sought to deceive him. But it is clear that Goethe was himself at this time, under the discipline of his court duties and the calming influence of Frau von Stein, seeking to discover harmony and serenity and to avoid the tragic.[60] Given also the recurrent avoidance of tragic endings in contemporary adaptations of Shakespeare, it is unlikely that Goethe would have imagined that a piece with a violent and unhappy ending would succeed on the Weimar stage.

In his reworking of the Euripidean original Goethe was not unaware of the darker elements of the piece, however, (Orestes' crazed guilt after his matricide, the recognition of human suffering in 'The story of the Parcae', and Iphigenia's almost impossible choice), but he opted to contain these within a classical form that in many ways intensified rather than weakened their impact.

THE AMATEUR STAGING OF
IPHIGENIA ON TAURIS

The first performance of *Iphigenia on Tauris* took place in the ballroom of Hauptmann's home on 6 April 1779, just nine days after Goethe had finished writing the first version. Only two rehearsals are recorded in Goethe's diary, but probably more took place, since a fair amount of care was devoted to these amateur performances, and especially since *Iphigenia on Tauris* represented the only work of real literary quality to be staged at Weimar between 1775 and 1783.

Significantly, Goethe himself took the role of Orestes, and he entrusted the part of Iphigenia to Corona Schröter (see Plate 12), who had come to Weimar from Leipzig two and a half years previously, and whose talent Goethe admired greatly. Indeed, the composer of the incidental music for *Iphigenia*, Johann Friedrich Reichardt, asserted that Goethe had written the play 'for the noble Corona'.[61] In his poem commemorating the carpenter of the amateur theatre, 'On Mieding's death', Goethe wrote of her:[62]

> Es gönnten ihr die Musen jede Gunst,
> Und die Natur erschuf in ihr die Kunst.
> [The Muses granted her every favour,
> And Nature created Art within her.]

Von Knebel played Thoas, Seidler played Arcas, and Prince Constantin took the role of Pylades. The same cast performed again on 12 April, but when the play was revived for the summer season in Ettersburg on 12 July 1779, Duke Carl August himself took over the role of Pylades.

From the evidence collected by Gisela Sichardt,[63] a reasonable amount is known about the amateur première in 1779. An invoice of 1 April 1779 from the court painter Schumann shows that he repainted four pairs of wing-flats (almost certainly with a foliage design that curved inwards at the top to give an impression of the grove), he coloured the borders blue to suggest bright Mediterranean sky, and painted the proscenium arch green with a marble effect to reflect the classical quality of the piece. The front-curtain was decorated with a landscape to prepare the audience for the idyllic ambience of the piece before the play started. The back-cloth which carried the design of the temple was at least a quarter larger than was usual in the amateur theatre (101 square ells compared with the normal 70 to 80 square ells). This means that it must have been some two metres wider than usual, which suggests that it may have been hung curved rather than straight, an early version of the cyclorama. There is also the unexplained item of a red curtain, which might have been hung to the rear of the stage to represent the entrance to the temple.

The stage was, for the first time, covered in green baize, which would have rendered moves silent on the boards of this temporary stage. It is also almost certain that the statue of Diana was made specially for this performance, at a cost of four Talers.

The engraving by Facius (Plate 13) gives no more than an idealized impression of the stage-set, since the actors are seen

Plate 13 Corona Schröter as Iphigenia, Goethe as Orestes (1779).

within the setting rather than against the backdrop, but it is a good record of the ornateness of the décor and of Goethe's formal gesture with his left hand.

In it we may also observe the elaborate costumes worn by the performers. Goethe was always keen that costumes should make a strong statement. In a note to Merck about costumes on 18 March 1778 he wrote: 'Think of all the actors with physiognomic clarity to the point of caricature.'[64] As Orestes,

Goethe wore a brick-red tunic, grey-blue lorica with gold bars and leather skirt, a bright blue cloak, belt, gilt sword, and boots. Even this picture-book costume was outshone by the flowing robes of Corona Schröter as Iphigenia, which were made up from 50½ ells (28¼ metres) of white muslin for her veil, 34 ells (19 metres) of white linen for her dress, 11 ells (6 metres) of white taffeta for her cloak, and 21 ells (11¾ metres) of silk ribbon. Two helmets were also gilded for the performance, and were probably worn by Thoas and Arcas in the fifth act to indicate their preparedness for battle.

The brightness of the setting, the ornateness of the décor, the richness of the costumes and the powerful image of the armed king and his follower must have added a strong visual dimension to what might otherwise appear a visually rather barren piece.

Few details are recorded of the performance, although we have some indication of the acting style from contemporary accounts. For instance, Schiller wrote to Körner in 1788 of Goethe as a performer: 'He . . . holds himself stiffly and walks in the same way; his face is impassive, but his eyes are full of life and expression.'[65] Amalie Voigt-Ludecus, writing in the *Zeitung für die elegante Welt (Journal for the Elegant World)*, similarly spoke of his stiff movements despite the energy of his performance. It is quite likely that Goethe's own stiffness helped to determine his preference for the formal style of his actors at the Court Theatre. His one great asset, it seems, was his fine voice. As Friedrich Wilhelm Riemer wrote of him: 'Goethe had a beautiful voice. He explored its full range – from the softest nuance of feeling to a voice of thunder.'[66]

For Corona Schröter, on the other hand, there was unreserved praise. Johannes Falk said of her: 'The Junoesque quality of her presence, the majesty of her grace, stature and gestures, beside so many other rare qualities of gracefulness that combined within her, had made her more suited than many others to be a priestess of Diana.'[67] And Wieland, writing to Merck on 3 June 1778, spoke of the 'infinitely noble Greek elegance of her whole being',[68] while the *Zeitung für die elegante Welt* observed that 'She looked her best in Greek costume'.[69] The same journal spoke favourably of von Knebel, who had initially declined a part in the play: 'Herr von Knebel declaimed excellently with his fine organ, and was completely at home in

Plate 14 Sketch of the 1802 production with Friederike Vohs as Iphigenia.

roles that require dignity, like Thoas in *Iphigenia*.'[70]

Apart from one revival of the play for the Duchess's birthday on 30 January 1781, of which no further details are recorded, the prose version of *Iphigenia on Tauris* was never again staged in Weimar.

Partly prompted by Wieland, who, on hearing *Iphigenia* performed, imagined that it was already written in iambics, Goethe began in 1780 to rewrite the play in verse, but he was dissatisfied with the resulting free verse version, and the following year wrote it again in prose. Although some of the irregularities of this earlier free verse are still discernible in the final version (as in III, 2, 1281f), it was only after his famous

Italian journey that Goethe finally recast the work in blank verse, a project he completed in January 1787.

PROFESSIONAL PRODUCTIONS OF
IPHIGENIA ON TAURIS

The première of the blank-verse version of *Iphigenia* did not take place until 1800, although it had been available in print for over two years, and when it was finally performed, it was not at the Court Theatre of Weimar but at the Burgtheater in Vienna. Friederike Bethmann played the title-role in the production which opened on 7 January 1800 and again in Iffland's Berlin production of 27 December 1802. Friedrich Schulz wrote of her:[71]

> Bethmann . . . was the perfect embodiment of Goethe's Iphigenia, not just the angelically pure Iphigenia who brings about total reconciliation but also the Greek woman, who, when the need arises, displays her courage, determination and enthusiasm for the highest ideals. The Song of the Parcae, in the rhythm with which she spoke it, still pounds in my head.

Weimar did indeed see a performance of *Iphigenia in Tauris* in 1800, but it was the opera by Gluck, directed by Goethe, with Furies whose primitive costumes were based on Greek vase-paintings. Significantly, when Goethe's *Iphigenia on Tauris* was finally presented at Weimar on 15 May 1802 (see Plate 14), Schiller as director tried to insist that Furies should be introduced, especially into Orestes' 'mad scene' (III,2), but Goethe firmly rejected the proposal. It was a sound decision, since the crass physicalization of these creatures of darkness would have circumscribed the imaginative breadth of the piece.

Schiller, who had come to Weimar in 1796, had a far less formal relationship with his actors than Goethe had. For example, he was so delighted by the première of *Wallenstein* that he smuggled some bottles of champagne on to the stage and drank it with the actors in the interval after the third act. It was perhaps predictable that this première of *Iphigenia* did not receive the disciplined treatment that it requires. Certainly,

Plate 15 Friedrich Haide.

because of the difficulties Mme Vohs had with the title-role, the performance had to be postponed for over a week.

Friederike Vohs was a slightly built, sensitive actress, who was regarded by the temperamental Karoline Jagemann as her chief rival. There had already been some dispute over who should play the title-role in Schiller's *Mary Stuart* in 1800.

Sensibly, the role was given to Vohs, of whom it was said: 'She united charm, gentleness, and suffering with royal dignity and bearing.'[72] Fortunately, Jagemann was a great success as the coldly political Elizabeth, and so it was predictable and wise that Jagemann should not be asked to play the spiritual role of Iphigenia.

Friedrich Cordemann, of whom the Duke had written that he had 'a lovely voice and a rather Arabic look',[73] was pleasing in the role of Orestes. Thoas was played by Johann Jakob Graff (1769–1848), who had come to Weimar in 1793, where he had played several leading roles, including the first Götz and the first Alba in *Egmont*. Pylades was performed by Friedrich Haide (see Plate 15), whose excessive hand gestures and strained vocal delivery had made him somewhat unpopular with Weimar audiences and who had on one occasion caused even the good-natured Schiller to explode at his mannerisms. Arcas was played by Heinrich Becker, a veteran of the Weimar stage who had performed there since the formation of the new troupe in 1791. His mobile and expressive face made him best suited to comic roles, and he was also notorious for his temperament, having once boxed the ears of a fellow-actress, conduct which earned him house-arrest from Goethe.

It was a sad reflection on the professional actors of the day that this première was less successful than the original amateur production, and lent substance to Goethe's rueful statement that he had never seen 'a perfect production of . . . *Iphigenia*'.[74] Sadly, too, Corona Schröter was too unwell to attend the première of the masterpiece which she had helped to launch thirteen years earlier.

Fortunately, a stronger cast was selected for the revival in 1807, which opened in Leipzig on 31 August, although significantly Jagemann again was not offered the main role. It was in fact taken by Amalie Wolff (1780–1851) (see Plate 16), who had first performed at Weimar at the age of fourteen. Gotthardi wrote of her:[75]

Amalia [*sic*] was a Junoesque figure, full and harmoniously proportioned, as noble as she was graceful, with a lightness of movement, with fiery, powerful yet gentle eyes, and a compellingly aristocratic quality in her appearance and bearing. For Goethe she was 'in her

Plate 16   Amalie Wolff.

imaginativeness and energy' such a significant artist that she was considered the model of the greatness of the Ancient Greeks. Her voice could not be said to have outstanding volume or range, but she commanded her limited abilities with considerable skill. Zelter says of her:

'Now one can observe with great pleasure the way this woman knows how to husband her resources so that one assumes a power behind the mild surface, a power which she watches over like Aeolus.'

A detail of Amalie Wolff's performance, recorded by Adolf Müllner, is of interest:[76]

People have objected to the fact that Wolff [Orestes] at the words: 'Here is the sword, with which he [Agamemnon] slew the brave men of Troy', etc. [V,6,2035f.] drew his sword, and Iphigenia, who stood between Orestes and Thoas, seized hold of it and held it out to Thoas. There is no need to do this; there is no mention of it in Goethe, and it would be fairly tasteless if this movement were designed merely to emphasize the recognition of the royal sword. But when Iphigenia takes hold of this sword with an expression of reverence which the hero's sword possesses for her and Orestes, and holds it out to Thoas, then I should like to know what objection there could be? People have also objected to the gesture of blessing in the scene between Iphigenia and Pylades as being inappropriate to the ancient world – but are not the words she speaks also modern: 'May you be blessed', etc.? [IV,4,1546] Rather than quibbling about such details, people should recognize with what greatness a German actress inhabits such an alien world . . . how, for example, she delivers the Song of the Parcae with haunting power.

Müllner's comments refer to a later production, in which Amalie Wolff's husband played Orestes, but in 1807 this role was taken by Karl Oels (1780–1831) (see Plate 17), who had come to Weimar in 1803. Oels was renowned for his good appearance and for his smooth delivery, but Goethe had had problems with his somewhat nonchalant style, on one occasion shouting at him: 'Herr Oels! We've seen enough of your rear, show us your face again!'.[77]

Thoas was again played by Graff, and Arcas was performed by Deny, the actor who had had such difficulty in being allowed to marry. Pylades was given to Pius Alexander Wolff (1782–1828) (see Plate 18), whom Amalie had married in

Plate 17 Karl Ludwig Oels.

December 1804. Goethe said of him that he was the only actor
to have wholly absorbed his methods: 'Speaking precisely,
Wolff alone could be called my pupil',[78] and it was to Wolff
that Goethe dictated his 'Rules for actors' in 1803. To his
natural dignity and grace he added the discipline of Goethe's
principles, both in movement and speech. It was he who, after
secretly working on *Torquato Tasso*, organized its première in
Weimar on 16 February 1807. After 1816 he and his wife

worked in Berlin, where he played Orestes to her Iphigenia, and together they helped to spread what was valuable in the Weimar style.

From these early performances, two things emerge clearly: first, mention is made again and again of the power of the piece and of its leading performer. Especially in the Song of the Parcae,[79] it is clear that Goethe's work, despite its classical trappings, serene atmosphere, beautiful verse and Utopian conclusion, is no plaster-of-Paris version of the ancient world but has deep undercurrents of passion.

Second, details of gesture assume considerable importance within the otherwise static style of the piece; so the handling of a sword can become a matter of considerable moment. As we shall see, Goethe uses minimal action together with subtle shaping of the scenes and of the verse to explore the full theatrical range of his confined but not confining form.

THE DRAMATIC STRUCTURE OF
IPHIGENIA ON TAURIS

Evidence of Goethe's strong formal concerns in *Iphigenia on Tauris* is provided by an examination of its accomplished structure. This can of course be perceived by the reader but can perhaps be fully experienced only by a theatre audience.

The central development of the piece is the healing of Orestes. Significantly, his mind is at its most disturbed in the middle scene of the middle act: Act Three, Scene Two, where, alone on stage, he has a vision of the underworld. The action leads up to and away from this turning-point. Within the acts themselves there is also a strong sense of rhythmic structure: the first act, which contains exposition and the first development, Thoas' renewed demand that Iphigenia should marry him, is embraced by an opening and a final monologue by the heroine. In Act Two the arrival of Orestes and Pylades is the major development, and it is they who take the stage. Iphigenia speaks only 22 of the 365 lines of the act, and it ends with a monologue by Pylades. The third act charts the process of Orestes' healing: Scene One brings Iphigenia and Orestes together for the first time; his collapse introduces the mono- logue in Scene Two; and Scene Three brings together the three Greek characters in a new spirit of closeness and optimism, the

Plate 18 Pius Alexander Wolff.

first scene in which more than two characters share the stage.

As Iphigenia now has to face the demands of their plan to steal the statue of Diana, her inner conflicts come to the fore, and in Act Four she soliloquizes at the beginning, the middle and the end (Scenes One, Three and Five). The dénouement proceeds in the fifth act by means of mainly very short scenes, except for the carefully placed dialogues between Iphigenia and Thoas (Scene Three) and between Iphigenia, Orestes and Thoas (Scene Six, the final scene).

Other structural devices increase the theatrical impact of the piece. Unlike Euripides, where Iphigenia begins with a formal prologue detailing her ancestry, Goethe opens with a soliloquy describing her innermost feelings, her yearning to return to Greece and her unhappiness at having to serve Diana on Tauris. Goethe immediately looks behind the external situation of Iphigenia to her feelings, an altogether more modern concern, that prepares the audience for the concentration on internal conflicts to follow.

It is a piece of cruel irony and a moment of great dramatic effectiveness that immediately after Iphigenia has uttered her prayer to Diana to be freed from Tauris, Arcas arrives to issue the ultimatum that threatens to bind her forever to the island in unwanted slavery either to the king or to the goddess. Thoas himself does not enter until the third scene, and so acquires a theatrical 'build-up' which lends him the stature appropriate to his role in the play, since he is, after all, the figure in the piece who comes closest to experiencing a tragic outcome.

Another departure from Euripides is the placing of the first meeting between Orestes and Iphigenia off-stage between Acts Two and Three. This removes the interest from the external encounter of two Greeks as yet unknown to each other to the much more significant recognition of each other as brother and sister (III,1).

VERSE STRUCTURE

There are similar strong effects created by the rhythms of the verse.

Stichomythia, though used considerably more sparingly than in the Greek original, is employed to strengthen the cut and thrust of debate (as in the interchanges between Iphigenia and Arcas, I,2,74–7 and 172–8; IV,2,1444–50 and – the longest – 1456–64).

Stichomythia quickens the pace but still operates within the regular structure of the verse. Regularity of rhythm establishes the serenity and calm of the piece; indeed, for over 300 lines the iambic metre maintains its steady beat, strengthened by the predominantly masculine line-endings. Then suddenly, as

Iphigenia recounts to the king the horrors of the Tantalids, just at the point where she speaks of the desperate suicide of an innocent woman, the line is cut short:

Der Vater wähnet Hippodamien
Die Mörderin, und grimmig fordert er
Von ihr der Sohn zurück, und sie entleibt
Sich selbst – [I,3,346–9]
[The father believing Hippodamia to be the murderess fiercely demands his son's return, and she takes her own life –]

The tremor of horror that causes both narration and metre to break off so abruptly creates a much greater impact in its silence than words could achieve. The same effect is created when Orestes breaks off, unable to speak of his father's murder (II,1,628).

Significantly, with the arrival of Orestes and Pylades the predominantly end-stopped lines give way to a much higher incidence of run-on lines, suggesting the undermining of the calm of Tauris with the renewed threat of human sacrifice. This characteristic is adopted by Iphigenia in her first meeting with Orestes (III,1), as her serenity is also threatened:

Und wehe dem, der, ungeduldig sie
Ertrotzend, saure Speise sich zum Tod
Geniesst. [III,1,1112–14]
[And woe to him, who defying them impatiently, enjoys sour food until his death]

It is as though the excess of emotion breaks out of the confines of the pentameter.

It is also in this scene that the Shakespearean device of the short line is twice employed:

Wie gärend stieg aus der Erschlagnen Blut
Der Mutter Geist
Und ruft der Nacht uralten Töchtern zu . . . [III,1,1052–4]
[As though in ferment the spirit of his mother arose from the blood of the murdered victim and calls to the primeval daughters of the night. . .]

                        zwischen uns
Sei Wahrheit!
Ich bin Orest! und dieses schuld'ge Haupt
Senkt nach der Grube sich und sucht den Tod.
[III,1,1080–3]
[Let truth rule between us! I am Orestes! And this guilty
head bows to the grave and seeks death]

The short line allows the actor a moment to express Orestes'
horrified recollection of the pursuit by the Furies and then the
bracing of himself before confessing his identity.

The disintegration of calm is reflected in the increasing
irregularity of the verse structure to the point where the blank
verse is abandoned entirely. In Orestes' vision of Hades (III,2),
as he witnesses the procession of his ancestors, the iambic
pentameter gives way to four-stress lines, iambs jostling with
anapaests and dactyls, as the ghostly figures shuffle past:

So bín auch ích willkómmen, und ich
dárf
In éuern féierlichen Zúg mich míschen.
Willkómmen, Váter, euch grüsst Orést
Von éurem Stámme der létzte Mánn;
Was íhr gesát, hat ér geérntet:
Mit Flúch beláden stíeg er heráb.
Doch léichter trágt sich hier jéde Búrde:
Néhmt ihn, o néhmt ihn in éuern Kréis!
[III,2,1279–86]
[Then I too am welcome, and I may join in your solemn
procession. Welcome, ancestors, Orestes greets you, the
last man of your family. What you sowed, he has
harvested. Laden with curses, he has descended. But
here each burden weighs less: take him, oh take him into
your circle!]

Once again it is Iphigenia who adopts the excited rhythm of
these shorter lines: Act Four opens with the throbbing metre of
dactyls that then erupt into the clatter of trochees and
anapaests, until the verse settles once more to iambic
pentameters, as Iphigenia composes herself to pray for
Pylades:

Dénken die Hímmlischen
Eínem der Érdgebórnen
Víele Verwírrungen zú,
Und beréiten sie íhm
In der Náhe der Stádt,
Oder am férnen Gestáde,
Daß in Stúnden der Nót
Auch die Hílfe beréit séi,
Einen rúhigen Fréund.
O ségnet, Götter, únsern Pýlades
Und   wás   er   ímmer   unternéhmen   mág!
[IV,1,1369–83]
[If the gods apportion confusion to any mortal, then they
also provide a calm friend, whether near his city or on a
foreign shore, so that help may be at hand in the hour of
need. Oh gods, bless our Pylades and whatever he may
undertake!]

The other decisive rupture of the regular rhythm of the blank
verse occurs in Iphigenia's recital of the Song of the Parcae at
the most intense moment of her emotional crisis:

Es fúrchte die Gótter
Das Ménschengeschlécht! . . . [IV,5,1726–7]
[May the human race fear the gods! . . .]

Here again the short lines and anapaestic metre seem almost
breathless compared with the secure and reassured rhythms of
the iambic pentameters that introduce the song.

From this nadir of Iphigenia's calm the versification is
gradually restored to the iambic flow of the opening. Finally,
the last expansive speeches of Orestes and Iphigenia contrast
with Thoas' grudging farewell expressed in the two short lines:

So geht! [V,6,2151]
Lebt wohl! [V,6,2174]
[Then go! Fare well!]

This brief analysis of the verse structure of *Iphigenia on Tauris*
indicates how Goethe discovered a further theatrical dimension
by transposing his prose drama of 1779 into its final
predominantly blank verse version of 1787. The subtle changes

of rhythm can be best appreciated when heard in performance; they are not there merely as aesthetic embellishments but provide clear indicators of the emotional developments within the action and stand as further proof of Goethe's powerful theatrical awareness.

ACTUAL STAGE DIRECTIONS

In Goethe's prose-version of *Iphigenia on Tauris* there are hardly any stage directions at all, no doubt because he went into rehearsal immediately on completing the play and so worked out moves with his actors. Even in the final verse version there are very few stage directions provided by Goethe. Since there is a single setting, each scene is prefaced simply by the names of the characters on stage at the beginning of the scene. There are generally not even directions for entrances and exits, and no adverbial directions indicating the manner in which a speech should be delivered, since, as with most poetic drama, this is anyway explicit in the text.

As with the minimal nature of the whole piece, those stage directions that are provided are thrown into greater relief by their scarcity. The first, the indication of the setting, reads: 'Grove before the temple of Diana'. This already establishes a different tone from the Euripidean original. In the Greek tragedy the setting is reminiscent of a slaughterhouse: the forecourt of the temple, dominated by an altar stained with the blood of human sacrifice, and, clearly visible, the trophies of the slaughtered victims. It is also a communal place, where the Chorus's presence is felt to be entirely acceptable. In Goethe the leafy grove at once suggests a more serene and intimate setting, with no sign of the bloody business formerly practised in the temple. It represents also, more even than in Euripides, the meeting-point between the palace and the sea. This assumes a particular significance in Act Four, Scene Five, where Iphigenia stands torn between her desire to follow Pylades' plan (the route to the sea) or to behave honourably towards Thoas (the path to the palace).

The few stage directions describing the action of the characters operate as strong visual signifiers within the otherwise fairly static framework. The first, in the second act, requires Iphigenia, as in Euripides, to remove Pylades' fetters soon after their first meeting, at once establishing Iphigenia's courage and compassion, whereas in the Greek original it is religious observance that demands his being unchained. Another stage direction referring to the use of a stage-property establishes again Goethe's more humane treatment of the original. This occurs shortly before the final resolution. Orestes rushes on to the stage 'armed' (V,4), but in response to Iphigenia's appeal, 'sheathes his sword'. This clear sign of Orestes' willingness to trust his sister contrasts with the fist-fight in which Euripides' character indulges in order to secure their freedom.

Perhaps the most significant and certainly the longest stage direction was a later addition in the process of composition. Pylades has just proposed that he should steal the statue from the temple: 'He goes towards the temple as he speaks these last words, without noticing that Iphigenia is not following. He finally turns round' (IV,4, after l.1565). Clearly, Goethe felt it important to emphasize Iphigenia's unwillingness to be involved in a dishonourable act, since her hesitation is already implied in the text. This stage direction and the one pause indicated by Goethe ('after a silence', V,3, before l.1892) interrupt the iambic flow of the blank verse at two crucial points – the first when Iphigenia finds it impossible to agree to the theft of the statue and the second when she resolves to reveal the truth to Thoas.

These moments of stillness speak with a considerable eloquence.

IMPLIED STAGE DIRECTIONS

Most of the physical action of the play is implied in the text rather than presented in actual stage directions.

The opening words already imply movement:

> Heraus in eure Schatten, rege Wipfel
> Des alten, heil'gen, dichtbelaubten Haines,
> Wie in der Göttin stilles Heiligtum,
> Tret' ich noch jetzt mit schauderndem Gefühl,
> Als wenn ich sie zum erstenmal beträte,
> Und es gewöhnt sich nicht mein Geist hierher.[I,1,1–6]
> [Out into your shade, you stirring trees
> Of this ancient, sacred, leafy grove,

As though into the silent sanctum of the goddess,
Still I step with a thrill of awe,
As if entering it for the first time,
And my soul has not grown accustomed to this place.]

The lines clearly indicate movement from the temple at the rear of the stage forwards to the front. Since the stage was just over nine metres deep, fifteen firm but graceful steps of thirty centimetres on each of the stressed syllables would bring the actress exactly to the centre of the stage, as she reaches the main verb of her opening sentence and, with it, the first irregular foot of the speech ('Trét' ich' – a trochee). The remaining three lines with their further fifteen stresses would allow the actress to achieve her normal downstage position at the footlights, just as she completes her opening sentence and begins a more reflective comment on her situation.

It is significant how many of the scenes begin, as here, with verbs of movement: 'sends' (I,2); 'tread' (II,1); 'come' (II,2); 'descended' (III,3); 'Hasten' (IV,2); 'follow' (IV,5); 'brings' (V,3); 'Do not linger!' (V,5). All of these indicate a far more dynamic quality than might otherwise be assumed from the neo-classical structure of the piece.

Balancing this dynamic quality was the use of tableaux, live paintings framed by the proscenium arch. It is probable that, although there was no need to change the set, the curtain would have fallen between acts, giving the opportunity for the playing of incidental music and sometimes to suggest the passing of time. Act One ends with Iphigenia's soliloquy. Since this is principally a prayer to Diana, and the speech ends with falling trochaic rhythms ('Eine Weile gönnen und lássen' – I,4,560), it seems likely that Iphigenia would return to the temple, from which she will again emerge in the course of the second act. As Act Two opens with the entrance of Orestes and Pylades, there would be no need for the curtain to fall here, since the action may be regarded as continuous. However, the dropping of the curtain would have lent a sense of completeness to each of the acts, and a moment of stillness after Iphigenia's return to the temple, while the audience contemplated the empty stage, would have given an opportunity for reflection and expectation.

Act Two would have ended on the exit of Pylades ('and let

us sail prudently with happy heart towards the star of hope that beckons' – II,2,925–6). Act Three begins with a tableau of Iphigenia loosening Orestes' fetters. It is possible that the curtain would rise on the two actors, Orestes standing, haunted and distressed, Iphigenia kneeling, Magdalen-like at his feet, while she unclasped his chains. By contrast, the act ends with Pylades' breathless exhortation to leave.

Act Four could begin with Iphigenia discovered on stage; alternatively, the excited rhythm of the short lines might suggest that she is again moving forward from the temple, where one presumes her to have been making preparations with the statue between the acts. The act ends with the Song of the Parcae, at a point of decision and despair, no doubt with Iphigenia immobile, in a virtual state of collapse.

The final act opens with Arcas and Thoas in conversation, but it is unclear whether in a tableau or entering on their first lines. There is no doubt however about the strong ending of the act: the striking picture of Thoas bidding farewell to Iphigenia and Orestes. The curtain would fall slowly on this final image of reluctant reconciliation.

There are also several textual indicators towards the posture and gesture of characters on stage. From her first apostrophe to the tree-tops of the sacred grove, Iphigenia's eyes are repeatedly lifted up from earthly things. Most of her soliloquies consist of prayers, and so would dictate an upward lifting of the gaze, an appropriate posture to emphasize Iphigenia's spirituality. When, however, she learns of her father's death or is brought into conflict by Pylades' plan for escape, her countenance darkens and the posture becomes one of suffering: 'Yes, you honour this king's house! I see how your breast struggles in vain with this unexpectedly monstrous account!' (II,2,883–5); 'Suddenly a quiet trace of sadness passes over your clear brow' (IV,4,1634).

Other implied stage directions create moments of great theatrical effectiveness. An example is the end of Act Five, Scene Three, where Iphigenia encourages Thoas to give his blessing to her plan to return to Greece: 'Oh, give me your hand as a sign of peace' (V,4,1990). During the concluding five lines of the scene she would hold out her hand in a gesture of friendship, while Thoas hesitates to take it. Just at the point where he might begin to lift his hand to hers, Orestes bursts on to the scene, armed and shouting to his followers off-stage. The first violent entrance of the piece destroys the brittle truce that Iphigenia and Thoas were about to establish.

Orestes' call to his off-stage followers is one of the many ways in which Goethe extends our sense of space beyond the confines of the actual set. In particular, several references are made to the sea and to the royal army, creating virtual sound-effects in the imagination. There are also repeated references to the Furies, glowering in the wings: they dare not enter Diana's grove (II,1,730), but their horrible laughter can be heard (III,1,1126f.).

Just as there are implied sound-effects, so too the level of illumination is suggested in the text. In fact the lighting would have remained the same throughout, but as in the daylight staging of Shakespeare, different light quality is inferred. Initially, the language tends to refer to darkness, from the 'shade' of the first line to the repeated mentions of 'night' (I,4,547; II,1,590; II,1,679; II,1,780). Where reference is made to 'light', it is to the light of the moon (I,4,547) or to the light of the sun which Orestes will renounce in death (II,1,573). Eventually, out of this darkness the bright voice of Iphigenia prays not to Diana, goddess of the moon, but to the 'golden sun' (III,1,982), and, despite Orestes' visions of the under-world, the language is suffused with ever brighter images, as Iphigenia's healing powers work upon her brother and the conflicts of the action. So by Act Four, Scene Four, Orestes' head is surrounded by a 'beautiful flame' (l.1541), his eyes 'glow' (l.1542), a 'beautiful fire' shall surround the dwellings of the paternal gods (l.1613), Iphigenia's soul turns towards the 'rays' of Pylades' words like 'a flower towards the sun' (ll.1620–1), and Iphigenia's doubts are like 'light clouds crossing the sun' (l.1635). Finally, in the closing lines of the play, Orestes speaks of his healing at the hands of Iphigenia: 'Through you I enjoy anew the vast light of day' (V,6,2124–6). The play seems to end in glorious light.

CONCLUSION

Just as the actual light levels of the stage are transformed by Goethe's imaginative powers, so the outcome of the play is lifted on to a preposterously beautiful and Utopian plane. As

Erich Heller says,[80] there can be no 'cure' for matricide. But the power of Goethe's poetry and stagecraft invite us to accept the successful workings of Iphigenia's purity and humanity.

We must remember that Goethe originally wrote *Iphigenia on Tauris* while touring the Duchy in order to conscript soldiers, and we recall that the theatre at Weimar continued its performances even while the guns of Napoleon's army were within earshot. This might be construed as an ostrich-like unwillingness to confront reality. On the other hand, the magical island of Tauris which permits humanity to prevail may stand as a courageous act of faith in a world of rationality amidst the last troubled decades of the eighteenth century.

Goethe's supreme achievement was to take a theme remote in time and concern, to confine it within the narrow limits of the neo-classical form and yet through the force of his poetry and theatrical imagination to allow us to glimpse a world of unrealized truth. In this process he is not blowing the dead ashes of neo-classicism into a last flickering flame. On the contrary, he provides an important link in the history of idealist and minimalist theatre.

As the theatre became more democratic and its concerns more closely related to those of its immediate audience, so it lost much of the remoteness, clarity and austerity of its earliest European manifestation, Greek tragedy. Racine discovered the means of allying the extremes of passion to the containment of the classical form, a tension which, after the writing of *Phèdre*, apparently caused him to abandon the theatre for over a decade. Goethe followed in Racine's footsteps, without any cultural hegemony to support him, and having to create a theatre to perform in with sufficient sensitivity and discipline.

In using the stage to reveal some higher reality, Goethe had formed curious alliances. As Eggert shows,[81] some of Goethe's thoughts on performance echo the ideas of Diderot, in fact a writer of bourgeois domestic drama. In *Paradoxe sur le comédien* Diderot wrote:[82]

Consider a moment what one calls truth in the theatre. Is it showing things as they are in nature? Not at all. Truth, in this sense, would be the commonplace. What then is truth on stage? It is the conforming of action, speech, facial expression, voice, movement and gesture with an ideal imagined by the poet and often exaggerated by the actor.

This accords almost exactly with Goethe's view of the function of the theatre, summarized in his words from his novel *Dichtung und Wahrheit (Poetry and Truth)*: 'The highest object of any art is to present the illusion of a higher reality through artifice' [Schein].[83]

Goethe knew that his world of Tauris was a fiction. He knew that a barbarian king would be unlikely to respond to appeals to his humanity as surely as he knew that there would be little sense in appealing to the good nature of an invading French soldier and ask him nicely to desist from killing. But Goethe was not running away from reality; he himself said: 'I can't force the King of Tauris to speak as though no textile workers were going hungry.'[84] But instead of placing starving textile workers on stage, he portrayed a world teetering on the edge of chaos and violence redeemed by the purity of a woman. It is a bold metaphor and one that is exploited theatrically in the subtlest of ways.

3

FROM THE EIGHTEENTH INTO THE NINETEENTH CENTURY

In common with other nations in Europe the German-speaking peoples grew more prosperous towards the end of the eighteenth century. The financial growth was not as striking as in Britain, nor were the political consequences as devastating as in France, but changes occurred no less certainly. The distinction between rich and poor became more pronounced: Cologne, a city of 42,000 inhabitants, boasted 6,000 *Bürger* (merchant freemen of the city) but had no less than 20,000 beggars. In other countries of the Rhineland there were per 1,000 inhabitants 50 priests and 260 beggars.[1]

The growing importance and wealth of the bourgeoisie led also to a growth in the demand for more freely available entertainment. There was now a market for performances that belonged neither to the refined circles of the court nor to the crude displays of the market-place. In music the new genre of *Lieder* was soon to become popular, and operatic entertainment was no longer the preserve of the court theatres. Popular and supposingly edifying spectacle became the order of the day: by the turn of the century major German towns boasted 'panoramas', 'perspective presentations' and 'mechanical theatres', all different names for a presentation involving an elaborately realistic set, with ingenious lighting effects and mechanical figures, usually depicting some historical event or exotic location. In 1812 Berlin had four such establishments, with frequently changing programmes, which, because of their popularity and low running costs, were able to sell their tickets more cheaply than theatres. There were also less educational presentations, for example, mechanical fortune-tellers, ghostly apparitions and waxworks, usually satisfying a prurient

111

fascination with the morbid while purporting to offer a sound moral lesson. There were mime-shows, acrobatic displays, rope-walkers and *Declamatoria*, at which third-rate sentimental or bombastic writing was recited as an uplifting experience for the audience. Especially popular were balloon displays, at which garish hot-air balloons were launched. One in Berlin in 1796 was attended by the Prussian Crown Prince and a crowd of 40,000, and caused the theatres to delay their opening by one and a half hours.

Needless to say, a delayed curtain was not the only effect this change in public affluence and taste had on the theatre. The cold wind of commercial competition was keenly felt by virtually all theatres. Attempts were made to force the 'panoramas' to remain closed at times when the theatres were open, and, when this did not succeed, the theatres themselves adopted something of the history lesson/travelogue function of the panorama. Sets became more elaborate, and it became common for the décor itself to be applauded and for the scene-painter to be called out. Costumes and props strove for authenticity, albeit idealized, and every effort was made to satisfy the public love for both spectacle and self-improvement.

New theatres were built and old buildings were converted, usually being leased out to any entrepreneur willing to take on the financial risk. Even the formerly well subsidized court theatres were more and more being run as commercial undertakings. We have already seen that at Weimar there was never sufficient funding to attract the best acting talents except for occasional guest-performances, and that Goethe's rupture with the Court Theatre in 1817 was due in part to a row over a performing dog. When the National Theatre was opened in Berlin in 1786 it was granted an annual subsidy by Friedrich Wilhelm II of 12,000 Talers a year. By 1787 this had been reduced to 6,000, and by 1790 it was further reduced to 5,400 Talers per annum, just enough to cover the free admission to the royal box and the courtiers' seating. Only in Stuttgart were generous subsidies offered to the Court Theatre after the turn of the century, and even here, when in 1819 an account for 115,000 Gulden was presented, the state representatives on the theatre management resigned in protest, eventually relenting by granting a regular annual subsidy of 50,000 Gulden.

An indicator of the changed character of the theatre is the

fact that in Prussia, after a brief period from 16 December 1808, when theatre was officially declared an organ of public education and therefore subordinate to the Ministry of Education and Culture, the new Trading Laws of 11 September 1810 firmly established the theatre as a primarily commercial enterprise. Under these laws, which were to prove the model for nearly all German states, theatre licences could be issued only by the police, who granted permission for any applicant, regardless of his or her knowledge of theatre, to manage a place of public entertainment for a certain period and in a specific place.

With state control came state censorship. The court theatres had imposed a high level of decorum upon themselves, directors seldom being inclined to risk the displeasure of their rulers by offending against good taste. But now censorship was no longer self-imposed. Maria Theresa, Empress of Austria, was the first to set up a central censorship authority with the declared intent of encouraging serious theatre in Vienna in opposition to popular coarse entertainment. Actors were to refrain from 'all indecency and nonsensical expressions'. A first offence would attract a warning; a second offence two weeks' prison; and a third a life sentence. The power of censorship will be witnessed in the failed attempts to have Kleist's *Prinz von Homburg* performed in Berlin.

A further sign of the entrepreneurial nature of early nineteenth-century theatre was the increased size of its administration. When Iffland took over the direction of the Berlin theatres in the winter of 1796, he managed them from one room with the assistance of a few clerks. Fifteen years later the theatre administration occupied a whole building. The bureaucracy responsible for overseeing theatrical entertainment expanded considerably too, to the point that it was rumoured that there was a separate inspectorate for left and right boots!

Artistic directors suffered constant interference from their administrators. Pius Alexander Wolff, the former Weimar actor, and Ludwig Devrient, one of the most important theatre personalities of the nineteenth century, soon gave up directing because of the daily trivia which interrupted their creative work. Authors also had to cope with the new bureaucratic machinery. Gone was the kind of personal relationship enjoyed by Schiller and Dalberg; instead authors submitted playscripts to a faceless organization, whose acceptance had to be regarded as a gracious favour.

In terms of economic and social importance the German theatre had never had it so good. By the turn of the century there were approximately fifty standing German theatre companies offering regular employment (although formal actor training was still unknown). Theatregoing was central to the life of the cultured; it was not uncommon for the well-to-do to go to the theatre, opera or ballet every night of the week. In 1790 Friedrich Wilhelm II saw three of the first four performances of Kotzebue's *Die Sonnenjungfrau (The Sun Virgin)* within six days, and a Berlin critic once complained that only a few Berliners made the effort to see the same play six times.[2]

By the 1820s the popularity of the theatre had turned leading actors and actresses into public celebrities, and Iffland was even decorated by the Prussian King for his work in the theatre. The social standing of the actor was now assured, but by the same token careers were dependent on public favour and on the ever more influential voice of the critics. As Max Martersteig commented: 'The newspapers were so full of theatre mania that one could be forgiven for believing that Germany was ruled from the stage and from the desks of the critics.'[3]

Predictably, the repertoires of these theatres were undemanding. Even in Weimar, as we have seen, the proportion of pieces of literary value was not high. Despite its promising beginnings, the fare at Mannheim was not much better: between 1781 and 1808, 37 plays by Iffland were produced (a total of 476 performances), 116 plays by Kotzebue (1,728 performances), while Schiller's *Die Räuber* was staged 15 times, his *Kabale und Liebe* 7 times, and *Fiesko* and *Don Carlos* only 3 times each. Statistics for Dresden in the years 1789–1813 are similar: Iffland and Kotzebue alone accounted for 33 per cent of performances, while Lessing, Goethe and Schiller together represented a mere 4 per cent of the repertoire, and there was hardly any Shakespeare. Apart from musical theatre the most popular offerings were the historical pageants of the *Ritterstück*, many written under the influence of the novels of Walter Scott (for example, one Ernst Raupach (1784–1852), who was a favourite of the German theatres in the 1820s and 1830s, had no less than 120 such plays performed); then there were melodramas and domestic dramas (like those of Iffland and Kotzebue), which, until the importation of Scribe in the 1830s, had little to commend them.

Against this background it comes as no surprise that, for the most part, leading literary figures of the day turned their backs on the theatre. Despite his successes at Weimar, Schiller had grown weary of the lack of sensitivity and intelligence of the actors he had to work with, writing to Goethe on 28 April 1801:[4]

> I want nothing more to do with actors, for it is impossible to achieve anything with reason and amiability. There is only one way of relating to them, and that is by issuing curt orders, which is simply not my way of working.

Goethe himself suffered growing disillusionment with the theatre, repeatedly begging Carl August to relieve him of the responsibility of running the Weimar Court Theatre, and when in May 1805 Schiller died, Goethe lost most of his enthusiasm for the stage. It is significant that *Faust*, and especially the second part, was written without the intention of having it performed, and we witness at the start of the nineteenth century a growing divorce between literature and the theatre. Most of the Romantic writers of the period did not write for the stage, preferring lyric poetry and the *Novelle*. For one thing, their intense individualism was poorly suited to drama, in which, to use Tom Stoppard's phrase, one of the joys is that one can 'contradict oneself in public'; for another, the tawdry, compromising nature of the commercial theatre would have got in the way of the high-flown vision of the Romantics: the 'blue flower' would have wilted in the smell of greasepaint.

By becoming primarily a form of commercial entertainment, the theatre almost entirely lost its former role as an artistic and political forum, and the latter part of the eighteenth century was mourned by several as a great age of German theatre which had now passed. In the first third of the nineteenth century, the Austrian Grillparzer, by discovering poetic tragedy within flamboyantly operatic historical material, was the major exception to the dearth of good writing for the stage, and even his heroic figures, by repenting of their misdeeds, lack the complexity and robustness of the truly tragic.

Dashed too were the eighteenth century hopes of seeing the

theatre as the rallying point for uniting all Germans. Schiller had written in his essay on 'The theatre regarded as a moral institution' that the theatre 'brings together all social degrees and classes'.[5] But now the Romantic author Eichendorff had to admit: 'It is the separation between the people and the cultured that prevents us from having a national theatre.'[6]

So we shall see, in the case of the two most important German playwrights of the first half of the nineteenth century, Heinrich von Kleist and Georg Büchner, that their works for the stage were either entirely neglected by the theatres of the day or were presented in bowdlerized versions. For Kleist it was a source of despair; for Büchner the freedom to ignore the constraints of the contemporary stage may well have contributed to his writing the most innovative piece of European theatre of the century.

There was, however, one figure of literary importance, who remained committed to the theatre and whose work shines like a beacon through the cultural gloom of the period. His name was Ludwig Tieck.

LUDWIG TIECK

Born in 1773, two years before Goethe went to Weimar, Ludwig Tieck was one of the few to attempt to resist the commercial pressures on the theatre, a theatre whose intention, according to Max Martersteig,[7] was

> not to debate problems, but to distract from them . . . it set out to portray only men with extraordinary lives – but in the Bengal lighting of phantastic Romanticism. Reality was banned – people were hardly interested: in both the serious and the comic the extraordinary and the sensational prevailed.

Despite looking back on the two decades from 1770 to 1790 as the highpoint of German theatre, Tieck had been disappointed as a young man by Weimar classicism. Arriving at the Court in 1800 in his third failed attempt to become an actor, he found the production of *Maria Stuart* bombastic and tedious. The formality of the actors and their slow, hollow delivery dismayed him: 'there was no longer any trace of character portrayal, of genuine intensity, of the emphasis or underplaying of this or that passage.'[8]

Predictably, too, Tieck was unimpressed by the popular melodramas of Iffland and Kotzebue. Their moralistic tone had about them 'the stench of a field-hospital'. On the other hand, he was opposed to the 'naturalistic' style of the Mannheim tradition. He condemned the appointment of Iffland, whose own acting style he had described as 'tragic gurgling'[9] as Director of the Berlin Royal Theatre in 1796, feeling that it had ushered in a style of flat and tedious naturalism in the theatres of the Prussian capital:[10]

> We have had to endure a great deal from these dreary actors who think themselves natural when they are merely trivial, actors who throw away important lines and great thoughts, constantly break up the flow of the dialogue and chop the meaning, regarding every elevated feeling as emotional bombast and all majesty and dignity as unnatural. In plays such bombastic performers have often been imitated and made to look ridiculous, seldom however these worshippers of impoverished naturalism, who deserve it every bit as much.

In place of the bombastic, the bathetic and the banal, Tieck urged a return to 'naturalness' on stage. As a Romantic author, he rejected all that was distorted by civilization and championed instead the 'naive', as defined in Schiller's seminal essay of 1795, *Über naive und sentimentalische Dichtung (On Naive and Sentimental Poetry)*. Fichte's *Wissenschaftslehre (Scientific Teaching*, 1794) and Friedrich Schlegel's *Fragmente* further championed the primacy of the individual imagination and declared the absolute autonomy of the artist to create according to his or her own subjectivity. Another philosophical influence on the acting of the day came from Hume. Johann Jakob Engel published *Ideen zu einer Mimik (Thoughts about Acting)*, first in 1785 and then in a more popular expanded edition in 1802, in which he referred to Hume's treatise 'On the passions'. Here Hume compares the soul with a 'string-instrument, where, after each stroke, the vibrations still retain some sound, which gradually and insensibly decays'. In this way, 'one passion will always be mixed and confounded with the other'. From this Engel draws the conclusion that 'emotions which arise quickly after one another, never arise as pure emotions.'[11] In place of the external emotions of Weimar classicism and the often underplayed emotion of Mannheim naturalism, the new actor of the nineteenth century was searching for much greater truthfulness in performance.

For Tieck, the ideal actor would embody a role with total conviction, allowing the emotional expression to flow from within. The actor should be inspired by 'beautiful madness', portraying 'passions in their finest nuances'.[12] In a way that anticipates Stanislavskian theory, Tieck believed that emotion genuinely felt on stage would yield a truthful expression of that emotion.

One actor who achieved this ideal for Tieck was Johann Friedrich Fleck (1757–1801). Fleck had been a pupil of Schröder in Hamburg and then in 1783 moved to Berlin, where from 1796 until his death in 1801 he performed under Iffland. Despite Iffland's professional jealousy of Fleck, he had to admit to his qualities,[13] praising

> the quality of his soul, whose melody irresistibly won the hearts of the audience, lifting everyone to the heights and plunging them into the depths according to the rush of his passion. . . . He scorned any assistance from stagecraft, he was the intimate of Nature and firmly and vigorously pursued his artistic career under her guidance.

Perhaps predictably, Fleck was particularly impressive as Karl Moor. As Tieck wrote of his performance:[14]

> The triumph of his greatness, however great he may have been in other roles, was the Robber Moor. This Titan-like creation of a young and bold imagination was invested [in Fleck's performance] with such terrible truth and noble dedication, the wildness was mixed with such moving tenderness that, on beholding it, doubtless the author himself would have been astonished at his own creation.

Needless to say, the intense subjectivity of Fleck's performance easily led to a lack of discipline, and one could never be certain that he would be sufficiently in the mood to act well; whether, as Eduard Devrient put it, one would be seeing 'the great Fleck or the little Fleck'. Devrient tells how, during a performance of Die Räuber, Fleck had been so annoyed by the muted applause at the end of the first act that he began to lose all interest in his role, muttered his lines and during one monologue nonchalantly balanced his musket on the end of his finger. The audience's patience became exhausted, and they began to stamp and hiss.[15]

> Fleck paused, took one step towards the footlights and looked round the stalls with his wonderful fiery eyes. Everything went quiet, an eyewitness said that this terrible look took his breath away, that the very dust in the theatre must have trembled. Fleck now stepped back, and, suddenly transformed, continued his role, playing with such fiery passion that his most devoted followers could not recall such an impression and the audience were driven to an utter mania of applause.

While as a young man Tieck may have been excited by these Romantic extravagances, in later life he clearly felt untutored talent was not in itself enough. In conversation with Heinrich Laube shortly before his death in 1853, Tieck said: 'There is just one lesson to be observed: learn to speak! It is my lasting regret that our actors do not learn to speak.'[16] Another major influence on Tieck was that of Shakespeare, but, significantly, much more as a man of the theatre rather than as the playwright that had so enthused the previous generation. Already in 1795 Tieck had translated *The Tempest* and was later to help complete the outstanding series of Shakespeare translations begun by August Wilhelm Schlegel, arguably the best translations of Shakespeare into any language in the world. It was on a visit to England in 1817, however, that Tieck became fully acquainted with what was known of the structure of the Elizabethan playhouse, and indeed in 1836 collaborated with the architect Gottfried Semper on a theoretical reconstruction of the Fortune Theatre.

He did not learn much from the contemporary London theatre: he was unimpressed by the declamatory style of Kemble, and found Kean too erratic, although he did commend Garrick's realistic technique of playing scenes in profile rather than the conventional style of facing out towards the audience. He found the stages at Drury Lane and Covent Garden too vast and the companies lacking in any sense of ensemble playing.

It was in the Elizabethan theatre that Tieck discovered his

Plate 19 Tieck's production of *A Midsummer Night's Dream*.

sought-after model of a great theatre which had evolved 'naturally' from the common populace itself, bringing together all strata of society in the kind of theatrical community for which attempts to establish a German National Theatre had striven.

Moreover the physical arrangement of the Elizabethan stage and its use could still provide a model for the contemporary theatre. For one thing, Tieck urged the abandonment of elaborate scenery and obsessively authentic costumes in favour of involving the imagination of the audience more deeply: 'In all artistic enjoyment the mind must enliven and expand the representation; for a performance to become real the imagination of the spectator must contribute half.'[17]

Other qualities of the Shakespearean theatre to be emulated were the unbroken flow of performance and the intimacy of the playing space. Tieck found it ludicrous that the trend in theatre building was towards ever greater stages, when five-sixths of the stage space was usually unused, except for mountains, battlements, and the like. He also deplored the contemporary habit of actors performing at the footlights, and argued that by using the full depth of the stage much more significant stage arrangements could be achieved, as, for example, when a servant addresses his master upstage (a suggestion that had to await better stage lighting to be fully implemented). All these theatrical elements could be achieved by replacing the picture-book stage with the presumed layout of the Elizabethan theatre. There should be a forestage, a rear-stage, which could be curtained off, and an upper stage reached by steps. This would offer a more effective use of stage space by allowing performers to occupy the upper level, it would permit an unbroken flow in performance and would militate against the tendency to dress the stage too elaborately.

In 1819 Tieck went to Dresden, where he was appointed *Dramaturg* at the Court Theatre from 1825 to 1832. Here he would attempt – without great success – to put into practice some of his innovatory ideas. He was responsible for a number of Shakespearean productions, *Hamlet* in 1820, *King Lear* in 1824 and *Macbeth* in 1836. As a necessary concession to the decorum of the Court Theatre audience, omissions still had to be made, like the blinding of Gloucester, most of the Porter's speech, and the carrying in of Macbeth's severed head. But it was in Berlin on 18 October 1843 that Tieck came closest to realizing his ideal stage in his own production of *A Midsummer Night's Dream* (see Plate 19). He used a shallow stage with an upper level reached by two flights of steps. This first represented Theseus's palace, and then, with woodland decoration, was used for the forest scenes. To create the mechanicals' area, a mid-curtain, painted with a design of the workshop, was lowered in front of the steps. This led to a fluid and simple production, a forerunner of the kind of staging common in the twentieth century, but which, in 1843, could be regarded only as a curious experiment.

It was earlier in his career, while still in Dresden, that Tieck had been involved in another innovative project, the staging of Heinrich von Kleist's *Prinz Friedrich von Homburg* (*The Prince of Homburg*). As we shall see, the theatrical fortunes of Kleist represent only too forcefully the dilemma faced by any playwright with literary aspirations as the nineteenth century dawned and the first German theatre had to cope with the fruits of its own success.

4

KLEIST IN PERFORMANCE
The Prince of Homburg

THE EARLY STAGE HISTORY OF *THE PRINCE OF HOMBURG*

With Kleist we encounter a major and dismaying example of the split between the popular and the literary in the German theatre of the period. Despite being a playwright whose worth has been finally recognized, and who was arguably the greatest dramatist of any nation writing in the first decade of the nineteenth century, and despite cherishing some very positive and challenging views about the nature of theatre, his relationship with the stage of his own day can only be described as disastrous.

Unlike Goethe and Schiller, he was never in any way attached to a working theatre, and indeed initially seems to have shown little interest in the contemporary stage. It is known that he received tuition in declamation at the University of Leipzig in March 1803; it is probable that he saw Iffland as Wallenstein, and he definitely saw Fleck; but we have no reports by Kleist about these experiences, nor of his visits to the theatre in Weimar or Paris. In one of his few references to theatre in his letters, he treats it as a form of entertainment amongst many. Writing from Berlin on 23 March 1801, he confessed to his sister: 'an inner turmoil gives me no rest, I run to coffee-shops and tobacconists, go to concerts and plays, and to distract and anaesthetize myself I do idiotic things that I would be ashamed to set down in writing.'[1] For Kleist, theatre seemed to be equated with time-wasting. It was no wonder then that at first he felt his own writings too precious to be released in as public a forum as the commercial theatre of his day. As he wrote from Paris to his fiancée on 10 October 1801: 'Writing for money – a thousand times no! . . . I cannot understand how a writer can hand over the child of his love to such a rough horde as men are.'[2]

Thus it was that Kleist presented his first play, *Die Familie Schroffenstein* (*The Schroffenstein Family*, 1801–2), in a private reading to a circle of friends. This strange piece, which leads to a grotesquely tragic ending through mistaken identities, was greeted with uncontrolled hilarity by Kleist's auditors, although a version did reach the stage of the Graz National Theatre on 9 January 1804. His next play, *Robert Guiskard*, like the majority of his plays, was not performed until many years after his death (*Robert Guiskard* in 1901, *Amphitryon* in 1899, *Penthesilea* in 1876, *Die Hermannsschlacht* in 1860).

His folk-comedy, *Der zerbrochene Krug* (*The Broken Jug*, 1802–5), did at least achieve the distinction of Goethe's offering it a production at Weimar. In the event, however, the performance on 2 March 1808 proved a further disaster: the court audience were distinctly hostile, and it was even the occasion for a courtier who had whistled his disapproval to be put under house-arrest for his bad manners. What could have possibly led to a productive collaboration in Weimar ended instead in an irrevocable rupture with Goethe, worsened by Goethe's dismissal of *Penthesilea* as 'morbid'.

When Kleist attempted to have *Das Kätchen von Heilbronn* performed in Berlin, Iffland responded: 'while acknowledging its poetic qualities, [it] could not work on stage without total rewriting'.[3] It was in fact premièred in a bowdlerized version in Vienna on 17 March 1810. The following year it was transformed by Franz von Holbein into a conventional *Ritterstück*, a pretext for an elaborate historical set (see Plate 20) and much display of knights in armour while the title-figure was relegated to being a man-crazy oddity. It was this version which was to be played for some fifty years on the stages of Germany, until the Meininger restored the original in 1876.[4]

From 1810 until it was forced, largely by government censorship, to close the following year, Kleist used the *Berliner Abendblätter*, Berlin's first daily newspaper (founded by Kleist himself) to write articles on the theatre and so found a platform for his hostility towards Iffland and the commercialized theatre of Berlin. By this time Prussia was little more than a

Plate 20 The set for the Berlin production of *Das Kätchen von Heilbronn.*

Napoleonic satellite, and the theatre repertoire of its capital was overburdened by trivial French pieces in translation. In one article, purporting to be written by a Berliner to a foreign friend, Kleist treats Iffland's achievements with heavy irony:[5]

> Since he has been in charge of the theatre here, Herr Theatre Director Iffland has, according to the views of most Berliners, determined and transformed its nature and standing in a remarkable and extraordinary manner which has certainly astonished all art-lovers. . . . It is true, however, that not all art-lovers, especially those who come from the modern school, agree with the principles by which he operates.

He also fulminated in print against the commercialism of the German theatre:[6]

> If one asks why the works of Goethe are so seldom performed on stage, then one receives the answer that, as repeated experience has shown, these plays, however excellent they may be, attract only a modest revenue at the box office. . . . For, just as the baker, according to Adam Smith, can tell that his rolls are good without any chemical knowledge of the reason, but simply because they sell well, so the theatre management can, without any regard for the critics, conclude that they are staging good plays, if the boxes and seats are filled at every performance.

Therefore when Kleist sought to have his last and best play, *The Prince of Homburg*, staged in Berlin, he once again turned his back on the commercial theatre and hoped, as he informed his sister in a letter of 19 March 1810, to see it performed in the private theatre of Prince Radziwill. There is no record of such a performance having taken place, and this was no doubt yet another of a long line of disappointments that led to Kleist's suicide beside the Wannsee on 21 November 1811.

It was Tieck who recognized Kleist's genius and who in 1816 planned publication of his complete works, which appeared in 1821. He also urged the Dresden Court Theatre to stage *The Prince of Homburg*. The première, however, took place at the Burgtheater in Vienna, under the direction of Josef Schreyvogel (1768–1832).

Like Tieck, Schreyvogel came from a literary background, and his first attempts at directing at the Burgtheater (1802–4) proved unsuccessful. His theatre career effectively began after his return to the Burgtheater in 1813, where, in the ponderous words of Heinz Kindermann, he displayed a 'quite strange synthesis of the conditionality of acting and the clarity of Kant'.[7] The première of *The Prince of Homburg* took place on 3 October 1821,[8] but had to be given the new title of *Die Schlacht von Fehrbellin (The Battle of Fehrbellin)*, in order not to offend a number of Austrian officers by the name of Homburg. Otherwise there were surprisingly few alterations to the text: a number of cuts, a predictable watering down of the scene in which Homburg is terrified at the thought of his own execution, and the significant change of the final patriotic shout: 'Into the dust with all the enemies of Brandenburg!', to read: 'Into battle! On to victory!'.

Visually, with its battle scenes and authentic military costumes, the production should have succeeded well, but the Viennese audience hooted with laughter at the introverted North German figure of Homburg. Particular merriment greeted the contentious line: 'O dieser Fehltritt, blond mit blauen Augen' (literally: 'Oh, this misdemeanour, blond with blue eyes', translated by Diana and Frederick Peters as 'Oh, it was a little error . . . innocent as his blond hair and blue eyes').[9] Much of the failure was caused by miscasting. Maximilian Korn, who played Homburg, was in his late forties and usually played drawing-room lovers. Koberwein, who was well known for his comic roles, played Homburg's antagonist, the Kurfürst. Princess Natalie was also played by an actress well advanced in years (Julie-Sophie Löwe), and it seems that only Gotthelf Koch as Kottwitz was convincing. Schreyvogel's diary for 3 October 1821 records simply that the première was 'a total flop'. The production was repeated five times, until it was closed by the police under orders from the Archduke, who disapproved of the unheroic display of an army officer shuddering before death – a concern that was to bedevil attempts to stage the play in Berlin.

The Dresden première on 6 December 1821 was altogether more successful. This version, prepared by Tieck, was even more faithful to the original than the Viennese text (here changing the ending to: 'Into the dust with all the enemies of

Germania!'). It was directed by Friedrich Julius (whose real name happened to be von Kleist), who also played the lead-role. The staging, and especially the groupings, were highly praised, as was the music, composed in the manner of Beethoven by Heinrich Marschner. This production was revived eighteen times over the following years.

A successful production, opening on 15 October 1821 and repeated six times, was mounted in Breslau, with Mme Unzelmann in the role of the Kurfürstin, while the play flopped in Frankfurt am Main (5 November 1821) and in Karlsruhe (18 December 1821). There were also productions in 1821 in Königsberg, Brünn and Prague, but no information is available about these.

Franz von Holbein, who had already bowdlerized *Das Kätchen von Heilbronn*, now turned his attention to this increasingly popular last play by Kleist. Holbein transformed the Kurfürst into an unsubtle despot, and Homburg, here free of any fear of death, became a brave hero. This version was used, and often further adapted, in Munich, Hamburg, Stuttgart and Hanover, all in 1822.

This drama, already in its different manifestations gaining so much recognition across the German-speaking world, and seemingly written in praise of the Prussian military ethos, still found no acceptance in Berlin. Already in 1799 Schiller's *Wallensteins Lager (Wallenstein's Camp)* could not be performed there because of its critical attitude towards the military.[10] So, despite the support of the Brothers Grimm, Grillparzer and Heine, Tieck's attempts to stage *The Prince of Homburg* in Berlin were thwarted. In 1826 Karl von Holtei tried to smuggle in the piece as a melodrama but failed, so it was not until 26 July 1828 that *The Prince of Homburg* reached the stage of the Berlin Royal Theatre. Even then the piece was considerably adapted, the first scene, for example, being entirely omitted. Some changes to the language were made to avoid the striking verbal risks taken by Kleist: hence 'blond with blue eyes' was changed to: 'as pure as the eyes of a child'.

Once again, it was the Duke of Saxe-Meiningen who first performed *The Prince of Homburg* in its original version, though with some cuts, opening on 28 March 1878.[11]. Since then, it has remained a part of the classical repertoire of German theatre, 'the ultimate test of every actor', as Wagner called it. It enjoyed unfortunate popularity in the Nazi period, because of its apparent nationalistic message, although, as we shall see, Kleist uses theatrical means to make a much more ambiguous statement.

THE PRINCE OF HOMBURG AS A PIECE FOR THE THEATRE

Given Kleist's sceptical attitude towards the theatre of his day, it is unsurprising that his plays do not make many concessions to contemporary stage practice. Neither *The Broken Jug* nor *Penthesilea*, for example, have any act divisions. This is not to say, however, that Kleist does not possess a great theatrical awareness, and it is significant that, despite all his disappointments with the stage and despite his achievements as a writer of *Novellen*, he continued to write major plays throughout his life.

Scenically *The Prince of Homburg* does not make great demands on the theatre, and indeed the 1822 Hamburg version by Holbein and Friedrich Ludwig Schmidt managed, without too great difficulty, to maintain the unity of place. All the battle scenes and deaths are reported, and for a historical piece there are relatively few changes of scene. In the original the plot unfolds as follows:

Act 1, Scenes 1–4 – 'Night' [before dawn on 28 June 1675]
Fehrbellin. Garden of the Castle
Homburg, exhausted from battle against the Swedes, is discovered in a somnambulistic state by the court of the Kurfürst (Elector) of Brandenburg, the antecedent of Prussia. When he awakes, he recalls as in a dream that a beautiful woman, whose glove he has seized, was with him. He is unaware that she was Princess Natalie, the niece of the Kurfürst.
Act 1, Scenes 5–6 – Consecutive on Scene 4 [early morning]
A hall in the Castle
While the officers are being given orders for battle, Homburg discovers that it is Natalie's glove that is missing. He is so overwhelmed that he does not listen to the orders.

Act 2, Scenes 1–2 – [Later that morning]
Battlefield by Fehrbellin
Contrary to orders to await the signal for attack,
Homburg leads his cavalry in a charge against the
Swedes.

Act 2, Scenes 3–8 – [Later the same day]
Room in a village
The Kurfürstin (Wife of the Elector) and Natalie are
brought to a peasant household after their carriage has
met with an accident. Homburg arrives, flushed with
victory, and, on learning that the Kurfürst has been
killed in battle, pledges to defend the women and his
country henceforth. The news of the Kurfürst's death
proves false, however, and Homburg leaves for Berlin
with the women.

Act 2, Scenes 9–10 – [After dusk on the same day]
Berlin. Garden of the Old Castle
with illuminated church
Despite his resounding victory against the Swedes, the
Kurfürst orders Homburg to be court-martialled for
disobeying orders.

Act 3, Scenes 1–2 – [The next day – 29 June 1675]
Fehrbellin. A prison
Homburg, condemned to death by the court-martial,
resolves to see the Kurfürstin to renounce his love for
Natalie, in the hope that this will persuade the Kurfürst
to relent.

Act 3, Scenes 3–5 – [Consecutive on Scene 2]
The Kurfürstin's chamber
On his way to the Kurfürstin, Homburg passes the
grave that is being prepared for him. Now terrified of
death, he renounces Natalie and begs the women to
intercede for his life.

Act 4, Scene 1 – [Consecutive on Act 3 – evening]
The Kurfürst's chamber
Natalie pleads for Homburg's life. The Kurfürst says
that Homburg may go free, if he thinks he has been
unjustly treated.

Act 4, Scene 2 – [Consecutive on Scene 1]
Natalie's chamber
Natalie learns that the officers have signed a petition for
Homburg's release.

Act 4, Scenes 3–4 – [Consecutive on Scene 2]
Homburg's prison
On learning that the condition for his release is to declare his sentence unjust, Homburg consents to his execution.

Act 5, Scenes 1–9 – [A few hours later]
Hall in the castle
The officers are on the verge of mutiny, but relent when they witness Homburg himself in support of the sentence of death passed on him. The Kurfürst is convinced that Homburg has learnt the lesson of obedience.

Act 5, Scenes 10–11 – 'Night' [consecutive on Act 5, Scene 9]
Garden of the Castle, as in Act 1
Homburg is taken out to his place of execution, where his blindfold is suddenly removed to reveal the whole court acclaiming him as the victor of Fehrbellin.

As may be seen, the action almost observes the unity of time, since the plot unfolds over the course of two nights and two days, with the last three acts taking place within the course of a few hours, the only delay being occasioned by the need for Kottwitz's regiment to journey to Fehrbellin. There are three different exterior scenes and six different interior scenes, all of them in the Castle of Fehrbellin, with the exception of the peasant household in Act Two. The battle-scenes are created by sound-effects and dialogue alone, and the only scene of spectacle is Act 2, Scenes 9–10, where, before a crowd 'of all ages and both sexes', the body of a fallen officer is carried in and laid on 'a magnificent catafalque', followed by the captured Swedish standards, borne by officers and accompanied by soldiers.

The piece would therefore have demanded a large cast and would have required a number of scene-changes, especially in Acts Three and Four. However, with the use of a mid-curtain to make the stage shallower for Homburg's prison scenes, Act Three could play without a break by opening the mid-curtain to reveal the more opulent surroundings of the Kurfürstin's chamber. The only difficult change would be for the three short scenes with which Act Four opens, unless one were to resort again to the device of a mid-curtain for the Kurfürst's chamber

– perhaps appropriate for the Spartan character of this military figure, although militating against the stage direction: 'Natalie enters by the middle door'.

The staging of *The Prince of Homburg* was thus well within the resources of an early nineteenth-century theatre. Indeed, one of its failings in the eyes of contemporary theatre managements was its very lack of spectacle and exciting action. The psychological did not sell as well as the physical.

Within the parameters of this fairly simple staging, which may be seen as a synthesis of the historical robustness of the *Sturm und Drang* drama and the cool precision of Goethe's neo-classical pieces, Kleist succeeded in introducing several strongly theatrical elements. First, he displays a good sense of the power of lighting to create a mood. The play opens and closes at night, and much of the fairy-tale atmosphere of the first scene is achieved by the use of torches (five of the first six stage directions refer to their use). There is also the implication that the doorway of the castle in the background is brightly lit, so that when the court withdraws, slamming the door in Homburg's face, he is suddenly plunged into darkness, as though banished from paradise:

> What a strange dream I had! It seemed as though a royal castle, agleam with gold and silver, suddenly opened wide its portals. . . . The ramp to the castle, as I began to mount it, stretched endlessly to the very gates of heaven. . . . And the portals clanged shut again. (Act 1, Scene 4)

With the rising fortunes of Homburg, the day dawns, and the sun shines on the battlefield, as the following lines with their Shakespearean ring testify: 'A beautiful day, as true as I live! A day made by God, the great lord of the world, for better things than fighting! The sun shines reddish through the clouds' (Act 2, Scene 1). The victory concluded, the play returns to darkness with the decision to prosecute Homburg for insubordination. The rest of the piece is sombrely played by the light of candles or of single torches, until the final scene of redemption, when Natalie appears 'surrounded by torches' and the castle is flooded with light. No doubt, although Kleist does not suggest it, the lighting designer could throw in the first glimmer of dawn for good measure.

Underlining the atmospheric quality of the lighting, Kleist makes abundant but careful use of sound-effects and music. After the silence of the opening scenes in the garden, broken only by the clanging shut of the castle door, the 'orders' scene opens to the sound of distant gunfire. The second act also alternates sounds with stillness. The battle scenes, full of the noise of cannons, muskets and shouts of victory, are followed by the subdued scenes in the peasants' home, which in turn are followed by the obsequies and victory celebrations in Berlin with the ringing of church bells and the playing of funeral music.

The play continues in the silent walls of the Castle of Fehrbellin, until the final scenes of the 'execution'. These begin with 'the death march' played on distant drums. Then, when Homburg collapses on discovering that he is being honoured instead of being shot, a march is played; first a single voice hails him, then the officers, and finally all on stage cheer him. There follows a 'moment of silence' broken by Homburg's bewildered question: 'No, tell me! Is this a dream?', after which the shouts build to a crescendo once more. The rhythmic pattern of sound is brilliantly conceived, with the momentary pause an essential element in its shaping.

Kleist in fact makes frequent use of pauses in his text, a technique more usually associated now with modern writers like Beckett and Pinter. To my knowledge, Kleist was the first playwright to place pauses in his dialogue with such precision, in recognition of the fact that silence on stage can be as eloquent as speech. In *The Prince of Homburg* Kleist prescribes twenty 'pauses', two 'short pauses', 'a momentary pause', 'a moment of silence', one 'long pause', and otherwise indicates breaks in the dialogue: 'he stops speaking' ('er hält inne') seven times, 'lost in a dream', 'lost in thought', 'he stares for a while', 'after some thought', and ' he reflects', once each. Thus the play contains no less than thirty-seven different instructions to the actors to interrupt their speech in favour of silent performance.

The visual impact of actors' moves and gestures is particularly significant in *The Prince of Homburg* and witnesses again to Kleist's strong sense of theatre. One scene, Act 1, Scene 2, consists merely of a single stage direction, and often a performer's actions say as much as words. One may cite the sleepwalking of Homburg at the opening, his violent disarming of an insubordinate officer (Act 2, Scene 2) or the intense response by Natalie on learning that the Kurfürst is in fact alive: 'She throws herself at the feet of the Kurfürstin and embraces her body' (Act 2, Scene 7). When Homburg is arrested, the Kurfürst indicates his disinterest by reading despatches (Act 2, Scene 10), Natalie reacts to Homburg's terror of death wordlessly, and 'lowers herself, deeply moved by these words, to sit weeping at a table' (Act 3, Scene 5), and, when Homburg begins to discover some composure in the face of death, 'he lowers himself nonchalantly on to a cushion spread on the floor' (Act 4, Scene 3), reminding one of Napoleon's dictum that it is impossible to be tragic sitting down.

Two pieces of gestic action are particularly striking: one occurs in Act 4, Scene 4, when Natalie brings Homburg the letter from the Kurfürst, saying that he may go free if he considers the sentence unjust. A writer with less sense of theatre would have depended on a verbal debate, before the Prince consents to his death sentence. Here, however, the conflict is externalized in theatrical action. Natalie brings the letter with its conditional promise of pardon, and Homburg reads it. Natalie presses his hand in joy, and herself places a chair for him to sit and pen a letter accepting his pardon. When he attempts to read the wording of the letter again, she tears the letter out of his grasp, and he at last sits, and calls for pen, paper, wax and seal. When a servant has brought these, he begins to write, pauses, then tears up the letter and throws it away. He begins another letter, while Natalie picks up the crumpled sheet and urges him to retain this wording. He pauses again, then tries to seize the Kurfürst's letter to check its content. She withholds it from him, an almost childish game ensues, until he succeeds in grabbing the Kurfürst's letter off her. He reads it again, rises from his chair, sits again, reflects, takes up the pen and at last begins writing once more. He finishes writing, folds and seals the letter, rises and finally hands it to a servant to deliver. Apart from the actual condition set out in the letter, the dynamics of the whole scene could be followed by a deaf member of the audience, so clear is Kleist's theatrical statement.

The other striking example is of a repeated gesture. When in

Act 2, Scene 6, Homburg learns of the Kurfürst's death, he offers consolation to Natalie by taking her hand and placing it on his breast. After a while she withdraws her hand; his desire to become her protector is a little premature for the modest Princess. When, in the final scene, Natalie honours Homburg as the victor of Fehrbellin, the gesture is echoed in reverse: she 'presses his hand on her heart'; he has at last become worthy of her.

The same visual sense is revealed in Kleist's recommendations about costume. For the scene in which Homburg expresses his terror of death, he is required to don the faintly absurd garb of coat and feather-hat over his more manly military uniform. Costume is also used effectively as a signifier at the start of Act Five. The Kurfürst appears 'half undressed' (although propriety usually did not permit this in the theatres of the 1820s) – a daring image though an appropriate one, since it is night-time. On hearing of Kottwitz's apparent mutiny, he 'dresses himself and puts on his official regalia' (Act 5, Scene 4) during the start of the next scene. Thus, in a way that anticipates the scene in Brecht's *Life of Galileo*, where the Pope changes from interested scientist to authoritarian pontiff as he puts on his papal dress, so here the Kurfürst assumes his role of leader as he becomes encased in uniform and regalia.

The piece of costume which comes closest to fulfilling a truly symbolic function is Homburg's blindfold in the final scenes. It exists in its own right as the normal requisite for a prisoner being led to execution, but beyond this it serves also as an indicator of Homburg's lack of awareness of what is really happening in the two scenes, and further still of his conversion from the 'blindness' of an immature and impulsive young man to the clear-sightedness of the mature individual he has now become, a theme to which we shall return later.

It is not only in his strong visual sense that Kleist shows himself to have a genuinely theatrical imagination and to be pioneer of developments in modern drama. His language is also very innovative. In some respects, it looks back rather than forwards: the play is written in blank verse, and, just as in Schiller's verse dramas, the linguistic register remains the same for all characters, be they the Kurfürst or the peasant couple in Act 2, Scene 3.

In other ways, Kleist's dialogue is astonishing. The opening speech of the play consists of a single question, ten lines in length (the Peters' prose translation not unreasonably converts this to two statements and two questions).[12] In other places the expression is so dense that any translation has to be in the nature of a paraphrase, e.g.:

> Du könntest an Verderbens Abgrund stehn,
> Dass er, um dir zu helfen, dich zu retten,
> Auch nicht das Schwert mehr zückte, ungerufen! (Act 5, Scene 9)
> (Literally: You could stand at the abyss of destruction, that he, to help you, to save you, would not even reach for his sword, uncalled for! The Peters' translation: 'you could be standing at the edge of doom and the Prince wouldn't lift a finger to help you: he wouldn't save your life unless you gave the order.'[13])

The literal translation contains twenty-five words, the stage version twenty-nine, and Kleist's original makes do with twenty-two.

The most modern element in Kleist's dialogue is the way he uses it not as a source of communication but as a source of misunderstanding. Again, to my knowledge, Kleist was the first playwright to explore, in a way that we now associate especially with Pinter, the phenomenon that everyday conversation often does not pursue any logical development but frequently consists of parallel monologues with each participant speaking past the other. In an essay of 1805 'On the gradual formulation of thoughts while speaking' he had already rejected the assertion of the rationalist that invariably a thought is formed in the mind and then uttered by the tongue, by referring to one's common experience that thoughts in fact often only present themselves while speaking. Indeed one can virtually 'overhear' oneself saying something which seems to have formulated itself without conscious participation. This recognition often gives Kleist's dialogue, within the constraints of his blank verse, an astonishing spontaneity. A good example is provided by the opening lines of Act Three:

> THE PRINCE OF HOMBURG So there you are, my good friend Heinrich! Welcome! Now, have I been released then?

HOHENZOLLERN *(astonished)* God be praised in the highest!

THE PRINCE OF HOMBURG What are you saying?

HOHENZOLLERN Released? Has he returned your sword to you?

THE PRINCE OF HOMBURG To me? No.

HOHENZOLLERN Not?

THE PRINCE OF HOMBURG No!

HOHENZOLLERN Then why do you think you have been released?

THE PRINCE OF HOMBURG *(after a pause)* I thought that you, you were bringing it to me. – Never mind!

HOHENZOLLERN I know nothing.

THE PRINCE OF HOMBURG Never mind! Do you hear! Never mind! (Act 3, Scene 1)

There are seven questions in these opening lines, as the two men re-establish a channel of communication in the muddied waters of their misunderstanding.

It was complexities like this which hindered Kleist in his efforts to find a theatre to produce *The Prince of Homburg*. More importantly still, a piece which deals with a heroic German victory was shot through with unheroic elements. The death in battle of the leader of Brandenburg is announced in the poor and intimate surroundings of a peasants' cottage, and the title figure is something less than the manly Prussian warrior that nineteenth-century audiences would have favoured. The Prince of Homburg is in fact quite a feminine character; with his blond curls and dreamy intuitive nature he projects more the image of a sensitive artist figure, such as Kleist would have easily identified with, rather than the general of a cavalry regiment. He is the last in a line of Kleist's characters who operate from some guiding instinct rather than from rational deliberation (e.g. Alkmene in *Amphitryon*, Eva in *The Broken Jug*, Kätchen von Heilbronn and the Marquise von O. in the *Novelle* of that name). 'Orders!' cries Homburg, as he prepares to lead the cavalry charge. 'Haven't you received them from your heart?' (Act 2, Scene 2).

The instinctual behaviour which allows these characters to remain convinced of the rightness of their behaviour in the face of all evidence to the contrary, finds philosophical justification in Kleist's most important contribution to the *Berliner Abend-blätter*, the essay 'Über das Marionettentheater' ('On the marionette theatre', 1810). This article, which must have influenced Craig almost a hundred years later in his formulation of the notion of the *Übermarionette*, argues that a marionette is more graceful than a human dancer, because all its movements necessarily follow an inner centre of gravity. This is a rather silly assertion, and seems to display an ignorance of the actual working of marionettes. The argument develops interestingly, however: it is the lack of consciousness of puppets that makes them so graceful, just as it may be observed that humans lose their poise if they raise their natural grace to a conscious level. Kleist gives the example of the destruction of innocence of a beautiful young man, who, drying himself after bathing, was praised for the beautiful pose he had adopted. He tried to repeat the pose, but in vain:[14]

> From that day, from that very moment, a strange transformation came over the young man. He began to spend days in front of the mirror, and his charm diminished bit by bit. An invisible and incomprehensible power seemed like an iron net to be laid over the freedom of his gestures, and after a year had passed no further trace could be discovered of the loveliness which had previously delighted the eyes of all who beheld him.

From this and other examples the conclusion is drawn: 'in the organic world gracefulness emerges more brightly and confidently in proportion to the dulling and weakening of reflection'.[15] Clearly, the attempt to eliminate conscious effort, to banish all striving for effect, contains important lessons for the actor, and gave a philosophical seal of approval to a performer like Fleck, whose inspirational genius Tieck had admired so much.

It also offers an important gloss on the theme of *The Prince of Homburg*. Initially, Homburg is just such a graceful character, free of conscious deliberation, but unlike Kleist's earlier plays this trust in his own instincts is not vindicated by events. He is forced into an educative process by the strict discipline of the Kurfürst. It is not clear however whether, as National Socialist theatre directors would have concluded, this embracing of the Prussian military ideal of unconditional obedience is viewed as entirely positive by Kleist or whether we may infer that, after the jubilation has died away, Homburg will become merely an efficient part of the Prussian fighting-machine, a man of whom it may also be said that 'no further trace could be discovered of the loveliness which had previously delighted the eyes of all who beheld him'.

Clearly, the law of the state has prevailed over the intuition of the individual, but one may question how valid this law is. It may be argued that the orders of the Kurfürst are as arbitrary as the orders that Homburg receives from his heart (after all, objectively the Kurfürst has won a colossal victory through Homburg's action; it is the Kurfürst who pursues the dream of a greater victory). Does the 'happy end' engineered by the too-good-to-be-true autocrat not throw into question what happens in real political life?

Certainly, the celebration of the ending is undercut by its context. For his 'execution' the blindfold Prince returns to the fairy-tale garden of the opening scene, a garden with mysterious flowers, lit by torchlight. On recovering from his faint, he asks: 'No, tell me, is it a dream?', and the level-headed Kottwitz replies: 'A dream, what else?'.

The play is then not a simple celebration of Prussian military ethos, and certainly no piece of Fascist propaganda. It is rather a deeply pessimistic statement about moral and political uncertainties.

This is perhaps why, despite all his disappointments, Kleist remained so committed to the theatre as a medium of expression and displayed such a good theatrical sense in his playwriting; for the theatre lives from the tension between reality and illusion. By writing plays, Kleist could reflect on the nature of reality and our perception of it in a form which is based on the presentation to an audience of an illusion purporting to be reality. The tragedy of Kleist's life was that he so seldom had access to an actual audience.

5

BÜCHNER IN PERFORMANCE
Woyzeck

One of the many extraordinary aspects of Büchner as a playwright is the fact that this widely acknowledged 'father of modern theatre' seems to have had very little first-hand acquaintance with the theatre of his day. He is reputed to have had an affair with an actress in Darmstadt, and it is inconceivable that he did not visit the theatre while studying in Strasbourg. However, in his surviving letters there is not a single mention of any visits to the theatre. He writes of his studies, of his friends, of walking tours in the countryside, of his political views, and, of course, of his writings. It may have been that, as for Kleist, the theatre was a form of entertainment one took for granted, so that he thought it not worth mentioning in his correspondence, any more than a student of today would write to tell her parents that she had watched television the previous evening. But one can affirm that there is no certain evidence that Büchner was even an occasional theatre-goer.

Significantly, too, when in 1835 he wrote his first play, *Dantons Tod* (*Danton's Death*), he apparently made no attempt to have it performed, but submitted it to Karl Gutzkow for publication as a reading text. That it did not receive its première until 67 years later, and that his two other extant dramas, *Leonce und Lena* and *Woyzeck*, were also not performed until decades after his death, are commonplaces of theatre history.

Once again we observe that the growing commercialism of contemporary theatre militated against the presentation of serious plays across the whole of Europe.[1] The nineteenth century saw the rise of the novel and a relative dearth of significant playwriting until the revival in Scandinavia towards the end of the century.

In this sense Büchner both closes a chapter and opens a new one. As a creative writer he still chose to express himself in dramatic form. There is no reason why the historical material of *Danton's Death* or of *Woyzeck* could not be presented as well, perhaps better, in a novel, but Büchner looked to Shakespeare and the theatre of the *Sturm und Drang* for inspiration. Clearly, he held the theatre of the past in the highest regard. It was the theatre of his own day, which, as with Kleist, failed to give him any confidence in it as a medium. So, it seems, his plays were not conceived as pieces for performance but rather as texts to be read, and as such anticipate the publication of, for example, Bernard Shaw's plays with their lengthy stage directions and prefaces.

However, precisely because Büchner did not need to consider how his plays would be staged, he could afford to be theatrically innovatory. The visual literalness of the nineteenth-century stage would have been quite unable to cope with the demands of *Danton's Death*, let alone of the much more fragmentary *Woyzeck*. Except in the inventively staged productions of Tieck, Shakespeare could be performed only by cutting several scenes and rearranging others. The fluidity of the Elizabethan stage had given way to the unwieldy settings of the proscenium-arch stage, and any scene that had a playing time of less than ten minutes would have seemed hardly worth setting up for. Even the makeshift of playing scenes in front of a painted curtain, which was possible for Schiller's *Robbers*, was now becoming increasingly unsatisfactory in view of the public taste for authenticity and spectacle. What a theatre director of the 1830s would have made of the minimal scenes of *Woyzeck* can only be guessed at, but almost certainly he would have regarded the play as an unstageable monstrosity. As it was, even as late as 1913, at the Berlin première of *Woyzeck*, the audience had to sit almost as long staring at the closed curtains behind which the set was being changed as at the action itself.

In considering Büchner's *Woyzeck* as a text for performance it is therefore not possible even to guess at the way it might have been staged at the time it was written, and it is in this respect quite unlike the other pieces we have so far examined. What will emerge is that Büchner, lacking the instant success that the young Schiller had had with *The Robbers*, enjoyed the freedom to consider ways in which theatre might function. As a socialist and an associate of the left-wing *Junges Deutschland* movement, it was predictable that he would decisively reject the neo-classicism of the later Schiller and Goethe, what Büchner refers to as the 'Idealistic school'. In his unfinished novella *Lenz*, he describes the visit of Lenz (1751–1792), the *Sturm und Drang* playwright, to a parsonage in Alsace. One evening at table the conversation turns to literature.[2]

> The Idealistic period was then just beginning; . . . Lenz was strongly opposed. He said that writers of whom it was said that they imitated reality in fact had no conception of it, but at least they were more tolerable than writers who sought to idealize it.
>
> He said: God has created the world the way it should be, and we cannot cobble together anything better, we should just try to copy it as best we can. I demand in all things – life, the possibility of existence, and then all is well. There is then no point in asking whether something is beautiful or ugly; the feeling that something that has been created possesses life, stands above both these qualities and is the only criterion in matters of art. Besides, this is quite a rarity; you can find it in Shakespeare, and we encounter it totally in folk-songs and sometimes in Goethe. All the rest can be thrown in the fire. They cannot even draw a dog's kennel. They try to create idealistic figures, but all that I have seen are wooden dolls. This Idealism reflects the most despicable contempt for human nature. People should try to plunge themselves into real life and to reproduce it in the tiny movements, the little hints, and in the fine, almost imperceptible play of features.

Despite the token praise for Goethe (which refers to a youthful piece like *Götz von Berlichingen*), this is a clear statement in favour of realism as opposed to the idealizing tendencies of neo-classicism, most obviously represented by Goethe's own *Iphigenia*. The sentence, 'There is then no point in asking whether something is beautiful or ugly', would have made Goethe shudder. For Goethe, as we have seen, the search for beauty in his theatre work was not only desirable but essential.

To discover beauty and order in the flux and apparent disorder of the world was the highest achievement of the creative imagination. For Lenz the realist, however, truth was much more important than beauty.

The question must be asked, how far does Lenz's view represent that of Büchner? It must be acknowledged that this alleged conversation takes place in 1778, almost 60 years before the writing of *Danton's Death* and *Woyzeck*, and that the exponent of realism here is otherwise shown in the story to be constantly on the verge of insanity. However, despite these considerations we may observe a close correspondence between Lenz's ideas and those of Büchner as revealed in his letters. There is a striking similarity of phrase between a letter of 1834 to his family ('Elitism is the most despicable contempt for the holy spirit in man')[3] and one of Lenz's observations: 'This Idealism reflects the most despicable contempt for human nature.' Even more conclusively, Büchner writes in a letter to his family after the publication of *Danton's Death*:[4]

> And as for the so-called Idealist poets, I find that they have created marionettes with sky-blue noses and affected emotions, but not human beings of flesh and blood whose sufferings and joy make me feel with them and whose deeds and actions fill me with revulsion or admiration. In a word, I have a high regard for Goethe or Shakespeare, but very little respect for Schiller.

Clearly, Idealism was still alive and well and living in the 1830s, and Büchner felt it necessary to defend the harsh realism of *Danton's Death* against the implied preference for a more 'beautiful' treatment of history, as, for example, in Schiller's version of the Joan of Arc story, in which the heroine dies gloriously on the battlefield.[5]

On the other hand, Büchner did not wholeheartedly embrace realism in his playwriting, and in fact stands much more in the Romantic tradition of Tieck than is commonly supposed. For, like Tieck, he rejected crass naturalism as the way forward and often shows a lack of interest in the kind of authenticity and factual detail that are the stuff of naturalism. As Richard Littlejohns has pointed out,[6] in *Danton's Death* there is no sense of Paris as a specific city, and the common people have little substance, exchanging Shakespearean quibbles with one another: 'Literature shapes Büchner's work far more than reality.' Even in *Woyzeck*, the so-called 'first working-class tragedy', there is considerable vagueness about the specific location or the timing of events, although the latter may be deduced with some confidence.[7]

What Büchner discovered in drama, despite his lack of access to actual performance, was a supremely effective medium for combining his scientific interest in human behaviour, which he might have pursued in the novel, with the immediacy of experience peculiar to the theatre. By exploring this medium without the constraint of considering the practicalities of staging, Büchner not only drew on what was best in the *Sturm und Drang* and the writing of Kleist, but also prepared a way for the future of theatre. So, as we shall see, the theatrical style inherent in *Woyzeck* anticipates the seemingly contradictory movements of both naturalism and expressionism, presenting the central figure as both conditioned by his environment and a prey to irrational forces, and achieving this in images that could be realized in either a realistic or a non-realistic mode. That Gerhart Hauptmann, the leading naturalist playwright, on the one hand, and most German expressionists on the other, acknowledged their debt to Büchner is testimony to the richness of theatrical style contained in *Woyzeck*.

THE TEXT OF *WOYZECK*

There is no definitive text of *Woyzeck*, since the manuscript was unfinished at the time of the author's death. What remains are two drafts (H1 and H2), a further two isolated scenes (H3), and what the eminent Büchner scholar Werner Lehmann[8] has called a 'provisional fair-copy' (H4). From Büchner's last letter written to his fiancée it is almost certain that he intended to complete his play within eight days, and so it would seem that this 'fair-copy' is the most accurate record of his intentions regarding the piece that can now be reconstructed. There are three problems, however: first, the fair-copy breaks off before the murder, so that it is uncertain how the piece is meant to end; second, even in the fair-copy there are gaps (e.g. in the Fairground scene) which Büchner clearly intended to fill later; and finally, and perhaps most controversially, Büchner has omitted from his fair-copy lines and even whole passages which one might well wish to see restored to any working script.

I do not propose to debate all the arguments surrounding the ordering of the text; this has been pursued elsewhere.[9] But the question is of interest not only to Büchner scholars but to anyone wishing to consider the theatrical possibilities of the text.

Let us begin with the opening of the play. For many years it was thought that the play opened with the scene of Woyzeck shaving the Captain, and many published versions and translations begin in this way. This is due to the fact that the first critical edition of Büchner's works in 1922 by Bergemann set the shaving scene at the start of the play. It was not an unreasonable surmise by Bergemann in his attempt to order the fragments of the manuscript. The shaving scene is the one that contains the most information about Woyzeck. From it we learn that he is a military subordinate, aged about thirty ('you've got a good thirty years left'[10]), that he has an illegitimate child, is poor, is rather dull-witted but seems to possess a certain native wisdom, and that he tends always to rush. There are also two further attractive characteristics of this scene. It contains the most pointed social criticism of the play ('if I was a gentleman and I had a watch and a big coat and all the proper words, I'd be virtuous alright'); it is also tantalizing in that the Captain may in fact be the focus of the scene. It is an interesting theatrical development to discover that it is the subordinate, the servant who waits on him, who is the protagonist and that the Captain's role is peripheral.

By deciding that *Woyzeck* should open in this way, Bergemann was understandably following his own notions of what conventional dramaturgy would demand in terms of exposition. The information conveyed in the shaving scene lends clarity; we discover who Woyzeck is, and we are invited to adopt certain attitudes both in terms of preferring his simple statements to the blustering cleverness and pompous moralizing of the Captain and in sympathizing with his poverty. Moreover, we are in a congenial interior setting, with 'the fourth wall removed'. This could easily be the opening of a naturalist play.

Thanks to Lehmann, however, we now know that *Woyzeck* actually opens with the scene in which Woyzeck is cutting sticks with Andres. The effect is quite different. We are outdoors, at sunset. There are two figures dressed as soldiers cutting sticks in the grass. One whistles, whether nonchalantly or to reassure himself is not clear. The other speaks of the mysteriousness of the place, of the curse of the ghostly head, of the Freemasons, of movement in the hollow earth beneath him, of the strange silence of the evening, and finally, in Biblical language, of the fiery sunset ('A fire raging in the sky and a clamour there below like trumpets'). Even his more sober companion sings a desolate song, is infected by Woyzeck's terror and allows himself to be dragged into the bushes to hide from the awful vision. In terms of actual information we learn little. Indeed, Woyzeck remains unnamed until almost the end of the scene. Who these men are and why they are cutting sticks remains unclear; what is important is the atmosphere of the place. With its emphasis on mood rather than exposition, this scene could easily be the opening of a symbolist or expressionist play.

At once we confront the major problem of *Woyzeck* in performance: is the play a piece of realist theatre or is it a non-naturalistic drama? The opening preferred by Bergemann suggests the former; the undoubtedly more authentic opening the latter.

The same difficulty is a feature of the ending. It is impossible to say how Büchner intended to end his play. The provisional fair-copy was unfinished, and the evidence from the first draft is ambiguous. On the one hand, this H1 draft shows Woyzeck (here called Louis) returning to the scene of the murder to dispose of the knife with which he has killed Marie. He throws the knife into a pond, but is immediately anxious that it might be discovered in the shallows, and so wades in to throw it further out into the deep water. This scene has led to the assumption that the play would have ended with Woyzeck's gradual descent into the water until he drowned either accidentally or as a suicidal act.

In addition though there is a further fragment in H1 which shows a court usher commenting with satisfaction on the 'good murder' in the presence of a doctor, judge and barber. Because the 'Barber' is described here as 'tall, thin', it has often been asserted that this must be Woyzeck himself, but the Barber is also described as a 'dogmatic atheist' which would be a totally inappropriate description of Woyzeck. It seems much more likely that the Barber was to be introduced to comment on the murder in a way that might counter the moralizing tendencies of the court. This fragment could have pointed towards ending the play with either an inquest or a trial, and so in no way helps to resolve the problem of what happens to Woyzeck.[11]

My own guess is that Büchner himself was not at all sure how to conclude his play, since it would be otherwise remarkable that so few fragments survive that indicate his intentions. On the one hand, he would no doubt have been drawn towards the possibility of remaining faithful to his source (the historical Woyzeck was beheaded in 1824 after a trial for murder) and would also have welcomed the possibility of debating the issues in a courtroom scene; on the other hand, such a trial scene would have been a cumbersome and discursive addition to the tightly constructed and dense quality of the existing scenes. For the record, most stage versions of *Woyzeck* have ended with Woyzeck's death instead of his being brought to trial.

What matters to us here, though, is not so much the impossible attempt to unravel Büchner's intentions regarding the ending as to note again the different theatrical impetus that would result from choosing one conclusion in favour of another. If the decision is taken to end the play with a trial, then there will be a greater concentration on the social aspects of the play and on Woyzeck's motivation; such a trial ending would be more appropriate to a naturalist piece. If, however, the play were to culminate in the drowning of Woyzeck, then the sense of tragic waste will be much greater, our preoccupation will be much more with the fate of the individual than with social causes.

Here then we have a curious phenomenon, a theatrical text so full of varying possibilities that even the ordering of the scenes and the decision regarding its ending will have an effect on the style of performance. The director will to a certain extent be obliged to construct his or her own text, which will then strongly influence all subsequent theatrical decisions.

THE STRUCTURE

The fact that there can be so much debate about the possible ordering of the scenes in *Woyzeck* is an indicator that they do not develop the action in conventional terms of plot with the Aristotelian 'beginning, middle and end'. The beginning and end are in doubt, and the scenes of the 'middle' could be presented in many different sequences without upsetting the telling of the story – the hall-mark of what in this century has become known as an 'epic' structure. Whether it was in fact Büchner's intention that *Woyzeck* should remain in its present fragmentary, elliptical state also can no longer be known. *Danton's Death* had already included several short scenes, so there is no reason why the montage quality of *Woyzeck* with its very modern feel should not have been intentional.

Once again, however, it is difficult to interpret this intention in terms of theatrical style. On the one hand, the kaleidoscopic quality of the many short scenes creates the impression of a dream. By illuminating aspects of Woyzeck's story by flashes rather than in the linear development of conventional dramaturgy, Büchner conveys all the disconnectedness familiar from the structure of expressionist drama.

On the other hand, it may be argued that such a dramatic structure in fact more nearly accords with our perceptions of reality than that of the 'well-made' play. Both our apprehension of the world and the manner in which the brain recalls the past are more in the nature of a series of fragments than the continuum which is suggested by the coherent development of the conventional dramatic plot. In the same way a realistic painting or photograph in effect distorts reality by suggesting that everything we see, foreground and background alike, are perfectly in focus, when actually they cannot be. Just as our brain forms coherent images by piecing together fragmentary images, so we may find that the montage structure of Büchner's play in fact more closely corresponds to our concept of the 'real' than do the so-called realist plays of, say, Ibsen, in which, in Brecht's words, 'each scene leads into the next'.

The same observation may be made about the structure of individual scenes. In the scene where Woyzeck sees Marie dancing with the Drum-Major (Scene 11 in H4, Mackendrick's Scene 12), for example, there are various elements which coexist autonomously: the drunken speeches of the Journeymen, the sermon of the First Journeyman, the singing, the erotic utterances of Marie and the Drum-Major, and the jealous agonizings of Woyzeck himself. Any of these elements could be set in time before any other or exist in isolation from the rest. Again, there is no suggestion of a linear development in the dialogue. It is at once intensely naturalistic, for this is indeed how the sounds of a tavern may be perceived, and yet it again shares the quality of the dream – or a nightmare.

Here again we are faced with a paradox regarding the realization of *Woyzeck* in performance: the structure suggests not only the dream-like distortions of expressionist theatre but also a super-realism that anticipates the most extreme forms of naturalism.

THE CHARACTERS

A similar problem surfaces when considering the characters of *Woyzeck*. When we examine the protagonist himself, we can speak in terms of a naturalist character: we are told a little of his past, a fair amount about his economic and social situation, and are allowed as many insights into his psychological motivation as we may reasonably expect from someone as inarticulate as Woyzeck. We learn his precise age, his rank, his marital situation, details of his income, we know that he has a sister and an invalid mother, and so on. In Stanislavskian terminology, the actor is provided with quite a number of 'given circumstances', and those he is not provided with can be fairly easily constructed from the social context of the piece.

When we consider the Captain or Doctor, however, we can only surmise about their past and can say little about their present situation. We know nothing about their existence outside the roles they play of military officer and experimenter/teacher.[12] They are flat, two-dimensional characters, and in this regard anticipate the cipher-like figures of expressionist drama and the social representatives of Brecht.

It would be tempting to conclude that Büchner has made a division between the named characters (e.g. Woyzeck, Marie) and the unnamed figures (Doctor, Captain, Drum-Major, Showman, etc.). However, the named characters like Andres and Margaret have no more substance than the anonymous characters. What does distinguish the Drum-Major from Andres, though, is that the latter clearly has Büchner's sympathy, whereas the Drum-Major (and even more obviously the Captain and Doctor) are not only two-dimensional but are given parodistic treatment. Unimaginative as Andres may be, we nevertheless witness him sharing Woyzeck's fears, trying to dissuade Woyzeck from becoming obsessed with Marie and encouraging him to seek a cure for his 'fever'. Andres is neither a rounded nor a particularly positive character, but there is nothing about him which invites us to dismiss him as an individual. A play like Woyzeck is hardly replete with jokes, but what laugh lines there are, are all invariably at the expense of figures like the Captain, the Doctor and the Drum-Major:

CAPTAIN. It makes me worried about the world, the thought of eternity. It's some business, Woyzeck, some business! Eternity . . . is eternity . . . is eternity – you can see that. But it's also not eternity, it's a single moment, Woyzeck, yes, a single moment. It's frightening, how the world turns round in a day. What a waste of time![13]

DOCTOR. I'd just stuck my nose out of the window and was letting the sunbeams play on it in order to observe the phenomenon of the sneeze.[14]

DRUM-MAJOR. You should see me Sundays with my plume and gauntlets. That's really something. 'He's my idea of a soldier,' the prince always says, 'A real man.'[15]

The essential distinction between Büchner's characters is then governed by the level of sympathy they engender. On the one hand, there are the named characters, all belonging to the common people, who even though they may not be very praiseworthy (Margaret, for example, is hardly an exemplary neighbour), at least do not participate in the exploitation of Woyzeck. On the other hand, there are the anonymous figures, who are either mere functionaries in the plot (Showman, Journeymen, Jew) or, as we have seen, are treated parodistically. This distinction reflects Büchner's socialist thinking, revealed in the letter he wrote to his family in February 1834:[16]

I despise nobody, least of all because of their intellect or education, because nobody can determine not to become a fool or a criminal – because if our circumstances were the same, we should surely all become the same, and our circumstances lie beyond our control. *Intellect* is after all only a very small aspect of our spiritual being, and education only an arbitrary form of it. . . . People say that I turn everything to mockery. It is true, I often laugh, but I don't laugh at what *kind* of man someone is but simply that he *is* a man, something he can't do anything about, and I laugh at myself at the same time because I share his fate. . . . Admittedly, I do have another kind of mockery, but it is not of contempt but of hatred. Hatred is as acceptable as love, and I nurture it in abundance against those very people *that are contemptuous.* There is a great number of them, who possess laughable extraneous qualities which is called education or a load of dead lumber which goes by the name of learning, and who lay out the great mass of their fellow beings on the altar of their own contemptuous egotism. Elitism is the most despicable contempt for the holy spirit in man, and I turn its own weapons against it: arrogance against arrogance, mockery against mockery. – You might do best to check with the man who polishes my boots. If I were arrogant or contemptuous towards people without much intellect or education, then he would be a perfect object. Please just ask him some time. . . . I hope you don't believe me capable of looking down my nose at people. And I hope too that I have cast more looks of pity towards those that suffer and are oppressed than I have said bitter words to those whose hearts are genteel and cold.

What we encounter here is a wholly new concept of characterization and a reversal of traditional notions of which characters deserve our sympathy. Throughout the history of European drama the convention had been that only noble figures were worthy of sympathy; slaves and peasants were at best a source of humour. Now Büchner invites our concern for precisely those formerly despised figures – the Woyzecks and the men who polish boots – while the educated classes – or those like the Drum-Major who are perverted by their superiors – are treated with contempt.

This opens up intriguing possibilities in theatrical performance: Woyzeck, Marie, Andres, Margaret, and Käthe might all approach their roles in a naturalist manner, employing Stanislavskian principles, sharing with the audience the necessary empathy that the performer must develop towards the character. All the other roles might be created in a more distanced and critical manner, using techniques associated with the creation of comic roles, or the 'alienated' style of Brechtian acting, or what I have elsewhere described as the 'abstractionist' mode of expressionist performance.[17] It might even be appropriate for this latter category of characters to wear masks, a strong theatrical signifier of a role that fulfils a generalized function rather than presents an individual.

THE SETTING

As might be expected, most of Büchner's stage directions are minimal, merely defining the location – Marie's room, tavern, etc. Of the twenty-four scenes of the 'provisional fair-copy', eleven are set outdoors, eleven are interior scenes, and two are indeterminate. The high proportion of exterior scenes militates against a naturalistic treatment, for while it is easy enough to create the interior of a room on stage, it is a much more difficult undertaking to reproduce an outdoor scene, especially where this includes a fairground or a pond.

It is interesting too how Büchner shifts focus in a scene in a quite cinematic manner. In Scene Two, for example, the scene begins with Marie and her neighbour Margaret watching from Marie's window as the Drum-Major parades past. Margaret makes a hasty exit, and Marie sings a lullaby to her child; she is brought into close-up after the public scene of the march-past. Woyzeck then appears in the street and is invited in by Marie; once again we go into medium long-shot. After Woyzeck's exit, we then go into close-up as Marie addresses her child again, and it seems that we follow her into the room ('The streetlamp usually shines in all the time'[18]). Similarly, the fairground scene, which exists only in draft form, takes place both outside and in the Showman's tent.

One interesting case of this 'cinematic' treatment is provided by the scene in which Woyzeck sees Marie and the Drum-Major dancing together at the tavern. Büchner's stage direction reads: *'Tavern. The windows open, dancing. Benches in front of the tavern.'*[19] The long speeches of the Journeymen therefore take place outside the tavern, and the dancers are glimpsed only through the open window. This could be very effective using a camera in close-up, but it is hard to envisage how it would be possible to give sufficient focus to the dancing couple in the theatre.

It would seem that Büchner had strong visual images for his scenes but that he made no effort to consider how they might be realized on stage. Given the literalness of scenic interpretation prevalent in the theatre of his day, this is not surprising. The director and set designer of more recent times will have to seek imaginative solutions for the problems that Büchner's settings create and so almost inevitably will be impelled towards a non-naturalistic décor.

THE LANGUAGE

In many respects the language of *Woyzeck* anticipates naturalist speech in the theatre: utterances are curt and reproduce the ellipses of everyday speech, and dialect is used for the first time in German-language drama without any comic intent. The language is anything but literary; Büchner deliberately limits his expressive range by allowing his characters to articulate only what would be realistically possible for them to communicate. We sense that Woyzeck has significant insights, but Büchner does not cheat by affording Woyzeck the ability to describe these coherently (for example, Büchner omits from his fair-copy Woyzeck's sententious line: 'Everyone's an abyss. You get dizzy if you look down.'[20]). Instead, by setting his mumbled thoughts against the empty loquacity of the Captain and the Doctor, his ideas are given some credence without our being able to understand them:[21]

> WOYZECK.   Have you ever seen nature inside-out, Doctor? When the sun stands still at midday and it's 's if the world was going up in flames? That's when the terrible voice spoke to me.
> DOCTOR.   You've an aberration, Woyzeck.
> WOYZECK.   Yes. Nature, Doctor, when nature's out –
> DOCTOR.   What does that mean, 'when nature's out'?

WOYZECK. When nature's out, that's – when nature's *out*. When the world goes so dark you have to feel your way round it with your hands, till you think it's coming apart like a spider's web.

Logically, Woyzeck's observations do not add up to much: his apocalyptic vision contains the contradictory notions of blinding midday light and of total darkness, and his initial attempt to define 'nature's out' consists merely of more emphatic repetition. However, the Doctor's callous diagnosis, 'You've an aberration, Woyzeck', pre-empts any desire on our part to dismiss Woyzeck's words as insane ramblings. Instead, without our being able to attach any clear meaning to the phrase 'when nature's out', we would rather share in the manic visions of Woyzeck than identify with the unimaginative response of the Doctor.

Büchner has here discovered a new means of poetic expression: in place of the overtly poetic style, for example, of Goethe in his *Iphigenia*, he reveals the poetic potential of ordinary speech. The power of Woyzeck's utterances derive in large part from the rich Biblical and folk language that they contain. There are several direct quotations from the Bible in the play, and the speech of the First Journeyman is a parodistic treatment of Old Testament prophecies. The Grandmother's frightening fable is cast in the idiom of the folk-tale, and, generally, the simple language with frequent references to animals is reminiscent of peasant speech.

All of these characteristics again anticipate the practice of Brecht. This is seen above all in the gestural language of Büchner, which may be seen as a forerunner of Brecht's concern with what he was to call (after Lessing) 'Gestik'. There are few stage directions in *Woyzeck*, not, as with *Iphigenia*, because the poetic language does not require a strong visual dimension, but because moves and gestures and emotional attitudes are so often implied by the dialogue:[22]

WOYZECK *enters*. MARIE *starts and covers her ears*.
WOYZECK. [*stops, stares and points at her left ear*] What's that?
MARIE. [*clenching her hands tighter, turning her left ear away from him and so inadvertently revealing her right hand clamped over her other ear*] Nothing.

WOYZECK. [*still concentrating on her left ear*] Under your fingers; it's shining.

MARIE. [*forced to admit it, jutting her chin defiantly*] An earring. I found it.

WOYZECK. [*suspiciously*] I never found that kind of nothing. [*Now noticing her other hand, pulls it away from her right ear*] Two at once, too.

MARIE. [*still defiant*] So? What does that make me?

WOYZECK. [*considering whether to express his fears and accuse her of infidelity, slowly lets his hand drop from hers and withdraws from the confrontation*] You're alright, Marie. [*Changing the subject to something that they share*] Kid's well away, look at him. 'Ll just move this arm so he doesn't get cramp. [*He does so. Looking down at the sleeping child*] Shiny drops, all over his forehead. – Nothing but work under the sun; we even sweat in our sleep. The poor. [*Taking some money from his pocket and giving it to Marie*] – Some more money, Marie. My pay and the extra from the Captain.

MARIE. [*quietly, guiltily*] God reward you, Franz.

WOYZECK. [*Communication now restored, he hovers a moment, uncertain whether to address Marie directly again. Decides against it*] Got to go. See you tonight. (*He goes out.*)

In this passage only the first and last stage directions are Büchner's; all those in square brackets are my own. Büchner did not include them, for they are in fact redundant, the kind of stage direction authors might append only if they did not trust the director or reader. One might dispute my own interpretation of just what the dialogue implies in terms of movement, and there still remains some latitude for the performers to find the most appropriate moves: e.g. does Marie take the offered money in her hand, or does Woyzeck put it down beside her or in her lap? What is important, is that almost each line contains the suggestion of movement and attitude. In this way, Büchner compensates for the verbal inarticulacy of his characters by providing them with an extensive vocabulary of gesture.

In terms of the overall production style, the language that Büchner uses would suggest that there is no need to go beyond realistic staging to convey the meaning of the text. A well thought-out naturalistic production would reveal the subtleties of the subtext without recourse to expressionistic exaggeration or distortion.

CONCLUSION

As we can see, *Woyzeck* is a remarkable phenomenon. It is impossible to discuss it in the way one may consider most plays as texts for performance, since it cannot have been composed with immediate performance in mind. In this Büchner was not alone: many of the more progressive pieces of theatre of this period had to wait for the theatre to catch up with the demands some playwrights made on it. So, for example, Tieck's *Der gestiefelte Kater* (*Puss in Boots*), published 1797, was first performed in 1844, and the plays of Grabbe fared even worse: *Herzog Theodor*, published in 1827 was premièred in 1892; *Scherz, Satire, Ironie und tiefere Bedeutung*, 1827 and 1907; *Die Hohenstaufen*, 1829/30 and 1875; *Napoleon*, 1831 and 1869; *Hannibal*, 1835 and 1918; and *Die Hermannsschlacht*, 1838 and 1936!

Clearly, Büchner committed himself to realism as opposed to the idealizing tendency of neo-classicism, but we should not necessarily understand this realism to coincide with the extreme forms of naturalism that were to follow later in the century. For one thing, Büchner's realism accommodates the possibility of individual motivation that cannot be ascribed purely to personal psychology or to the effect of the social environment. It also allows our empathy and understanding for the common people, above all for Woyzeck himself, to be intensified by setting them against mask-like figures.

We cannot therefore conclude that a performance of Büchner should be approached as a piece of naturalism. Such an approach would be unhelpful for the actors playing the Captain and the Doctor; for the set-designer it would be an impossibility. On the other hand, a full-blooded expressionist treatment would be similarly unproductive. The subtleties of *Woyzeck* do not require overstatement. As Lenz urges, real life should be reproduced 'in the tiny movements, the little hints, and in the fine, almost imperceptible play of features'.

As with Shakespeare, whom Büchner so much admired, there is no right way of performing *Woyzeck*; with both writers there is a juxtaposition of the realistic with the non-realistic; directors, actors, set and costume designers have no contemporary model to match themselves against and have to find their own solutions. Perhaps in the search for these solutions, they might consider abandoning received notions of stylistic unity, just as Shakespeare's actors may have done;[23] in this search it is just possible that a new unity based on a synthesis of naturalism and expressionism may be found.

We cannot even know whether Büchner imagined that one day the theatre would be ready for *Woyzeck* or whether, as with *Danton's Death*, he was intending to publish the piece as a reading text. With his knowledge of and respect for Shakespeare, Büchner must have recognized that theatre was not necessarily limited by the literal conventions of his own day, and no doubt looked forward to a theatre that would accommodate his extraordinary piece. While this can only be surmise, since there are no extant comments of Büchner on theatre, we can at least assert with some confidence that he championed a revolution in theatre, a revolution that would concern itself with the attempt to bring into harmony the two opposing styles of *Woyzeck*. That this attempt still preoccupies the theatre of our own day may be witnessed in the statement by Peter Stein, the leading contemporary German theatre director, made in 1976:[24]

> There are two divergent strains in all theatre work: on the one hand there is an instinctive need for greater rationality, for greater precision, for 'scientification', as Herr Brecht called it; in a totally different direction there are questions about the irrationality of what theatre represents, about its immediate 'experientiality'. They are two aspects of current work which have become separated and which somehow must be brought together again.

That Büchner recognized this need over a century and a half ago is nothing short of remarkable.

CONCLUSION

The emergence of the first German theatre was as spectacular as the equally belated and rapid industrial revolution in Germany a century later, and, regrettably, eventually shared with it the same concern for profit.

It would have been impossible for a German actor of the mid-eighteenth century to conceive of what changes would take place in one generation: the shift from theatre as a fairground sideshow to a major part of cultural life; the erection of magnificent theatre buildings; the founding of the first National Theatre in 1767; the long-awaited convergence of literature and theatre in the plays of Lessing, Schiller, Goethe and the writers of the *Sturm und Drang*; the care and intelligence devoted to the training of actors, to the rehearsing of plays and to the design of costumes and sets; the social acceptance of actors; and especially the repeated assertion that the theatre would form the focus for German nationhood.

Sadly, with success developed commercial pressures, the need to fill seats and to satisfy the tastes of an increasingly prosperous bourgeoisie. Before long, literature and theatre diverged once more, Kleist finding it difficult to have his plays performed, Büchner, hailed by figures as divergent as Artaud and Brecht as the father of modern theatre, finding it impossible.

The story of the first German theatre is both glorious and disheartening, but the seeds sown then are still bearing fruit on the stages of Germany today. For despite all commercializing tendencies, the theatre in Germany has retained its status as a major aspect of cultural life. The tradition of court theatre, seen at its best in Mannheim and Weimar, and later at Meiningen,

158

has, despite all historical upheavals, lent German theatre a prestige that is envied in Anglo-Saxon nations.

A German finds it difficult to comprehend why a British audience should pay tax to see *Hamlet* in the theatre, when they pay no tax to buy the text in a book-shop. What is primarily culture to the German is 'entertainment' to the British.

Because of this cultural status, the theatre in Germany today often functions as a museum. Hence most theatres operate an expensive and demanding 'repertoire' system, with a different play being performed each evening. While this repertoire will embrace some contemporary writing, it will also inevitably include classical pieces of world theatre, so that performances of plays, say, by Sophocles, Lope de Vega, or Molière are not the rare occurrences they are on English-speaking stages. In order to propose and facilitate the production of world theatre, all theatres boast at least one *Dramaturg*, a direct link with the role performed by Lessing at Germany's first National Theatre in Hamburg.

The seriousness of German theatre work is also indicated by the economic structure of municipal and regional theatres. Supported by very generous public funding, managements can afford to maintain a standing ensemble of performers, just as Dalberg and Goethe did two centuries ago. The emphasis on ensemble acting and on corporate discipline, so praised, for example, by Beckett in his work at the Schiller-Theater in West Berlin, contrasts strongly with the individualistic style of American and British performers. Once again, it may be traced back to the practices of the court theatres, and especially to the model established by Goethe at Weimar.

If one looks back, then, at the achievements of the first German theatre, one sees much that, in terms of staging, now seems clumsy and naive; one sees a theatre under Goethe whose elevated style led to excessive formality; and eventually a commercial theatre that failed to recognize the talents of some of the finest playwrights of the day.

Nevertheless, these authors continued stubbornly to write for the theatre, and the bold style of writers like Kleist and Büchner established a tradition of experimentation which brought forth the Naturalists, the Expressionists, and the political theatre of Piscator and Brecht. Today Germany, with

159

directors like Peter Stein, Peter Zadek and Claus Peymann, continues to boast not only the best funded theatres of the world but also the most innovative.

The first German theatre was long in coming, a century or two after the golden ages of Spanish, English and French theatre, but, once arrived, it laid the foundations for what has arguably become the theatre nation of the world.

APPENDIX 1

THEATRE RULES FOR THE MANNHEIM NATIONAL THEATRE (1780)

In order further to improve the quality of a good piece of theatre, to add to the pleasure of the public, and to promote the goal of dramatic art itself, the Management of the Royal Theatre has thought it fit, following the praiseworthy example of several other well-organized German theatres, to draw up rules that will further these objectives and to which in future each member of this Royal Theatre shall have to adhere. They are as follows:

1   The monthly repertoire shall be shown to each member, and unless there are any well-founded objections which shall be provided immediately in writing, then nothing may be permitted to impede the performance of the pieces scheduled for that month, except in the case of illness which must always be attested by a medical certificate. Penalty for infringement the deduction of one quarter of the weekly wage.

2   Each member is required to arrive at read-throughs and rehearsals at precisely the hour determined by Director Seyler. Anyone who comes a quarter of an hour too late shall suffer the deduction of one sixth of the weekly wage.

3   Whoever misses a rehearsal or comes too late shall suffer the deduction of one quarter of the weekly wage.

4   At each dress-rehearsal, as well as at rehearsals for pieces that have already been performed, each member shall rehearse without a script and shall know his part thoroughly. Penalty for infringement the deduction of one

quarter of the weekly wage.

5 At each dress-rehearsal of a new play each member shall play their role in character and at least in such a way that a sketch of the character is clearly recognizable, so that any faults may be corrected. Penalty for infringement the deduction of one sixth of the weekly wage.

6 At no rehearsal shall anybody be on stage except those who are needed to perform, and all members are required to pay attention to their entrances. Penalty for infringement at a dress-rehearsal the deduction of one tenth of the weekly wage. Penalty for infringement during an actual performance the deduction of one eighth of the weekly wage.

7 No-one is permitted to indulge in an argument with any theatre personnel or to abuse anyone with words or actions, either in the theatre or wardrobe. Penalty for infringement the deduction of one sixth of the weekly wage.

8 Costumes that have been decided upon for a piece may not be changed, and, except in the greatest emergency and with the prior knowledge of Director Seyler, no alterations may be made to them. Penalty for infringement the deduction of one tenth of the weekly wage.

9 Domestic servants may enter the theatre only if they are needed to dress their employers; the same applies to hairdressers. Otherwise, they shall be shown to the upper gallery of the theatre, so that they may be on hand. Penalty for infringement, or for anyone bringing a stranger into the theatre or wardrobe, the deduction of one eighth of the weekly wage.

10 On no account will children be tolerated in the theatre; anyone bringing in a child shall pay 3 guilder.

11 Whoever through carelessness or malice ruins their costumes, throws them into grease or dirt or uses them for wiping off make-up or cleaning their shoes, shall pay not only for the damage but shall suffer a deduction of one twelfth of the weekly wage.

12 Whoever refuses a role that has been allocated by the Director and confirmed by the Management or sends the part back with some empty excuse and refuses to play it, shall be penalized by suffering the deduction of one

quarter of the weekly wage.

13 Whoever fails to follow the admonitions, instructions and orders of Director Seyler at read-throughs or other rehearsals whether inside or outside the theatre, or behaves in an improper manner towards him in word or action, shall suffer the deduction of one half of the weekly wage.

14 Whoever in their performance makes changes or additions to the detriment of the piece, or introduces unseemly business or slapstick, shall pay the eighth part of their weekly wage.

15 In the case of a proven obscene performance the contract shall be suspended.

16 No-one may leave the town for more than 24 hours without giving notice, even if they are free at this time. Penalty for infringement the deduction of one quarter of the weekly wage.

17 The Director shall inform the paymaster of all fines and arrange for their deduction.

18 To calculate the fines, each annual salary shall be averaged out per week.

19 All these fines shall be placed in a box designated for the purpose and are to be distributed among needy travelling actors.

So that no member is able to complain of partiality, Director Seyler is instructed, in especially doubtful cases or incidents or those that are not described above, to convene a committee of four members of the company, who shall be empowered to arbitrate on the doubtful case.

Each member of the company shall be called upon to serve on this committee in turn according to circumstances and appropriate fitness, but only in doubtful cases.

In the case of this committee failing to reach agreement on the questions placed before it, the Theatre Management shall have the final decision.

In the case of important incidents or with respect to such matters that affect the general welfare and are not laid down in the above rules, any member may demand a committee of different members who shall examine and decide upon the matter.

The Royal Theatre Management however reserve the right to approve such decisions.

Mannheim, 1780

The Royal Theatre Management

APPENDIX 2

INSTRUCTIONS REGARDING COMMITTEE MEETINGS (1782)

In each committee meeting the following items shall be addressed according to the agenda laid down here:

1 The minutes of the previous meeting shall be read out by the chairman.

2 The critique and the relevant written comments on the performances of each play which have taken place between one committee meeting and the next, shall be read out by each member of the committee.

It is understood that an actor can give a complete critique of a play only if s/he has not performed in it. If no actors were free, the critique shall be given by the Management itself.

In these critiques anonymity should be carefully preserved. Therefore they shall be submitted some days before the committee meeting, but without signing one's name.

3 Each member may have the opportunity of proposing new plays for performance, and must provide a written critique of any pieces which s/he has been given by the Management for consideration, or which members have experienced for themselves.

4 Each member must indicate any proposed necessary changes, omissions or additions to a role or a play and must provide the reasons for such amendments, so that judgment may be passed on them.

5 Any infringements of the theatre regulations shall be

announced, and proposals for improvement made.

6 The programme for the following fourteen days shall be decided upon, whereby preferably a comedy should be performed on Sundays, a tragedy on Tuesdays and an operetta on Thursdays.

7 All complaints that have been received shall be examined and judged impartially.

8 Articles in theatre journals that contain new or remarkable ideas shall be read out and assessed. The chairman shall be responsible for reading out such articles in addition to any correspondence that has been received.

9 The chairman, or in his absence the vice-chairman, shall also keep minutes.

10 At each meeting the Management shall pose a dramaturgical question, which each member is required to answer in writing at the next meeting. Whoever excels in such essays in the course of one year shall receive the prize of a medal of twelve ducats.

Mannheim, 23 August 1782   The Royal Theatre Management
                             Freiherr von Dalberg

CHRONOLOGY 1767–1837

This table lists the most significant play productions on German-language stages in the seventy years from the opening of the National Theatre in Hamburg in 1767 until the death of Büchner in 1837. After a summary of major historical and cultural events for each year the following information is given:

1 Date of première (where known)
2 Author and title of work performed. Long titles have been abbreviated. Titles of all non-German pieces are rendered into English.
3 Theatre and/or town where performed
4 Director and/or leader of troupe
5 Lead actors or actresses (given only in significant cases)

The following abbreviations are used:

Burgth Vienna – Burgtheater Vienna; Fft/Main – Frankfurt am Main; Kgl Th Berlin – Königliches Theater Berlin; Kurfürstl Th Bonn – Kurfürstliches Theater Bonn; Th in L Vienna – Theater in der Leopoldstadt Vienna; Weimar Am Th – Weimar Amateur Theatre

1767

Opening of National Theatre, Hamburg (22 April). Lessing begins *Hamburgische Dramaturgie*. Herder's *Fragmente*.

30.9	Lessing: *Minna von Barnhelm*	Hamburg	Ackermann
	Lessing: *Minna von Barnhelm*	Leipzig	Döbbelin

1768

Goethe: *Die Laune des Verliebten.*

Lessing: *Minna von Barnhelm*	Berlin	Döbbelin
Shakespeare/Weisse: *Richard III*	Hamburg	

1769

Invention of practical steam engine. National Theatre, Hamburg, forced to close. Klopstock: *Hermanns Schlacht.*

22.6	Gerstenberg: *Ugolino*	Berlin	Döbbelin

1770

Goethe: *Die Mitschuldigen.* Goethe completes studies in Strasbourg. Sonnenfels: *Programm eines Nationaltheaters.*

Shakespeare/Weisse: *Richard III*	Burgth Vienna

1771

Goethe: *Zum Schäkespears Tag.* J.P. Sulzer: *Allgemeine Theorie der schönen Künste.* On death of Konrad Ackermann, his troupe taken over by Schröder. Heinrich Koch takes over licence for Berlin theatres from Schuch. Ekhof goes to Weimar Court Theatre.

10.6	Lessing: *Miss Sara Sampson*	Kgl Th Berlin	Koch

1772

First partition of Poland by Russia, Austria and Prussia. Wieland takes post as tutor in Weimar.

13.3	Lessing: *Emilia Galotti*	Brunswick	Döbbelin	
6.4	Lessing: *Emilia Galotti*	Berlin	Koch	
14.5	Lessing: *Emilia Galotti*	Hamburg	Schröder	D. Ackermann
	Shakespeare/Weisse: *Romeo and Juliet*	Burgth Vienna		

168

1773

Herder: *Von deutscher Art und Kunst.* Goethe: *Götz.* Bürger: *Lenore.* Schiller goes to military academy. Birth of Tieck.

Shakespeare/Heufeld: *Hamlet*	Burgth Vienna	

1774

Death of Louis XV. Première of Gluck's *Iphigenia in Aulis* at Paris opera. Weimar court fire causes Ekhof-Seyler troupe to move to Gotha. Goethe: *Werther.* Lenz: *Anmerkungen über das Theater* and translations of Plautus. Goethe meets Carl August. Production of Goethe's *Götz von Berlichingen* establishes practice of dropping curtain between acts.

24.1	Lessing: *Philotas*	Kgl Th Berlin	Koch	
	Cumberland: *West Indian*	Burgth Vienna		
12.4	Goethe: *Götz*	Kgl Th Berlin	Koch	Brückner
23.8	Goethe: *Clavigo*	Hamburg	Schröder	Ch. Ackermann
Oct.	Goethe: *Götz*	Hamburg	Schröder	
	Shakespeare: *Othello*	Pressburg	Wahr	
	Shakespeare: *King Lear*	Pressburg	Wahr	

1775

Goethe goes to Weimar (7 November), begins scientific studies, writes *Urfaust.* Lavater: *Physiognomische Fragmente.* Charlotte Ackermann retires from stage. Death of Koch. Lichtenberg sees Garrick in London. Theater am Gendarmenplatz, Berlin, built. Beaumarchais' *Barber of Seville* premièred in Comédie Française.

5.12	Wagner: *Die Reue nach der Tat*	Hamburg	Schröder
11.12	Wagner: *Die Reue nach der Tat*	Berlin	

1776

American Declaration of Independence. Goethe takes over direction of Weimar Amateur theatre (until 1783). Herder in Weimar. Lenz goes to Weimar but is sent away. Lenz anonymously publishes *Die Soldaten* (first performed 1863). Burgtheater Vienna raised to National Theatre by Emperor

169

Joseph II. Hospital in Mannheim rebuilt as theatre. Schröder begins productions of Shakespeare.

8.2	Goethe: *Stella*	Hamburg	Schröder	D. Ackermann
23.2	Klinger: *Zwillinge*	Hamburg	Schröder	
13.3	Goethe: *Stella*	Kgl Th Berlin	Döbbelin	
19.6	Leisewitz: *Julius von Tarent*	Berlin	Döbbelin	
20.9	Shakespeare: *Hamlet*	Hamburg	Schröder	
	Shakespeare: *Othello*	Hamburg	Schröder	
21.11	Goethe: *Die Geschwister*	Weimar Am Th Goethe		Goethe

1777

Birth of Kleist. Sheridan: *School for Scandal*. Prince Maximilian III of Bavaria dies. Karl Theodor removes court from Mannheim to Munich, establishes National Theatre at Mannheim as compensation. Performance of Wagner's *Kindermörderin* banned in Berlin. First individual acting tour by Bock from Gotha.

	Shakespeare: *Measure for Measure*	Hamburg	Schröder
9.1	Goethe: *Die Mitschuldigen*	Weimar Am Th Goethe	Goethe
30.1	Goethe: *Lila*	Weimar Am Th Goethe	Goethe
1.4	Klinger: *Sturm und Drang*	Leipzig	Seyler
July	Wagner: *Die Kindermörderin*	Pressburg	Wahr
	Shakespeare: *Macbeth*	Hanover	Schröder

1778

Bürger: *Gedichte*. Herder: *Volkslieder*. Dorothea Ackermann retires from stage. Dalberg becomes Director of National Theatre Mannheim. Deaths of Voltaire, Rousseau and Ekhof. Johann Boeck replaces Ekhof as Director of Court Theatre at Gotha. Frederick the Great disbands French ensemble in Theater am Gendarmenmarkt.

13.1	Cumberland: *West Indian*	Weimar Am Th Goethe	Ekhof
30.1	Goethe: *Triumph der Empfindsamkeit*	Weimar Am Th Goethe	Goethe
12.4	Lenz: *Der Hofmeister*	Hamburg	Schröder
4.9	Wagner: *Evchen Humbrecht*	Fft/Main	Seyler

20.10	Goethe: *Plundersweilen*	Weimar Am Th Goethe	Goethe
	Shakespeare: *King*		
	Lear	Hamburg	Schröder
	Shakespeare:		
	Richard II	Hamburg	Schröder
	Shakespeare:		
	Richard III	Mannheim	

1779

Seyler, Iffland, Beck and Boeck go to Mannheim. End of Gotha Court Theatre. Death of Garrick.

6.4	Goethe: *Iphigenie*	Weimar Am Th Goethe	Goethe
20.5	Goethe: *Laune des*		
	Verliebten	Weimar Am Th Goethe	

1780

Death of Maria Theresa. Joseph II becomes Holy Roman Emperor. Goethe becomes Privy Councillor. Wieland: *Oberon*. Schiller regimental doctor. New theatre opened at Weimar.

| 10.1 | Lessing: *Philotas* | Hamburg | Schröder |

1781

Death of Lessing. Wieland: *Die Abderiten*. Kant: *Kritik der reinen Vernunft*. Sarah Siddons plays Hamlet. Schröder goes to Vienna. Première of Mozart's *Idomeneo* in Munich.

1782

Death of Schönemann. Première of Mozart's *Entführung aus dem Serail* in Vienna. Schiller takes flight from Stuttgart (22 October).

13.1	Schiller: *Die Räuber*	Mannheim	Dalberg	Iffland
22.7	Goethe: *Die Fischerin*	Weimar Am Th Goethe		Schröter
	Sheridan/Schröder:			
	School for Scandal	Burgth Vienna	Schröder	

1783

Treaty of Versailles: recognition of American independence. Schiller becomes writer in residence at Mannheim.

Beaumarchais' *Marriage of Figaro* privately premièred in France. Professional company under Bellomo takes up residence in Weimar. Johann Fleck joins Döbbelin as director.

1.1	Schiller: *Die Räuber*	Kgl Th Berlin	Döbbelin	
21.3	Gozzi: *Zobeis*	Weimar Am Th	Goethe	Schröter
14.4	Lessing: *Nathan der Weise*	Kgl Th Berlin	Döbbelin	Döbbelin
20.7	Schiller: *Fiesko*	Kurfürstl Th Bonn	Grossmann	

1784

First use of oil-lamps for stage-lighting at Comédie Française. First public performance of Beaumarchais' *Marriage of Figaro* at Comédie Française. Death of Diderot. Schiller: 'Die Schaubühne als eine moralische Anstalt betrachtet' as inaugural lecture to Deutsche Gesellschaft. Birth of Ludwig Devrient.

11.1	Schiller: *Fiesko*	Mannheim	Dalberg
8.3	Schiller: *Fiesko*	Kgl Th Berlin	Döbbelin
13.4	Schiller: *Kabale und Liebe*	Fft/Main	
15.4	Schiller: *Kabale und Liebe*	Mannheim	Dalberg
22.11	Schiller: *Kabale und Liebe*	Kgl Th Berlin	Döbbelin
	Goldsmith/Schröder: *She Stoops to Conquer*	Burgth Vienna	Schröder

1785

Alliance of Princes: Prussia, Hanover, Saxony and others unite against Austrian policy. Johann Jakob Engel: *Ideen zu einer Mimik*. Schröder returns from Vienna to Hamburg. Schiller leaves Mannheim for Leipzig. Mozart's *Entführung aus dem Serail* performed at Residenztheater Munich. Iffland: *Fragmente über Menschendarstellung auf den deutschen Bühnen*.

3.2	Goethe: *Clavigo*	Weimar	Bellomo

1786

Death of Frederick the Great (6 December). Döbbelin opens Königliches Nationaltheater Berlin. Goethe embarks on first

Italian journey. Bürger: *Baron Münchhausen*. Première of Mozart's *Hochzeit des Figaro* in Burgtheater Vienna.

1787

Schiller's first visit to Weimar. Talma's début in Comédie Française. Première of Mozart's *Don Giovanni* in Prague.

29.8	Schiller: *Don Carlos*	Hamburg	Schröder

1788

Schiller's first meeting with Goethe. Schiller becomes Professor of History in Jena. Kant: *Kritik der praktischen Vernunft*. Mozart's *Don Giovanni* performed in Burgtheater Vienna.

21.7	Goethe: *Die Geschwister*	Kgl Th Berlin	Döbbelin
	Kotzebue: *Menschenhaß und Reue*	Kgl Th Berlin	Döbbelin
	Schiller: *Don Carlos*	Mannheim	Dalberg

1789

Storming of Bastille. Brockmann becomes Director of Burgtheater Vienna.

9.1	Goethe: *Egmont*	Mainz	
15.5	Goethe: *Egmont*	Fft/Main	Koch
	Kotzebue: *Menschenhaß und Reue*	Burgth Vienna	

1790

Death of Kaiser Joseph II. Leopold II becomes 'Holy Roman Emperor'. Kant: *Kritik der Urteilskraft*. Goethe's second Italian journey, publishes *Faust, Ein Fragment*. Première of Mozart's *Così fan tutti* at Burgtheater Vienna. Schröder uses box-set for first time on German stage. Fleck becomes Director of Königliches Nationaltheater Berlin. Birth of Raimund.

173

1791

Goethe becomes Director of Weimar Court Theatre. Anton Genast goes to Weimar. Première of Mozart's *Zauberflöte* in Vienna.

31.3	Goethe: *Egmont*	Weimar	Bellomo
7.5	Iffland: *Die Jäger*	Weimar	Goethe
25.9	Schiller: *Don Carlos*	Erfurt	Fischer
29.11	Shakespeare: *King John*	Weimar	Goethe
17.12	Goethe: *Gross-Cophta*	Weimar	Goethe

1792

Death of Kaiser Leopold II. Franz II becomes 'Holy Roman Emperor'. First Coalition War: Austria and Prussia oppose France. Russia occupies Poland. French revolutionary army occupies left bank of Rhine and conquers Belgium. Goethe involved in campaign against French. Death of Lenz.

21.1	Goethe: *Die Geschwister*	Weimar	Goethe
28.1	Shakespeare: *Hamlet*	Weimar	Goethe
28.2	Schiller: *Don Carlos*	Weimar	
14 &	Shakespeare:		
21.4	*Henry IV, Pts I & II*	Weimar	Goethe
28.4	Schiller: *Die Räuber*	Weimar	
	Iffland: *Der Hagestolz*	Kgl Th Berlin	

1793

Britain declares war on France. Second Partition of Poland between Russia and Prussia. Execution of Louis XVI. Schiller: 'Über das Erhabene'. Death of Döbbelin.

1.4	Lessing: *Emilia Galotti*	Weimar	Goethe	Neumann
2.5	Goethe: *Der Bürger-general*	Weimar	Goethe	Beck
9.5	Lessing: *Minna von Barnhelm*	Weimar	Goethe	Neumann

1794

French conquer the Netherlands. Goethe begins friendship with Schiller; they collaborate on *Die Horen*, new literary journal. Amalie Wolff and the scene-painter Lorenzo Vincenzio go to Weimar. J.J. Engel performs Mozart's *Zauberflöte* in Royal

Theatre Berlin and is promptly dismissed by the Kaiser. Death of Johann David Beil.

1795

Third Partition of Poland between Russia, Austria and Prussia. Treaty of Basle between Prussia and France: left bank of Rhine conceded to France. France conquers Holland. Schiller: *Über die ästhetische Erziehung des Menschen*.

Cumberland/ Brockmann: *The Jew*	Burgth Vienna

1796

Goethe: *Wilhelm Meisters Lehrjahre*. Schiller: *Über naive und sentimentalische Dichtung*. Iffland gives guest-performances in Weimar and becomes Director of Königliches Nationaltheater (Royal Theatre), Berlin. Retirement of Schröder. Death of Dorothea Ackermann.

16.4	Schiller: *Die Räuber*	Weimar	Goethe
25.4	Goethe: *Egmont*	Weimar	Goethe
18.6	Shakespeare: *King Lear*	Weimar	Goethe

1797

Treaty of Campio Formio between Austria and France. Accession of William III of Prussia. Hölderlin: *Empedokles* fragment begun. Schelling: *Ideen zu einer Philosophie der Natur*. Tieck: *Der gestiefelte Kater* (first performed 1844). First of A.W. Schlegel's translations of Shakespeare published. Einsiedel: *Grundlinien zu einer Theorie der Schauspielkunst*. Jagemann goes to Weimar.

1798

Forming of new coalition between England, Russia and Austria. Prussia remains neutral. Weimar Court Theatre rebuilt. Schiller goes to Weimar. Hölderlin: *Gedichte*.

28.4	Kotzebue: *Menschenhaß und Reue*	Weimar	Goethe

12.10	Schiller: *Wallensteins*			
	Lager	Weimar	Goethe	Graff

1799

Second Coalition War starts. Napoleon elected First Consul. Novalis: *Die Christenheit oder Europa*. Death of Beaumarchais.

30.1	Schiller: *Die*			
	Piccolomini	Weimar	Schiller	Vohs
20.4	Schiller: *Wallensteins*			
	Tod	Weimar	Schiller	
17.5	Schiller: *Wallensteins*			
	Tod	Kgl Th Berlin	Iffland	
15.10	Shakespeare/Schlegel:			
	Hamlet	Kgl Th Berlin	Iffland	Wolff

1800

7.1	Goethe: *Iphigenie*	Burgth Vienna		Bethmann
30.1	Voltaire/Goethe:			
	Mahomet	Weimar	Goethe	
14.5	Shakespeare/Schiller:			
	Macbeth	Weimar	Schiller	
14.6	Schiller: *Maria Stuart*	Weimar	Schiller	Vohs
	Terence: *The Brothers*	Weimar	Goethe	

1801

Treaty of Lunéville between France and Austria. Prussia takes advantage of isolation of English to seize Hanover for Napoleon. Death of Fleck.

8.1	Schiller: *Maria Stuart*	Kgl Th Berlin	Iffland	
30.1	Voltaire/Goethe:			
	Tancred	Weimar	Goethe	Haide
25.2	Goethe: *Egmont*	Kgl Th Berlin	Iffland	
11.9	Schiller: *Jungfrau von*			
	Orleans	Leipzig		
21.9	Schiller: *Maria Stuart*	Weimar	Schiller	Unzelmann
24.10	Terence: *The Brothers*	Weimar	Goethe	
28.11	Lessing: *Nathan der*			
	Weise	Weimar	Goethe	
	Schiller: *Maria Stuart*	Kgl Th Berlin	Iffland	
	Schiller: *Jungfrau von*			
	Orleans	Kgl Th Berlin	Iffland	

1802

Treaty of Amiens between France and England. Introduction of

176

Code Napoleon. Kleist in Weimar. Novalis: *Heinrich von Ofterdingen*. Lauchstädt Theatre re-opened.

2.1	Euripides/Schlegel:			
	Ion	Weimar	Goethe	
30.1	Gozzi/Schiller:			
	Turandot	Weimar	Schiller	
15.5	Goethe: *Iphigenie*	Weimar	Schiller	Krüger
27.12	Goethe: *Iphigenie*	Kgl Th Berlin	Iffland	

1803

Reichsdeputationshauptschluss: ecclesiastical lands and many small German states apportioned to bigger states. Deaths of Gleim, Klopstock, Herder and Beck. Kleist attempts to join French army. P.A. Wolff goes to Weimar. Goethe's 'Regeln für Schauspieler' formulated.

19.3	Schiller: *Braut von*		
	Messina	Weimar	Goethe
2.4	Goethe: *Natürliche*		
	Tochter	Weimar	Goethe
23.4	Schiller: *Jungfrau von*		
	Orleans	Weimar	Schiller
14.6	Schiller: *Braut von*		
	Messina	Kgl Th Berlin	Iffland
12.7	Goethe: *Natürliche*		
	Tochter	Kgl Th Berlin	Iffland
1.10	Shakespeare/Schlegel:		
	Julius Caesar	Weimar	Goethe
28.11	Schiller: *Wallensteins*		
	Lager	Kgl Th Berlin	Iffland

1804

Napoleon becomes Emperor. Franz II becomes Emperor of Austria. Death of Kant.

9.1	Kleist: *Familie*	Nationaltheater	
	Schroffenstein	Graz	
30.1	Racine/Bode:		
	Mithridate	Weimar	
17.3	Schiller: *Wilhelm Tell*	Weimar	Schiller
4.7	Schiller: *Wilhelm Tell*	Kgl Th Berlin	Iffland
22.9 &			
13.10	Goethe: *Götz I & II*	Weimar	
	Shakespeare/Schlegel:		
	Julius Caesar	Kgl Th Berlin	Iffland

1805

Renewed Coalition against France, Prussia remaining neutral. Battle of Austerlitz: France defeats Russia and Austria, grants Hanover to Prussia and so establishes Napoleonic hegemony in Germany. Death of Schiller. Première of Beethoven's *Fidelio* (first version).

30.1	Racine/Schiller:	
	Phaedra	Weimar
8.6	Shakespeare/Voss:	
	Othello	Weimar

1806

Confederation of the Rhine: most German states, but not Prussia and Austria, in union under Napoleon's protection. Prussia declares war on France after French occupation of Bayreuth and Ansbach. Napoleon defeats Prussia at Jena and Auerstädt. Collapse of Prussian army. Napoleon in Berlin. Goethe marries. Under Napoleon's orders Königliches Nationaltheater Berlin renamed simply Königliches Theater Berlin. Death of Dalberg. Beethoven: *Fidelio* (second version).

15.1	Goethe: *Stella*	Weimar	Goethe
30.1	Corneille: *Le Cid*	Weimar	Goethe
3.5	Schiller: *Fiesko*	Weimar	Goethe
11.6	Werner: *Martin Luther*	Kgl Th Berlin	Iffland

1807

Undecided battle between French and Prussians at Preussisch-Eylau. Treaty of Tilsit: Russo-French alliance. Prussia loses many possessions. Beginning of Prussian reforms under Reichsfreiherr von Stein: end of serfdom, increased social mobility. Fichte: *Reden an die deutsche Nation*. Kleist: *Amphitryon* (first performed 1878). Iffland publishes *Almanach fürs Theater*.

16.2	Goethe: *Tasso* (1790)	Weimar	P.A. Wolff
24.5	Schiller: *Don Carlos*	Leipzig	
2.8	Schiller: *Maria Stuart*	Lauchstädt	
31.8	Goethe: *Iphigenie*	Leipzig	A.A. Wolff

1808

Stein introduces town-councils, elected by citizens, and

reforms bureaucracy. Removal of Stein on Napoleon's insistence. Reforms pursued however by Hardenberg. Goethe meets Napoleon. Schubert: *Nachtseite der Naturwissenschaft*. Goethe publishes first part of *Faust*. Kleist: *Penthesilea* (first performed 1876). Kleist: *Robert Guiskard* (first performed 1901). Talma visits Weimar. A.W. Schlegel lectures in Vienna on 'Dramatische Kunst und Literatur'.

2.3	Kleist: *Der zerbrochene Krug*	Weimar	Goethe

1809

Austrian revolt against France; no support from Prussia. Defeat of Austria. Treaty of Schönbrunn weakens Austria. New policy of Austro-French co-operation of Metternich. Other revolts in Tirol and Brunswick suppressed. Goethe: *Die Wahlverwandschaften*.

1.7	Schiller: *Wilhelm Tell*	Weimar

1810

Founding of Berlin University. Kleist: *Erzählungen*, 'Über das Marionettentheater'.

24.2	Werner: *Der 24. Februar*	Weimar	
17.3	Kleist: *Kätchen von Heilbronn*	Vienna	
29.3	Schiller: *Don Carlos*	Kgl Th Berlin	Iffland
	Goethe: *Götz*	Innsbruck	

1811

Reform of feudal system effectively adds to power of nobility: peasants lose smallholdings to big estates. Beethoven's *Egmont* premièred at Burgtheater Vienna. Iffland becomes Director General of all Berlin theatres. Stuttgart theatre renovated. Kleist commits suicide.

30.1	Calderon/Schlegel: *Constant Prince*	Weimar	Wolff
17.6	Goethe: *Iphigenie*	Weimar	
July	Schiller: *Die Räuber*	Weimar	

179

1.9	Kleist: *Kätchen von Heilbronn*	Bamberg	
25.11	Goethe: *Torquato Tasso*	Kgl Th Berlin	
	Goethe: *Egmont*	Burgth Vienna	

1812

Prussia: emancipation of Jews; reform of army under Scharnhorst, Gneisenau, and Clausewitz; Humboldt's educational reforms. Napoleon declares war on Russia, reaches Moscow, but retreats with huge losses. Prussia's own national revolt against France begins. First volume of Grimm's *Märchen*. Death of Brockmann.

1.2	Shakespeare/Schlegel: *Romeo & Juliet*	Weimar	Goethe
29.4	Calderon: *Life's a Dream*	Weimar	Goethe
12.11	Körner: *Der grüne Domino*	Kgl Th Berlin	
3.12	Körner: *Toni*	Kgl Th Berlin	

1813

Battle of Leipzig. Wars of liberation against Napoleon. Birth of Büchner. Schreyvogel becomes Director of Burgtheater Vienna.

8.12	Goethe: *Adalbert von Weislingen*	Weimar	Goethe
11.12	Goethe: *Götz*	Weimar	Goethe
	Müllner: *Die Schuld*	Stuttgart	

1814

Napoleon exiled to Elba. Louis XVIII becomes King of France. Death of Iffland. Graf Brühl becomes General Director of Berlin theatres. Beethoven: *Fidelio* (third and final version).

9.1	Körner: *Die Braut*	Weimar
29.1	Goethe: *Egmont*	Weimar
18.2	Brentano: *Ponce de Leon*	Vienna
31.10	Körner: *Vetter aus Bremen*	Kgl Th Berlin
2.12	Körner: *Die Braut*	Kgl Th Berlin

180

1815

Napoleon's 'hundred days'. 'Holy Alliance' between Russia, Prussia and Austria. Esslair joins Stuttgart Court Theatre.

1.2	Calderon/Gries:		
	Zenobia	Weimar	Goethe
14.4	Körner: Hedwig	Kgl Th Berlin	
20.4	Körner: Rosamunde	Kgl Th Berlin	
April	Schiller: Die Räuber	Kgl Th Berlin	Devrient

1816

Death of Schröder.

1817

Goethe resigns from Directorship of Weimar Theatre. Tieck visits London. Schauspielhaus Berlin destroyed by fire.

31.1	Grillparzer: Die	
	Ahnfrau	Th an der Wien Vienna

1818

Grillparzer becomes theatre poet at Burgtheater Vienna (until 1823).

21.4	Grillparzer: Sappho	Burgth Vienna

1819

Karlsbader Beschlüsse. Première of Rossini's Barber of Seville in Vienna. Tieck goes to Dresden.

Goethe: Faust I	Schloss	Brühl
	Monbijou	
	Berlin	
Goethe: Faust I	Weimar	

1820

Death of Napoleon. Wiener Schlussakte. Première of Weber's Freischütz in Vienna.

181

28.9	Kleist: *Der zerbrochene*		
	Krug	Hamburg	
	Kleist: *Kätchen von*		
	Heilbronn	Burgth Vienna	Schreyvogel
	Shakespeare: *Hamlet*	Dresden	Tieck

1821

Publication of Kleist's works by Tieck.

26./	Grillparzer: *Das*		
27.3	*goldene Vlies*	Burgth Vienna	
3.10	Kleist: *Prinz von*		
	Homburg	Burgth Vienna	Schreyvogel
6.12	Kleist: *Prinz von*		
	Homburg	Dresden	

1822

10.2	Kleist: *Prinz von*		
	Homburg	Hofth Munich	
8.3	Kleist: *Prinz von*	Stadtth	
	Homburg	Hamburg	
30.3	Kleist: *Prinz von*		
	Homburg	Hofth Stuttgart	
21.6	Kleist: *Prinz von*		
	Homburg	Hofth Hanover	

1823

Death of Kemble. Graz theatre destroyed by fire.

1824

Goethe's 'Regeln für Schauspieler' published by Eckermann.

21.4	Kleist: *Kätchen von*		
	Heilbronn	Kgl Th Berlin	
18.8	Kleist: *Familie*		
	Schroffenstein	Kgl Th Berlin	
17.12	Raimund: *Diamant des*		
	Geisterkönigs	Th in L Vienna	
	Shakespeare: *King*		
	Lear	Dresden	Tieck
	Grillparzer: *Die*		
	Ahnfrau	Burgth Vienna	Schreyvogel

1825

Weimar Court Theatre destroyed by fire. New theatre opened within six months. Tieck appointed *Dramaturg* at Dresden Court Theatre.

19.2	Grillparzer: *König Ottokar*	Burgth Vienna
7.11	Goethe: *Iphigenie*	Weimar

1826

Death of Talma.

1827

Schiller: *Wilhelm Tell*	Burgth Vienna	Schreyvogel

1828

Graf von Redern replaces Brühl as Director of the National-bühne Berlin.

28.2	Grillparzer: *Treuer Diener*	Burgth Vienna
26.7	Kleist: *Prinz von Homburg*	Kgl Th Berlin
17.10	Raimund: *Alpenkönig*	Th in L Vienna

1829

19.1	Goethe: *Faust*	Brunswick	Klingemann
29.3	Grabbe: *Don Juan & Faust*	Detmold	Pichler
	Goethe: *Faust*	Weimar	

1831

Death of Hegel.

5.4	Grillparzer: *Des Meeres und der Liebe Wellen*	Burgth Vienna

183

1832

Death of Goethe and Devrient. Schreyvogel dismissed as Director of Burgtheater Vienna. Dies soon after.

1833

10.4	Nestroy:	
	Lumpazivagabundus	Th an der Wien Vienna
26.4	Kleist: *Prinz von*	
	Homburg	Düsseldorf

1834

Laube imprisoned for two and a half years.

20.2	Raimund: *Der*	
	Verschwender	Th in d Josephstadt Vienna
4.10	Grillparzer: *Der*	
	Traum, ein Leben	Burgth Vienna

1835

Banning of *Das junge Deutschland*. Gutzkow imprisoned for his novel *Wally*. Büchner: *Dantons Tod*.

1836

Büchner appointed Professor of Anatomy in Zurich. Büchner: *Leonce und Lena*. Death of Raimund.

Shakespeare: *Macbeth*	Dresden	Tieck

1837

Death of Büchner on point of completing *Woyzeck*.

NOTES

INTRODUCTION

1 F.J. von Reden–Esbeck, *Caroline Neuber und ihre Zeitgenossen*, Leipzig, 1881, pp. 37–8, in Betsy Aikin-Sneath, *Comedy in Germany in the First Half of the Eighteenth Century*, Oxford University Press, 1936, p. 41.

2 A term taken from the French neo-classicists. Cf. Pierre Corneille, 'Discours des trois unités, d'action, de jour et de lieu', *Writings on Theatre*, ed. H.T. Barnwell, Oxford, 1965, p. 64.

3 C.L. Stieglitz, 'Schauspiel-Haus, Schauplatz, Opern-Haus, Comödien-Haus, Theater', *Enzyklopädie der bürgerlichen Baukunst*, 4, Leipzig, 1797, p. 684; Sibylle Maurer-Schmoock, *Deutsches Theater im 18. Jahrhundert*, Niemeyer, Tübingen, 1982, p. 35, n. 14.

4 Bernhard Diebold, *Das Rollenfach im deutschen Theaterbetrieb des 18. Jahrhunderts*, Theatergeschichtliche Forschungen 25, Leipzig, 1913, p. 61.

5 *Schauspieler–Anekdoten*, ed. T. Kellen, Stuttgart, n.d.[1909], p. 28.

6 G.E. Lessing, *Hamburgische Dramaturgie*, Stück 2, 5 May, 1767; *Lessings Werke*, Reclam, Leipzig, n.d., vol. 4, p. 8.

7 Hilde Haider-Pregler, *Des sittlichen Bürgers Abendschule, Bildungsanspruch und Bildungsauftrag des Berufstheaters im 18. Jahrhundert*, Jugend und Volk, Vienna, 1980.

8 J.W. Goethe, *Dichtung und Wahrheit*, Book 7, *Goethes Werke*, Hamburger Ausgabe, 1955, vol. 9, p. 281.

9 C.M. Wieland, 'Briefe an einen jungen Dichter', 3. Brief, *Werke*, Carl Hanser, Munich, 1967, vol. 3, p. 478.

10 J. Petersen, *Das deutsche Nationaltheater*, Leipzig, 1919, p. 59.

11 J.W. Goethe, 'Zum Schäkespears Tag', *Goethes Werke*, Hamburger Ausgabe, 1953, vol. 12, p. 225.

12 G.E. Lessing, *Hamburgische Dramaturgie*, Stück 4, 12 May 1767, *Lessings Werke*, Reclam, Leipzig, n.d., vol. 4, p. 14.

13 J.G. Robertson, *Lessing's Dramatic Theory*, Cambridge University Press, 1939, p. 471.

14 H. Kindermann, *Theatergeschichte Europas*, Otto Müller, Salzburg, 1961, vol. 4, p. 545.

15 In the two years of its life the Hamburg National Theatre gave 507 performances of 117 different plays (86 comedies, 24 tragedies, four *drames*, two pastoral comedies, and one *Festspiel*, a form of masque). 66 of these plays were French, 37 German, 5 Italian, 4 English, and 5 from other nations. The 8 most frequently performed pieces were:

1 Lessing: *Minna von Barnhelm* (16 performances)
2 Diderot: *Der Hausvater* (12)
3 Marivaux: *Der Bauer mit der Erbschaft* (11)
4 Beaumarchais: *Eugènie* (10)
5 Hippel: *Der Mann nach der Uhr* (9)
    Löwen: *Die neue Agnese* (9)
    Weisse: *Romeo und Julia* (9)
8 Corneille: *Rodogune* (8)

16 S. Maurer-Schmoock, op. cit., p. 137, n. 2.

17 J.J.A. vom Hagen, *Magazin zur Geschichte des Deutschen Theaters*, Erstes Stück, Halle, 1773, pp. 72f., in S. Maurer-Schmoock, op. cit., p. 174.

18 Significantly, the post in Weimar was defined as 'Poet und Souffleur' ('Poet and Prompter') (see S. Maurer-Schmoock, op. cit., p. 97).

19 *Journal des Luxus und der Moden*, Weimar, September 1791, p. 501. Cit. in Jörn Göres (ed.), *Gesang und Rede*, Düsseldorf, 1973, p. 68.

20 See below, pp. 76–84.

21 'Über Kleidertrachten auf der Bühne', *Dramaturgische Blätter*, ed. A.W. Schreiber, 1. Stük, Friedrich Esslinger, Frankfurt/Main, 2 October 1788.

1 SCHILLER AT MANNHEIM

1 Letter from Schiller to Schröder, 12 October 1786.

2 Anton Pichler, *Chronik des grossherzoglichen Hof- und National-Theaters in Mannheim*, Bensheimer, Mannheim, 1879, pp. 46–7.

3 Max Martersteig, *Die Protokolle des Mannheimer Nationaltheaters unter Dalberg aus den Jahren 1781 bis 1789*, Mannheim, 1890, pp. 53, 56f.; in Sibylle Maurer-Schmoock, *Deutsches Theater im 18. Jahrhundert*, Niemeyer, Tübingen, 1982, p. 181.

4 For a fuller account see Kurt Sommerfeld, *Die Bühneneinrichtungen des Mannheimer Nationaltheaters unter Dalbergs Leitung 1778–1803* (Schriften der Gesellschaft für Theatergeschichte 36), Berlin, 1927.

5 J.J.A. vom Hagen, *Magazin zur Geschichte des Deutschen Theaters*, 1. Stück, Halle, 1773, p. 72; S. Maurer-Schmoock, op. cit., p. 42.

6 Johann Christian Brandes, *Meine Lebensgeschichte*, 3 vols., Berlin, 1802–7, vol. 1, p. 158; S. Maurer-Schmoock, op. cit., p. 42, n. 33.

7 See M. Patterson, 'Reinhardt and theatrical Expressionism or the second wall removed', *Max Reinhardt. The Oxford Symposium*, ed. M. Jacobs and J. Warren, Oxford Polytechnic, 1986, pp. 52–4.

NOTES

8   Martersteig, op. cit., p. 46.
9   ibid., pp. 74–87. The German formulation is: 'Was ist Natur, und welches sind die wahren Grenzen derselben bei theatralischen Vorstellungen?'
10 Lessing, *Hamburgische Dramaturgie*, 29. Stück, 18 March 1768, *Sämtliche Schriften*, ed. K. Lachmann, Göschen, Stuttgart, 1894, vol. 10, p. 174.
11 S. Troitzkij, *Konrad Ekhof, Ludwig Schröder, August Wilhelm Iffland, Johann Friedrich Fleck, Ludwig Devrient, Karl Seydelmann. Die Anfänge der realistischen Schauspielkunst*, Bruno Henschel, Berlin, 1949, p. 54.
12 See below, p. 46.
13 Pichler, op. cit., pp. 67–8.
14 *Das Potpourri*, January 1782; cit. Pichler, op. cit., p. 70.
15 Pichler, op. cit., p. 68.
16 Bertolt Brecht, *Schriften zum Theater*, Frankfurt/Main, 1963, vol. 1, p. 39.
17 All information from the Mannheim prompt-book is taken from F. Walter, *Archiv und Bibliothek des Grossh. Hof- und Nationaltheaters in Mannheim 1779–1839*, Hirzel, Leipzig, 1899, vol. 2, pp. 224ff.
18 Martersteig, op. cit., p. 58.
19 Pichler, op. cit., p. 69.
20 J.W. Goethe, 'Rezension des Ifflandschen Almanachs für Theater und Theaterfreunde 1807', *Sämtliche Werke*, Jubiläums-Ausgabe, Cotta, Stuttgart, vol. 36, p. 296.
21 Pichler, op. cit., p. 69.
22 J.W. Goethe, op. cit., p. 296.
23 *Journal der Luxus und der Moden*, ed. F.J. Bertuch and G.M. Kraus, Weimar, 1796, vol. 11, p. 268.
24 J.C.F. Manso, Letter to W.G. Becker, 6 July 1799, in J. Göres, *Gesang und Rede*, Düsseldorf, 1973, p. 134.
25 C.A. Böttiger, *Entwicklung des Ifflandischen Spiels*, Göschen, Leipzig, 1796, pp. 292ff.
26 Schiller, 'Die Schaubühne als eine moralische Anstalt betrachtet', *Sämtliche Werke*, Säkular-Ausgabe, Cotta, Stuttgart, n.d., vol. 11, pp. 89–90.
27 ibid., p. 97.
28 ibid., p. 98.
29 Schiller, 'Über das Pathetische', op. cit., vol. 11, pp. 267–8; Schiller's italics.

2 GOETHE AT WEIMAR

1   Goethe, *Wilhelm Meisters theatralische Sendung*, vol.1, §15.
2   E. Genast, *Aus Weimars klassischer und nachklassischer Zeit*, 5th edn., Lutz, Stuttgart, n.d. [1906], p. 136.
3   'Saat von Göthe gesäht'; see W. Flemming, *Goethe und das Theater seiner Zeit*, Kohlhammer, Stuttgart, 1968, pp. 249f.

187

4   V. Tornius, 'Goethes Theaterleitung', *Jahrbuch des Freien Deutschen Hochstifts*, 1912, p. 202.
5   G. Hauptmann, *Die Ratten, Sämtliche Werke*, ed. H.-E. Hass, Propyläen Verlag, Berlin, 1965, vol. 2, p. 778.
6   Ronald Harwood, *All the World's a Stage*, episode 9, BBC Television, broadcast 25 March 1984. This assertion is not repeated in the book published to accompany the series.
7   *De l'Allemagne*, Nouvelle Edition, Hachette, Paris, 1959, vol. 3, pp. 215–16.
8   For a fuller account of the Weimar Court Theatre and Goethe's involvement in it, the reader is referred to the large body of works in the bibliography, especially M. Carlson, *Goethe and the Weimar Theatre*, and W. Flemming, *Goethe und das Theater seiner Zeit*.
9   Goethe to Eckermann, 22 March 1825; J.P. Eckermann, *Gespräche mit Goethe*, Brockhaus, Wiesbaden, 1959, p. 426.
10 Cf. W.H. Bruford, *Culture and Society in Classical Weimar 1775–1806*, Cambridge, Cambridge University Press, 1962, *passim*.
11 *Faust I*, 'Vorspiel auf dem Theater', Gedenkausgabe, ed. Ernst Beutler, Zurich, 1949, vol. 5, pp. 143–4.
12 Goethe to Cotta, 29 September 1798, cit. E. Scharrer-Santen, *Weimarische Dramaturgie*, Paetel, Berlin, 1927, p. 154.
13 C. Langhans, *Über Theater oder Bemerkungen über Katakustik in Beziehung auf Theater*, Gottfried Hayn, Berlin, 1810, p. 6; cit. A. Doebber, *Lauchstädt und Weimar*, Mittler, Berlin, 1908, p. 62.
14 *Gedenkausgabe*, vol. 19, p. 623.
15 To Eckermann, 25 December 1825; *Gespräche mit Goethe*, p. 128.
16 Flemming, op. cit., p. 218.
17 Genast, op. cit., p. 45.
18 Cf. H. Huesmann, 'Goethe als Theaterleiter', *Ein Theatermann*, ed. I. Nohl, Munich, 1977, p. 145.
19 The common story that Goethe resigned in protest is not strictly true. See Carlson, pp. 288–92.
20 Scharrer-Santen, op. cit., pp. 314–15.
21 To Eckermann, 14 April 1825; *Gespräche mit Goethe*, p. 434.
22 *Elegante Zeitung*, 1817, p. 1046.
23 In 1817 to Freiherr von Biedermann; G. Sichardt, *Das Weimarer Liebhabertheater*, Arion, Weimar, 1957, p. 113.
24 W. Gotthardi, *Weimarische Theaterbilder*, Costenoble, Jena, 1865, vol. 1, p. 162.
25 'Ueber das Heirathen der Schauspieler', clerk's MS; Göres, *Gesang und Rede*, Düsseldorf, 1973, exhibit no. 193/2, pp. 103–4.
26 Heinrich von Kleist, 'Korrespondenznachricht', *Sämtliche Werke und Briefe*, Hanser, Munich, 1961, vol. 2, p. 270.
27 Gotthardi, vol. 1, p. 90.
28 ibid., vol. 1, p. 92.
29 Genast, op. cit., pp. 120f.
30 W. Herwig, *Goethes Gespräche*, vol. 2, p. 985.
31 Flemming, op. cit., p. 267.
32 J. Wahle, *Das Weimarer Hoftheater*, Weimar, 1892, p. 79.

33 For a summary, see J. Prudhoe, *The Theatre of Goethe and Schiller*, pp. 91–6, and for a full translation see Carlson, pp. 309–18.
34 See R. Meyer, 'Goethes "Regeln für Schauspieler"', *Goethe-Jahrbuch*, vol. 31, pp. 117–35.
35 Cf. Goethe's memorandum to the actors, 8 January 1807, in Göres, exhibit no. 277, p. 150.
36 Göres, exhibit no. 195, p. 107.
37 'Über Wahrheit und Wahrscheinlichkeit der Kunstwerke', Gedenkausgabe, vol. 13, pp. 175–81.
38 To Eckermann, 10 April 1829; *Gespräche mit Goethe*, p. 271.
39 Sir Joshua Reynolds, *Discourses on Art*, ed. R.R. Wark, Huntington Library, San Marino, 1959, pp. 42–5.
40 'Rules for actors', §35; Gedenkausgabe, vol. 14, p. 80.
41 Genast, op. cit., p. 99.
42 Cf. *Gedenkausgabe*, vol. 13, pp. 119–20.
43 W. Hogarth, *The Analysis of Beauty*, ed. Joseph Burke, Clarendon, Oxford, 1955, title-page.
44 ibid., p. 149.
45 ibid., p. 154.
46 ibid., p. 161.
47 Genast, op. cit., p. 51.
48 Cf. 'Rules for actors', §83: 'The stage should be regarded as an empty picture for which the actors supply the figures.' *Gedenkausgabe*, vol. 14, p. 89.
49 Genast, op. cit., p. 51.
50 *Gedenkausgabe*, vol. 14, p. 83.
51 ibid., vol. 14, p. 90.
52 ibid., vol. 14, p. 64.
53 To Eckermann, 14 April 1825; *Gespräche mit Goethe*, p. 434.
54 *Gedenkausgabe*, vol. 14, p. 88.
55 *Gedenkausgabe*, vol. 20, p. 798.
56 *Gedenkausgabe*, vol. 14, p. 81.
57 F.W. Riemer, *Mitteilungen über Goethe*, Insel, Leipzig, 1921, p. 334.
58 Goethe to Eckermann, 1 April 1827; *Gespräche mit Goethe*, pp. 463–4.
59 To Eckermann, 4 February 1829; *Gespräche mit Goethe*, p. 237.
60 Cf. Erich Heller, 'Goethe and the avoidance of tragedy', *The Disinherited Mind*, Bowes & Bowes, London, 1975, pp. 35–63.
61 P. Stein, *Deutsche Schauspieler. Eine Bildnissammlung, Schriften der Gesellschaft für Theatergeschichte* 11, Parts 1–2, 2 vols, Berlin, 1907, p. 18.
62 'Auf Miedings Tod', *Gedenkausgabe*, vol. 2, p. 94.
63 G. Sichardt, *Das Weimarer Liebhabertheater unter Goethes Leitung*, Arion Verlag, Weimar, 1957.
64 Flemming, op. cit., p. 65.
65 Sichardt, op. cit., p. 117.
66 Riemer, op. cit., p. 397.
67 Stein, op. cit., p. 18.
68 Wieland to Merck, 3 June 1778.

69 *Zeitung für die elegante Welt*, no. 39, in Sichardt, op. cit., p. 122.
70 ibid., no. 40; Sichardt, op. cit., p. 122.
71 *Theater-Almanach auf das Jahr 1828*, ed. M.G. Saphir, Berlin, 1828, p. 145.
72 Carlson, op. cit., p. 145.
73 Duke Carl August to Goethe, 1800.
74 To Eckermann, 1 April 1827; *Gespräche mit Goethe*, p. 464.
75 Gotthardi, op. cit., p. 49.
76 Adolf Müllner, 'Hier ist das Schwert', *Morgenblatt für gebildete Stände*, 1822, no. 121, 21 May 1822, p. 42.
77 Reported in Flemming, op. cit., p. 160.
78 To Eckermann, 11 October 1828; *Gespräche mit Goethe*, p. 226.
79 Cf., for example, Alexander Freiherr von Sternberg's review of Auguste Crelinger's performance in Berlin, c. 1850: 'In the scene where she goes to the altar and speaks the Song of the Parcae in a dreamlike monotone of paralysed horror, a shudder ran through the silent auditorium. We hardly dared to breathe.' (*Erinnerungsblätter*, Berlin, 1856, vol. 2, p. 118).
80 Erich Heller, op. cit., p. 42.
81 C.A. Eggert, 'Goethe and Diderot on actors and acting', *Modern Language Notes*, vol. 11, no. 4, Baltimore, April, 1896, pp. 205–20.
82 D. Diderot, *Oeuvres Esthétiques*, Garnier, Paris, 1959, p. 317.
83 *Hamburger Ausgabe*, vol. 9, p. 95.
84 Carlson, op. cit., p. 34.

3 THE NINETEENTH CENTURY

1 Figures from Max Martersteig, *Das deutsche Theater im neunzehnten Jahrhundert*, Breitkopf und Härtel, Leipzig, 1904, pp. 8ff.
2 Rudolf Weil, *Das Berliner Theaterpublikum unter A.W. Ifflands Direktion (1796 bis 1814)*, Dr. Phil. dissertation, Cologne, 1930, p. 78.
3 Martersteig, op. cit., p. 205.
4 F.Schiller, *Werke*, Nationalausgabe, Weimar, 1985, vol. 31, p. 32.
5 F. Schiller, 'Die Schaubühne als eine moralische Anstalt betrachtet', *Sämtliche Werke*, Säkular-Ausgabe, Cotta, Stuttgart, vol. 11, p. 98.
6 Dr Edgar Gross, *Die ältere Romantik und das Theater*, Hamburg & Leipzig, 1910, p. 54.
7 Martersteig, op. cit., p. 204.
8 Ludwig Tieck, *Kleine Schriften*, Reimer, Berlin, 1854, vol. 2, p. 343.
9 Eduard Devrient, *Geschichte der deutschen Schauspielkunst*, Elsner, Berlin, 1905, vol. 2, p. 103.
10 Hans Oberländer, *Die geistige Entwicklung der deutschen Schauspielkunst im 18. Jahrhundert*, Voss, Hamburg, 1898, p. 200.
11 J.J. Engel, *Ideen zu einer Mimik*, Berlin, 1802, vol. 2, pp. 161–2.
12 Ludwig Tieck, 'Über Shakespeares Behandlung des Wunderbaren', *Werke*, ed. E. Berend, Berlin, n.d., vol. 5, p. 90.
13 Martersteig, op. cit., p. 149.
14 Ludwig Tieck, *Phantasus*, Berlin, 1812–16, vol. 3, p. 455.

15 Devrient, op. cit., vol. 3, p. 69.
16 Heinrich Laube, *Das norddeutsche Theater*, 1864; Gross, p. 56.
17 Tieck, *Kleine Schriften*, vol. 4, p. 86. In his 1836 production of *Macbeth* Tieck insisted that his actors should wear idealized armour rather than kilts.

4 KLEIST IN PERFORMANCE

1 Heinrich von Kleist, letter to Ulrike von Kleist, 23 March 1801, *Sämtliche Werke und Briefe*, Hanser, Munich, vol. 2, p. 694.
2 Kleist, letter to Wilhelmine von Zenge, 10 October 1801, ibid., p. 268.
3 Iffland, letter to Kleist, 13 August 1810; Curt Müller (ed.), *Ifflands Briefwechsel mit Schiller, Goethe, Kleist, Tieck und anderen Dramatikern*, Reclam, Leipzig, n.d.
4 See e.g. John Osborne, *The Meiningen Court Theatre 1866–1890*, Cambridge University Press, 1988, p. 146.
5 Kleist, 'Schreiben eines redlichen Berliners, das hiesige Theater betreffend, an einen Freund im Ausland', *Berliner Abendblätter*, 20 November 1810; *Sämtliche Werke und Briefe*, vol. 2, p. 415.
6 'Unmassgebliche Bemerkung', *Berliner Abendblätter*, *Sämtliche Werke und Briefe*, vol. 3, p. 491.
7 Heinz Kindermann, *Theatergeschichte Europas*, Müller, Salzburg, 1961–4, vol. 5, p. 332.
8 Not the 30th October, as is frequently asserted, nor 3 October 1820, as Kindermann states.
9 Heinrich von Kleist, *Prince Friedrich of Homburg*, transl. D.S. & F.G. Peters, New Directions, New York, 1978, p. 60.
10 See letter Iffland to Schiller, 10 February 1799; *Schillers Werke*, Nationalausgabe, Weimar, 1975, vol. 38, pp. 34–6.
11 See Osborne, pp. 111–40. For the description of a spectacular modern staging of *The Prince of Homburg*, see M. Patterson, *Peter Stein*, Cambridge University Press, 1981, pp. 90–7.
12 Peters, op. cit., p. 5.
13 Peters, op. cit., p. 89.
14 'Über das Marionettentheater', *Sämtliche Werke und Briefe*, vol. 2, p. 344.
15 ibid., vol. 2, p. 345.

5 BÜCHNER IN PERFORMANCE

1 Even in book form *Danton's Death* was given the subtitle, 'Dramatic pictures from France's Reign of Terror', in order to make the play a more saleable commodity.
2 Georg Büchner, *Complete Plays*, ed. M. Patterson, Methuen, London, 1987, pp. 256–7.
3 *Complete Plays*, p. 289.
4 *Complete Plays*, p. 295.
5 It would be unfair to judge Schiller by this example, however. His

treatment of Mary Stuart (*Maria Stuart*, 1800), for example, despite a certain 'idealization' of her execution, contains a good deal of insight into the world of 'real' politics. The received notion that Schiller was more of an Idealist than Goethe is due in part at least to Schiller's own seminal essay *Über naive und sentimentalische Dichtung* (*On Naive and Sentimental Poetry*, 1796), in which Schiller castigates himself for failing to share the 'naivety' of Goethe.

6   Richard Littlejohns, ' "God's creation, born anew every minute": dramatic form in Büchner's work', lecture delivered on 6 May 1989, The Theatre of Georg Büchner Conference, University of Birmingham.

7   Cf. M. Patterson, 'Contradictions concerning time in Büchner's *Woyzeck*', *German Life and Letters*, vol. 32, no. 2, January 1979, pp. 115–21.

8   Georg Büchner, *Sämtliche Werke und Briefe*, ed. W.R. Lehmann, Christian Wegner Verlag, Hamburg, n.d. [1967].

9   Cf. e.g. Georg Büchner, *Woyzeck*, trans. J. Mackendrick, Methuen, London, 1979, pp. xxi–xxvi; *Complete Plays*, pp. 167–72.

10 All quotations are from the Mackendrick translation in which this scene is Scene Five.

11 For a fuller discussion of this issue, see *Woyzeck*, pp. xxii–xxv; *Complete Plays*, pp. 168–70.

12 The reference to the Captain's wife in Scene Nine of Mackendrick's version is a mistranslation ('your wife will be dead inside four weeks'); the Doctor is in fact speaking about the patient he is rushing off to attend to (*Woyzeck*, p. 18; *Complete Plays*, p. 194).

13 *Woyzeck*, p. 11; *Complete Plays*, p. 187.

14 *Woyzeck*, pp. 13–14; *Complete Plays*, pp. 189–90.

15 *Woyzeck*, pp. 15–16; *Complete Plays*, pp. 191–2.

16 *Complete Plays*, pp. 288–9; Büchner's italics.

17 See M. Patterson, *The Revolution in German Theatre*, Routledge & Kegan Paul, London, 1981, pp. 73ff.

18 *Woyzeck*, p. 6; *Complete Plays*, p. 182.

19 *Complete Plays*, p. 219.

20 *Woyzeck*, p. 22; *Complete Plays*, p. 198.

21 *Woyzeck*, p. 14; *Complete Plays*, p. 190. 'Nature's out' in the original is 'doppelte Natur', literally 'double nature'.

22 *Woyzeck*, p. 10; *Complete Plays*, p. 186.

23 See Peter Thomson, *Shakespeare's Theatre*, Routledge, London, 1983, pp. 115ff.

24 Peter Stein, *Die Zeit*, 2 January 1976, in M. Patterson, *Peter Stein*, Cambridge University Press, 1981, p. 98.

BIBLIOGRAPHY

Aikin-Sneath, Betsy, *Comedy in Germany in the First Half of the Eighteenth Century*, Oxford University Press, 1936.

Arnold, Heinz Ludwig (ed.), *Georg Büchner*, 2 vols, Text & Kritik, Munich, 1979–81.

Baravalle, R., *Unbekannte Erst- und Frühaufführungen Kleistscher Dramen*, *Jahrbuch der Kleist-Gesellschaft*, 1929/30.

Berger, Alfred Freiherr von, 'Über Goethes Verhältnis zur Schauspielkunst', *Goethe-Jahrbuch* 25, Frankfurt/Main, 1904, pp. 1*–15*.

Bruford, Walter Horace, *Germany in the Eighteenth Century. The Social Background of the Literary Revival*, Cambridge University Press, 1935.

——, 'Goethe and the theatre', *Essays on Goethe*, ed. William Rose, Cassell, London, 1949, pp. 75–95.

——, *Theatre, Drama and Audience in Goethe's Germany*, Routledge & Kegan Paul, London, 1950.

——, *Culture and Society in Classical Weimar 1775–1806*, Cambridge University Press, 1962.

Burkhardt, Dr C.A.H., 'Goethes Werke auf der Weimarer Bühne 1775–1817', *Goethe-Jahrbuch* 4, Frankfurt/Main, 1883, pp. 107–26.

Burkhardt, C.A.H., *Das Repertoire des Weimarischen Theaters unter Goethes Leitung 1791–1817*, Voss, Hamburg, 1891.

Carlson, Marvin, *The German Stage in the Nineteenth Century*, Scarecrow Press, Metuchen, 1972.

——, *Goethe and the Weimar Theatre*, Cornell University Press, Ithaca, 1978.

Catholy, Eckehard, 'Bühnenraum und Schauspielkunst. Goethes Theaterkonzeption', *Bühnenformen – Bühnenräume – Bühnendekorationen*, Festschrift für Herbert A. Frenzel, ed. R. Badenhausen and H. Zielske, Schmidt, Berlin, 1974, pp. 136–47.

Coleville, Maurice, 'Goethe et le théâtre,' *Etudes Germaniques*, 1949, pp. 148–61.

Devrient, [Philipp] Eduard, *Geschichte der deutschen Schauspielkunst*, Neu-Ausgabe, 2 vols, Elsner, Berlin, 1905.

Doebber, Adolf, *Lauchstädt und Weimar. Eine theatergeschichtliche Studie*, Mittler, Berlin, 1908.

BIBLIOGRAPHY

Eckermann, Johann Peter, *Gespräche mit Goethe*, ed. H.H. Honben, Brockhaus, Wiesbaden, 1959.
Eggert, C.A., 'Goethe and Diderot on actors and acting,' *Modern Language Notes*, vol. 11, no. 4, Baltimore, April 1896, pp. 205–20.
Flemming, Willi, *Goethe und das Theater seiner Zeit*, Kohlhammer, Stuttgart, 1968.
Garland, H.B., 'Some observations on Schiller's stage-directions', *German Studies*, presented to W.H. Bruford, Harrap, London, 1962, pp. 153–62.
Genast, Eduard, *Aus Weimars klassischer und nachklassischer Zeit. Erinnerungen eines alten Schauspielers*, ed. R. Kohlrausch, 5th edn., Lutz, Stuttgart, n.d. [1906].
Göres, Jörn (ed.), *Gesang und Rede, sinniges Bewegen. Goethe als Theaterleiter. Eine Ausstellung des Goethe-Museums*, Düsseldorf, 1973.
Gotthardi, W.G., *Weimarische Theaterbilder aus Goethes Zeit*, 2 vols, Costenoble, Jena, 1865.
Gross, Dr Edgar, *Die ältere Romantik und das Theater*, Theatergeschichtliche Forschungen 22, Voss, Hamburg, 1910.
Güntter, Otto, 'Die ersten Darsteller der "Räuber"', *Marbacher Schillerbuch*, ed. O. Güntter, Cotta, Stuttgart, 1907, vol. 2, pp. 405–18.
Hinck, Walter, 'Der Bewegungsstil der Weimarer Bühne', *Goethe* 21, 1959, pp. 94–106.
——, 'Man of the theatre', *Goethe Revisited*, ed. E.A. Wilkinson, Calder, London, 1984, pp. 153–69.
Hinderer, Walter, *Büchner-Kommentar zum dichterischen Werk*, Winkler, Munich, 1977.
Hinton, Julian, *Georg Büchner*, Macmillan, London, 1982.
Huesmann, Heinrich, *Shakespeare-Inszenierungen unter Goethe in Weimar*, Österreichische Akademie der Wissenschaften, vol. 258, no. 2, Vienna, 1968.
——, 'Goethe als Theaterleiter. Historisches Umfeld und Grundzüge', *Ein Theatermann*, Festschrift zum 70. Geburtstag von Rolf Badenhausen, ed. I. Nohl, Munich, 1977, pp. 143–60.
Jacobs, Monty, *Deutsche Schauspielkunst*, Insel, Leipzig, 1913.
Jagemann, Karoline, *Erinnerungen*, ed. E. von Bamberg, 2 vols, Sibyllen-Verlag, Dresden, 1926.
Kellen, Tony (ed.), *Schauspieler-Anekdoten. Ernste und heitere Szenen aus dem Bühnenleben*, Lutz, Stuttgart, n.d. [1909].
Kindermann, Heinz, *Theatergeschichte der Goethezeit*, Bauer, Vienna, 1948.
——, *Theatergeschichte Europas*, vols 4–6, Müller, Salzburg, 1961–4.
Kliewer, Dr Erwin, *A.W. Iffland: ein Wegbereiter in der deutschen Schauspielkunst*, Germanische Studien 195, Ebering, Berlin, 1937.
Knudsen, Hans, *Goethes Welt des Theaters*, Tempelhof, Berlin, 1949.
——, *Deutsche Theater-Geschichte*, Kröner, Stuttgart, 1959.
Koischwitz, Otto, 'Das Bühnenbild im Sturm- und Drang-Drama. Eine theatergeschichtliche Skizze', *Germanic Review*, vol. 1, 1926, pp. 96–114.

Kosch, Wilhelm, *Das deutsche Theater und Drama im 19. Jahrhundert*, Dyksche Buchhandlung, Leipzig, 1913.

Kühn, W., *Heinrich von Kleist und das deutsche Theater*, Leipzig, 1911.

Lamport, F.J., *German Classical Drama, Theatre, Humanity and Nation 1750–1870*, Cambridge University Press, 1990.

Martersteig, Max (ed.), *Die Protokolle des Mannheimer Nationaltheaters unter Dalberg aus den Jahren 1781 bis 1789*, Bensheimer, Mannheim, 1890.

——, *Das deutsche Theater im neunzehnten Jahrhundert. Eine kulturgeschichtliche Darstellung*, Breitkopf & Härtel, Leipzig, 1904.

Maurer–Schmoock, Sibylle, *Deutsches Theater im 18. Jahrhundert*, Niemeyer, Tübingen, 1982.

Meyer, Richard M., 'Goethes "Regeln für Schauspieler"', *Goethe-Jahrbuch* 31, Frankfurt/Main, 1910, pp. 117–35.

Mirow, Dr Franz, *Zwischenaktmusik und Bühnenmusik des deutschen Theaters in der klassichen Zeit*, Schriften der Gesellschaft für Theatergeschichte 37, Berlin, 1927.

Müller, Curt (ed.), *Ifflands Briefwechsel mit Schiller, Goethe, Kleist, Tieck und anderen Dramatikern*, Reclam, Leipzig, n.d.

Oberländer, Hans, *Die geistige Entwicklung der deutschen Schauspielkunst im achtzehnten Jahrhundert*, Voss, Hamburg, 1898.

Pascal, Roy, *The German Sturm und Drang*, Manchester University Press, 1953.

Pasqué, Ernst, *Goethe's Theaterleitung in Weimar in Episoden und Urkunden*, 2 vols, Weber, Leipzig, 1863.

Petersen, Prof. Dr Julius, *Schiller und die Bühne*, Palaestra 32, Mayer & Müller, Berlin, 1904.

——, *Das deutsche Nationaltheater*, Zeitschrift für den deutschen Unterricht, 14. Ergänzungsheft, Teubner, Leipzig, 1919.

Pichler, Anton, *Chronik des grossherzoglichen Hof- und National-Theaters in Mannheim*, Bensheimer, Mannheim, 1879.

Prudhoe, John, *The Theatre of Goethe and Schiller*, Blackwell, Oxford, 1973.

Riemer, Friedrich Wilhelm, *Mitteilungen über Goethe*, ed. Pollmer, Insel, Leipzig, 1921.

Robertson, John George, *Lessing's Dramatic Theory*, Cambridge University Press, 1939.

Rudloff-Hille, Gertrud, *Schiller auf der deutschen Bühne seiner Zeit*, Aufbau-Verlag, Berlin, 1969.

Rullmann, Wilhelm, *Die Bearbeitungen, Fortsetzungen und Nachahmungen von Schillers 'Räubern' (1782–1802)*, Schriften der Gesellschaft für Theatergeschichte 15, Berlin, 1910.

Satori-Neumann, Bruno Th., *Die Frühzeit des Weimarischen Hoftheaters unter Goethes Leitung (1791 bis 1798)*, Schriften der Gesellschaft für Theatergeschichte 31, Berlin, 1922.

Scharrer-Santen, Dr Eduard, *Die Weimarische Dramaturgie aus Goethes Schriften gesammelt, erläutert und eingeleitet*, Paetel, Berlin, 1927.

Schaub, Martin, *Heinrich von Kleist und die Bühne*, Juris, Zurich, 1966.

Scheithauer, Lothar, 'Zu Goethes Auffassung von der Schauspielkunst', *Gestaltung Umgestaltung*, Festschrift für H.A. Korff, ed. J. Müller, Koehler & Amelang, Leipzig, 1957, pp. 108–17.

Schlenther, Paul, 'Das Weimarische Theaterjubiläum', *Theater im 19. Jahrhundert*, ed. H. Knudsen, Schriften der Gesellschaft für Theatergeschichte 40, Berlin, 1930.

Schloenbach, Arnold, *Beiträge zur Geschichte der Schillerperiode des Mannheimer Theaters, Schiller-Buch*, Blochmann, Dresden, 1860, pp. 113–283.

Schreyvogel, Josef, *Tagebücher 1810–1823*, ed. K. Glossy, Schriften der Gesellschaft für Theatergeschichte 2–3, Berlin, 1903.

Sichardt, Gisela, *Das Weimarer Liebhabertheater unter Goethes Leitung*, Arion, Weimar, 1957.

Sommerfeld, Dr Kurt, *Die Bühneneinrichtungen des Mannheimer Nationaltheaters unter Dalbergs Leitung 1778–1803*, Schriften der Gesellschaft für Theatergeschichte 36, Berlin, 1927.

Stein, Philipp, *Deutsche Schauspieler. Eine Bildnissammlung*, Schriften der Gesellschaft für Theatergeschichte 11, Parts 1–2, 2 vols, Berlin, 1907.

Terfloth, John H., 'The pre-Meiningen rise of the director in Germany and Austria', *Theatre Quarterly*, vol. 6, no. 21, 1976, pp. 65–86.

Tornius, Dr Valerian, 'Goethes Theaterleitung und die bildende Kunst', *Jahrbuch des Freien Deutschen Hochstifts*, Frankfurt/Main, 1912, pp. 191–211.

Troitzkij, S., *Konrad Ekhof, Ludwig Schröder, August Wilhelm Iffland, Johann Friedrich Fleck, Ludwig Devrient, Karl Seydelmann. Die Anfänge der realistischen Schauspielkunst*, Henschel, Berlin, 1949.

Wahle, Julius, *Das Weimarer Hoftheater unter Goethes Leitung*, Schriften der Goethe-Gesellschaft 6, Weimar, 1892.

Walter, Dr Friedrich, *Archiv und Bibliothek des Grossh. Hof- und Nationaltheaters in Mannheim 1779–1839*, 2 vols, Hirzel, Leipzig, 1899.

Weddigen, Dr Otto, *Geschichte der Theater Deutschlands*, 2 vols, Frensdorff, Berlin, n.d. [1904].

Weichberger, Alexander, *Goethe und das Komödienhaus in Weimar 1779–1825*, Theatergeschichtliche Forschungen 39, Voss, Leipzig, 1928; Kraus Reprint, Nendeln, Liechtenstein, 1977.

Weil, Rudolf, *Das Berliner Theaterpublikum unter A.W. Ifflands Direktion (1796 bis 1814)*, publ. Dr Phil. Diss., Cologne, 1930.

Ziegler, Günther, *Theater-Intendant Goethe*, Koehler & Amelang, Leipzig, 1954.

Unpublished D. Phil. dissertations:

Albrecht, Egon-Erich, 'Heinrich von Kleists "Prinz Friedrich von Homburg" auf der deutschen Bühne', Kiel, 1921.

Reiprich, G., 'Heinrich von Kleist und das Theater', Würzburg, 1922.

SOURCES OF ILLUSTRATIONS

Plate 1: *Theater-Kalender auf das Jahr 1794*, ed. H.A.O. Reichardt, Carl Wilhelm Ettinger, Gotha, 1794; Plates 2 and 3, Figs 1 and 2: *Die Bühneneinrichtungen des Mannheimer Nationaltheaters unter Dalbergs Leitung 1778–1803* by Dr Kurt Sommerfeld, Schriften de Gesellschaft für Theatergeschichte 36, Berlin, 1927; Plates 4, 8, 16, and 17: *Goethes Welt des Theaters* by Hans Knudsen, Tempelhof, Berlin, 1949; Plates 5 and 18: *Gesang und Rede, sinniges Bewegen. Goethe als Theaterleiter. Eine Ausstellung des Goethe-Museums*, ed. Jörn Göres, Düsseldorf, 1973; Plates 6, 11, 13, 14, and 15: *Deutsche Schauspieler. Eine Bildnissammlung*, by Philipp Stein, Schriften der Gesellschaft für Theatergeschichte 11, 2 vols, Berlin, 1907; Plates 7, 9, and 10: *Lauchstädt und Weimar. Eine theaterbaugeschichtliche Studie* by A. Doebber, Mittler, Berlin, 1908; Plate 12: *Goethe Jahrbuch*, vol. 9, Rütten & Loening, Frankfurt/Main, 1888; Plates 19 and 20: *Theatergeschichte Europas* by Heinz Kindermann, Müller, Salzburg, 1961–4; Figures 3, 4, and 5: *Goethe und das Komödienhaus in Weimar 1779–1825* by Alexander Weichberger, Theatergeschichtliche Forschungen 39, Voss, Leipzig, 1928; Figure 6: Nationale Forschungs– und Gedenkstätten der klassischen deutschen Literatur in Weimar.

INDEX

Académie Française 9
Ackermann, Charlotte (actress)
169
Ackermann, Dorothea (actress)
19, 168, 170
Ackermann, Konrad (actor) 7–9,
14, 16, 19, 167, 168
acting style: Büchner 152, 157;
disciplines v. individualistic
159; Ekhof 7; Ekhof and
Schröder 14; Goethe 54–6,
76–83, 90–1, 94–8; in London
119; Lessing 13, 14; Mannheim
33–7; Neuber 5; Tieck 116–19;
virtuosity 19; wandering
players 4–5
actor remuneration 15, 22–3, 71–2
actor training 7, 76–7, 114, 158
alexandrines 6
American War of Independence
169, 171
Amiens, Treaty of 176
Anna Amalia of Weimar,
Dowager Duchess 57, 91
Ansbach 178
Argand lamps 67
Artaud, Antonin 158
audience 17, 18, 60, 63, 65,
111–12
Auerstädt, Battle of 178
Austerlitz, Battle of 178
Austria 8, 168, 172–81 passim

Backhaus, Johann Wilhelm
(Mannheim actor) 22

Bamberg 180
Barry, James 79
Basle, Treaty of 175
Bastille, Storming of 173
Beaumarchais, Pierre-Augustin
16, 176; The Barber of Seville 169;
The Marriage of Figaro 172
Beck, Heinrich (Mannheim actor)
7, 22, 171, 174, 177
Becker, Heinrich (Weimar actor)
94
Beckett, Samuel 159
Beethoven, Ludwig van 128;
Egmont 179; Fidelio 178, 180
Beil, Johann David (Mannheim
actor) 7, 22, 35, 175
Belgium 174
Bellomo, Joseph (director) 58–9,
60, 69, 71, 172
Bergemann, Fritz (critic) 145
Berlin 8, 15, 18, 19, 57, 92, 98,
111, 112, 113, 114, 118, 121,
123, 128, 141, 168–83 passim;
Royal National Theatre 17, 112,
117, 128, 169–83 passim;
Schauspielhaus 181;
Schiller-Theater 159; Schloss
Monbijou 181; Theater am
Gendarmenmarkt 169, 170;
University 179; Wannsee 126
Bethmann, Friederike (Friederike
Unzelmann) (actress) 92, 176
Bismarck, Otto von (Prussian
statesman) 51
blank verse 92, 100–4, 135–6

Bock, Johan Christian (actor) 19, 170
Bode, Johann Joachim (writer) 177
Boeck, Johann Michael (Mannheim actor) 22, 23, 43–4, 170, 171
Böttiger, Carl August (critic) 47–50
Brandes, Charlotte (Mannheim actress) 20, 22
Brandes, Johann Christian (Mannheim actor and playwright) 16, 23, 30
Brandes, Minna (Mannheim actress) 22
Brawe, Joachim (playwright) 16
Brecht, Bertolt 3, 13, 39, 75, 81, 154, 158, 159
Brentano, Clemens (writer): *Ponce de Leon* 180
Breslau 128
Britain 111, 174; *see also* England
British National Theatre 9
Brockmann, Franz (actor) 15, 175, 180
Brown, John Russell xiii–xiv
Brückner, Johann Gottfried (actor) 169
Brühl, Karl Moritz Graf von (director) 180, 181, 183
Brünn (Brno) 18, 128
Brunswick 179, 183
Büchner, Georg xiii–xiv, 17, 116, 140–57 *passim*, 158, 159, 180, 184; *Danton's Death* 140, 141, 143–4, 157, 184; *Lenz* 142–3, 156; *Leonce and Lena* 140, 184; *Woyzeck* 140–57 *passim*, 184
Bühnensprache 9, 77
Bürger, Gottfried August (writer) 169, 170, 173

Calderón de la Barca, Pedro: *The Constant Prince* 76, 179; *Life's a Dream* 180; *Zenobia* 181
Campio Formio, Treaty of 175
Carl August of Weimar, Duke 55–6, 57, 60, 65, 72, 74, 88, 94, 115, 169

Carlson, Marvin xiv
Celle Court Theatre 18
censorship 113
Chekhov, Anton 77
Clausewitz, Karl von (Prussian general) 180
Colman, George, the Elder 16
Cologne 111
Constantin, Prince, of Weimar 88
Cordemann, Friedrich (Weimar actor) 94
Corneille, Pierre 6, 12, 16; *Le Cid* 178; *Rodogune* 186
costume 3, 4, 19–20, 31–3, 47, 77, 89–90, 112, 120, 158, 162, plates 4, 13
Craig, Edward Gordon 138
critics 17, 38, 114
Cronegk, Friedrich Freiherr von (playwright) 16
Cumberland, Richard: *The Jew* 175; *The West Indian* 58, 168, 170
curtain 2, 26, 38, 67, 131, 169

Dalberg, Wolfgang Heribert Freiherr von (director) 19, 21–46 *passim*, 113, 159, 166, 170, 171, 172, 173, 178
Danzy, Mannheim (composer) 38
Darmstadt 37
décor 65, 78–9, 88, 112, 120, 158, plates 2–3, 20; *see also* stage-sets
Deny, Johann Friedrich Wilhelm (Weimar actor) 74, 96
Destouches, Philippe, 16; *La Fausse Agnès* 6
Detmold 183
Devrient, Ludwig (actor) 113, 172, 184
Diderot, Denis 12, 16, 109, 172; *Le père de famille* 186; 'Paradoxe sur le comédien' 109–10
Döbbelin, Ludwig (actor and director) 57, 167–74 *passim*
Dramaturg 13, 14, 17, 121, 159, 183
Dresden 6, 114, 121, 122, 127, 181, 182; Court Theatre 126, 183

Düsseldorf 184

Eckermann, Johann Peter
(Weimar courtier) 72, 77, 79,
82, 84
Eggert, C.A. (critic) 109
Eichendorff, Joseph Freiherr von
(writer) 116
Einsiedel, Friedrich Hildebrand
von (writer) 175
Ekhof, Konrad (actor) 2, 7, 14, 15,
17, 19, 35, 57, 58, 168, 169, 170
Elba 180
Engel, Johann Jacob (director)
174–5; *Thoughts about Acting*
117–18, 172
England xiii, 27, 176; *see also*
Britain
ensemble acting 26, 55, 72, 74,
119, 159
Ernst August of Weimar, Duke 57
Esslair, Ferdinand (actor) 54, 181
Ettersburg 88
Euripides: *Ion* 177; *Iphigenia in
Tauris* 87, 100, 104, 105
Expressionism 144, 148, 159

Facius, Friedrich Wilhelm (artist)
88, plate 13
Falk, Johannes (Weimar critic) 90
Fichte, Johann Gottlieb (writer):
Speeches to the German nation
178; *Scientific Teaching* 117
Fischer, Franz Joseph (Weimar
actor) 72
Fleck, Johann Friedrich (actor)
118–19, 123, 172, 173, 176
Fortune Theatre 119
France xiii, 27, 111, 172, 174–80
passim; cultural domination by
1, 8, 53, 56, 62, 126, 170
Frankfurt am Main 8, 37, 128,
170, 172
Frankfurt an der Oder 12
Franz II, Emperor of Austria 177
Frederick the Great (Friedrich II)
of Prussia 1, 170, 172
Friedrich Wilhelm II of Prussia
112, 114, 175

Fuseli, Henry (Heinrich Füssli)
79, 80

Galli-Bibiena, Ferdinando (stage-
designer) 15
Garrick, David 119, 171
Gellert, Christian Fürchtegott
(writer) 12
Genast, Anton (Weimar actor) 15,
54, 71, 74, 75, 81, 174
German language 1, 8–9, 77
Gerstenberg, Heinrich Wilhelm
(playwright): *Ugolino* 168
Gleim, Ludwig (writer) 177
Gluck, Christoph Wilibald,
(composer): *Iphigenia in Aulis*
169; *Iphigenia in Tauris* 92
Gneisenau, August Wilhelm Graf
von (Prussian general) 180
Goethe, Johann Wolfgang von xiii-
xiv, 16, 17, 20, 23, 35, 36, 37,
46, 47, 53–110 *passim*, 112, 114,
142, 158, 159, 168–81 *passim*,
184; plate 13; *The Accomplices*
58, 168, 170; *Brother and Sister*
58, 170, 173; *Der Bürgergeneral*
174; *Clavigo* 15, 58, 169, 172;
Egmont 58, 76, 94, 174, 180;
Elective Affinities 179; *The Fair-
Day at Plundersweilen* 171; *Faust*
59, 69, 115, 181, 183; *The Fisher-
Maiden* 58, 171; *Götz von
Berlichingen* 11, 15, 20, 23, 94,
142, 169, 177, 179, 180; *Great
Cophta* 174; *Iphigenia on Tauris*
56, 58, 62, 69, 74, 76, 84–110
passim, 142, 154, 171, 176, 177,
178, 179; plates 13–14; *Lila* 170;
Mahomet 176; *The Mood of the
Lover* 168, 171; *The Natural
Daughter* 177; *On Shakespeare's
Name-Day* 12, 168; *Poetry and
Truth* 11, 110; *Propyläen* 78, 80;
'Rules for Actors' 19, 54–5,
76–83 *passim*, 97, 177, 182; *Stella*
170, 178; *Torquato Tasso* 56, 59,
69, 97, 178, 180; *The Triumph of
Loneliness* 170; *Urfaust* 169;
'Weimar Court Theatre' 82;

INDEX

Wilhelm Meister 53, 82, 175
Goldoni, Carlo 16, 57
Goldsmith, Oliver 16; *She Stoops
to Conquer* 172
Gotha Court Theatre 7, 15, 19, 20,
46, 57, 169, 170, 171
Gotthardi, W.G. (Weimar actor)
75
Göttingen 69
Gottsched, Johann Christoph
(writer) 5–6, 12; *The Dying Cato*
16, 20
Gozzi, Carlo: *Turandot* 177; *Zobeis*
172
Grabbe, Christian Dietrich
(playwright): *Don Juan and
Faust* 183; *Duke Theodore* 156;
*Fun, Satire, Irony and Deeper
Meaning* 156; *Hannibal* 156; *Die
Hermannsschlacht* 156; *The
Hohenstaufens* 156; *Napoleon* 156
Graff, Jakob (Weimar actor) 76,
94, 96, 176
Granville Barker, Harley xiv
Graz 59; National Theatre 124,
182
Gries, Johann Friedrich (writer)
181
Grillparzer, Franz (playwright)
56, 115, 128, 181; *Die Ahnfrau*
181, 182; *The Golden Fleece* 182;
Life's a Dream 184; *A Loyal
Servant of his Master* 183; *King
Ottokar* 183; *Sappo* 181; *Waves of
the Love and the Sea* 183
Grimm, Brothers Jacob and
Wilhelm (writers) 128, 180
Grossmann, Gustav (actor) 172
Grotowski, Jerzy 83
Grüner, Karl (Weimar actor) 77
Gutzkow, Karl (writer) 140, 184

Haferung, Mannheim (actor) 23
Hagen, J.J.A. vom (critic) 27
Haide, Friedrich (Weimar actor)
76, 94, 176, plate 15
Halle 54
Hamburg 6, 15, 56, 82, 118, 128,
129, 167–83 *passim*, 182;

National Theatre 8–11, 16, 158,
159, 167, 168, 186; Stadttheater
182
Hanover 71, 128, 172, 176; Court
Theatre 182
Hanswurst 4–5
Hardenberg, Karl August Fürst
von (Prussian statesman) 179
Harwood, Ronald 55
Hauptmann, Anton (Weimar
court-official) 58, 87
Hauptmann, Gerhart
(playwright) 144; *The Rats* 55
Hebbel, Friedrich (playwright) 56
Hegel, Georg Wilhelm Friedrich
(philosopher) 183
Heine, Heinrich (writer) 128
Heller, Erich 109
Herder, Johann Gottfried (writer)
167, 169, 170, 177
Herdt (actor) 18
Herter, Maximilian (Mannheim
actor) 23
Heufeld, Franz (writer) 169
Heygendorf, Frau von *see*
Jagemann, Karoline
Hildburghausen 9
Hippel, Theodor Gottlieb von
(playwright) 186
Hitler, Adolf 51
Hogarth, William 85; *The Analysis
of Beauty* 80–1
Holbein, Franz von (writer) 124,
128, 129
Hölderlin, Friederich (writer) 175
Holland *see* Netherlands, The
Holtei, Karl von (director) 128
Humboldt, Alexander von
(educationalist) 180
Hume, David 117

Iffland, August Wilhelm (actor,
director and playwright) 3, 7,
18, 22, 23, 26, 33, 35–6, 37,
46–52, 69, 72, 92, 113, 114, 171,
175–80 *passim*, plate 6; *The
Bachelor* 174; *Fragments on the
Representation of Characters on
the German Stage* 172; *The*

202

Huntsmen 69, 174
improvisation 4, 75, 164, plate 1
Innsbruck 179
Italian opera 1, 15, 57

Jagemann, Karoline 72, 94, 175,
   plate 11
Jena 63, 173; Battle of 178
Jesuit theatre xiii
Jospeh II, Holy Roman Emperor
   170, 171, 173
Julius, Friedrich (Friedrich von
   Kleist) (director) 128
Junges Deutschland 142, 184

Kant, Immanual (philosopher)
   77, 127, 171, 173, 177
Karlsbader Beschlüsse 181
Karlsruhe 128
Karl Theodor, Duke of
   Mannheim 21, 170
Kean, Edmund 119
Kemble, John Philip 79, 80, 119,
   182
Kindermann, Heinz (critic) 14,
   127
Kleist, Heinrich von xiii-xiv, 17,
   56, 75, 116, 122–39 passim, 144,
   159, 170, 177, 179, 182;
   Amphitryon 124, 137, 178; Die
   Hermannsschlacht 124; Berliner
   Abendblätter 124; The Broken Jug
   60, 124, 129, 137, 179, 182;
   Prince Friedrich von Homburg
   113, 122, 126–39, 182, 183, 184;
   Kätchen von Heilbronn 124, 128,
   137, 179, 180, 182, plate 20; 'On
   the marionette theatre' 138–9,
   179; 'Marquise von O' 137;
   Penthesilea 124, 129, 179; Robert
   Guiskard 124, 179; The
   Schroffenstein Family 124, 177
Klingemann, Ernst (director) 183
Klinger, Friedrich Maximilian
   (playwright): Storm and Stress
   170; The Twins 170
Klopstock, Friedrich Gottlieb
   (writer) 168, 177
Knebel, Carl Ludwig von

(Weimar courtier) 88, 90–1
Koberwein, Joseph (Viennese
   actor) 127
Koch, Gotthelf (Viennese actor)
   127
Koch, Heinrich (director) 17, 57,
   168, 169, 170
Königsberg 8, 75, 128
Korn, Maximilian (Viennese
   actor) 127
Körner, Christian Gottfried
   (playwright) 90; The Bride 180;
   The Cousin from Bremen 180; The
   Green Domino 180; Toni 180
Kotzebue, August von
   (playwright) 69, 74, 114, 115,
   117; Misanthropy and Remorse
   173, 175; The Sun Virgin 114
Krüger, Johann Christian
   (playwright) 16
Krüger, Sophie Christina
   (Weimar actress) 177
Kummerfeld, Mme (Mannheim
   actress) 22

La Chaussee, Nivelle de 12, 16
Landau (Weimar actor) 77
Langhans, C. (critic) 67
Latin xiii, 1
Laube, Heinrich (writer) 119, 184
Lauchstädt Theatre 60, 63, 67,
   177, 178, plates 9–10
Lavater, Johann Kaspar (writer)
   169
Lehmann, Werner (critic) 144, 145
Leibniz, Gottifried Wilhelm
   (philosopher) 1
Leipzig 5, 31, 83, 87, 94, 123, 167,
   172, 178; Battle of 180
Leisewitz, Johann Anton
   (playwright): Julius von Tarent
   170
Lenz, Johann Michael Reinhold
   (playwright) 142–3, 169; Notes
   on the Theatre 169; The Soldiers
   169; The Tutor 170
Leopold II, Holy Roman Emperor
   173, 174
Lessing, Gotthold Ephraim 7,

11–14, 16, 51, 57, 114, 154, 158, 159, 171; *Emilia Galotti* 12, 58, 168; *Hamburg Dramaturgy* 13–14, 34, 167; *Laokoon* 34; *Minna von Barnhelm* 8–11, 16, 17, 58, 167, 168, plate 1; *Miss Sara Sampson* 12, 13, 168; *Nathan the Wise* 12, 172; *Philotas* 169; 'Seventeenth Letter on Literature' 12; *The Young Scholar* 13
Lichtenberg, Georg Christoph (writer) 169
lighting 19, 27, 30–1, 43, 44, 45, 67, 108, 132, 172, plate 1
Lillo, George 16
Littlejohns, Richard 143
London 119, 181; Covent Garden Theatre 119; Drury Lane Theatre 119
Lorrain, Claude 79
Louis XV, King of France 169
Louis XVI, King of France 174
Louis XVIII, King of France 180
Löwe, Julie-Sophie (Viennese actress) 127
Löwen, Johan Friedrich von (playwright) 16, 186
Lunéville, Treaty of 176

Mainz 37
make-up 47
Mannheim National Theatre xiii, xiv, 7, 15, 19, 20, 21–46 *passim*, 72, 82, 114, 117, 118, 158, 161–6, 170–3 *passim*, figures 1 and 2, plates 2–3
Manso, Johann (critic) 47
Maria Theresa, Empress of Austria 113, 171
Marivaux, Pierre 16, 57, 186
Marschner, Heinrich (composer) 128
Martersteig, Max (critic) 114, 116
Mathilda of Denmark, Queen 18
Maximilian III, Prince of Bavaria 21, 170
Maximilian, Emperor 31
Mecklenburg, Duke of 6

Meiningen *see* Saxe-Meiningen, Duke of
Merck, Johann Heinrich (writer) 89, 90
Metternich, Prince von (Austrian statesman) 179
Meyer, Wilhelm (Mannheim actor and director) 22, 33–4
Mieding, Johann Martin (Weimer court carpenter) 58, 88
Moliere (Jean-Baptiste Poquelin) 16, 51, 57, 159
Moore, Edward 16
Moscow 180
Mozart, Wolfgang Amadeus 56; *Abduction from the Seraglio* 171, 172; *Cosi fan tutti* 173; *Don Giovanni* 173; *Idomeneo* 171; *The Magic Flute* 174; *The Marriage of Figaro* 173
Müllner, Adolf (playwright and critic) 96; *The Guilt* 180
Munich 15, 21, 128, 171; Court Theatre 182; Residenztheater 172
music 38, 42, 43, 133

Napoleon 109, 176–81 *passim*
Naturalism 55, 144, 159
Nestroy, Johann Nepomuck (playwright): *Lumpazivagabundus* 184
Netherlands, The 174, 175
Neuber, Karoline (director) 5–6, 13, 20
Neumann, Johanne Elisabeth (acress) 174
Noh theatre 3
Novalis, Friedrich (writer) 176, 177

Oels, Karl (Weimar actor) 96, plate 17
Opie, John 79

panoranas 111–12
Paris 123, 124, 169; Comèdie Française 9, 172, 173
Peters, Diana and Frederick 127

Peymann, Claus (director) 160
Pichler, Anton (director) 183
Piscator, Erwin (director) 159
Plato 77
Plautus 169
Poeschel, Mme (Mannheim actress) 22
Poland 168, 174, 175
Prague 71, 128
Pressburg 169, 170
Pretzsch, Alfred (artist) 63, figure 6
Preussisch-Eylau, Battle of 178
Proteus, Peregrinus 51
Prudhoe, John xiv
Prussia 8, 11, 112, 124, 168, 172, 174–81 *passim*

Racine, Jean 6, 12, 16, 109; *Mithridate* 177; *Phèdre* 109, 178
Radziwill, Prince 126
Raimund, Ferdinand (playwright) 173, 184; *The King of the Alps* 183; *The Spendthrift* 184
Raupach, Ernst (playwright) 114
realism 3–4, 7, 14, 34–7, 40, 78–80, 117, 142–3, 146–57
Redern, Friedrich Wilhelm Graf von (director) 183
rehearsals 7, 17–19, 36–7, 75–6, 158, 161–2
Reichardt, Friedrich (critic): *Theater-Kalender* 15
Reichardt, Johann Friedrich (Weimar composer) 88
Reichsdeputationshauptschluss 177
Reinhold, Karl (actor) 54
Rennschüb (Büchner), Johann Ludwig (Mannheim director) 34–5
repertoire: Bellomo's troupe at Weimar 58–9; early eighteenth century 16–17, 18; under Goethe at Weimar 67–71; Hamburg National Theatre 186; late eighteenth century 114–15; at Mannheim 114, 161, 166; in modern Germany 159
Reynolds, Sir Joshua 79

Rhine, Confederation of the 178
Rhineland 111, 174, 175
Riemer, Friedrich Wilhelm (Weimar courtier) 90
Ritterdramen 20, 58, 114, 124
Robertson, J.G. 13
Rollenfach (type-casting) 22–6, 72
Rossbach, Battle of 8
Rossini, Gioacchino Antonio: *The Barber of Seville* 181
Rousseau, Jean-Jacques 170
Russia 6, 168, 174, 175, 178, 180, 181

Sartorius, Georg (Professor of Politics) 69
Saxe-Meiningen, Duke George of 27, 56, 124, 128, 158
Saxony 11, 172
Scandinavia 141
Scharnhorst, Gerhard Johann von (Prussian general) 180
Schelling, Friedrich Wilhelm von (writer) 175
Schiebeler, Daniel (playwright) 16
Schiller, Friedrich xiii–xiv, 17, 20, 21–52, 56, 69, 76, 83, 90, 92, 94, 113, 114, 115, 142, 158, 169, 171–8 *passim*; *The Bride of Messina* 42, 177; *The Conspiracy of Fiesco in Genoa* 21, 41, 114, 172, 178; *Don Carlos* 56, 114, 173, 174, 178, 179; *Intrigue and Love* 21, 41, 114, 172; *Macbeth* adaptation 176; *The Maid of Orleans* 18, 26, 143, 176, 177; *Mary Stuart* 42, 94, 116, 176, 178; 'On naive and sentimental poetry' 117, 175; 'On the aesthetic education of mankind' 175; 'On the representation of suffering' 51; 'On the sublime' 174; *Phèdre* adaptation 178; *The Piccolomini* 176; *The Robbers* 16, 21–50 *passim*, 58, 60, 114, 118, 141, 142, 171, 172, 174, 175, 179, 181, plates 2–6; 'The theatre regarded as a moral institution' 9, 50–1, 116, 172;

Turandot adaptation 177; *Wallenstein* 92, 123, 128; *Wallenstein's Camp* 69, 177; *Wallenstein's Death* 176; *William Tell* 27, 177, 179, 183

Schlegel, August Wilhelm 56, 60, 119, 175; *The Constant Prince* adaptation 179; 'Dramatic art and literature' 179; *Fragments* 117; *Ion* adaptation 60, 177; *Julius Caesar* adaptation 177; *Romeo and Juliet* adaptation 180

Schlegel, Johann Elias 3, 16; *Hermann* 11

Schlosser, Pastor Friedrich Christoph (playwright) 16

Schmidt, Friedrich Ludwig (writer) 129

Schönbrunn, Treaty of 179

Schönemann, Johann Friedrich (actor and director) 7, 8, 13, 15, 171

Schreyvogel, Josef (director) 126–7, 180, 182, 183, 184

Schröder, Friedrich Ludwig (actor and director) 4, 14–15, 16, 18, 19, 27, 35, 56, 82, 118, 168–75 *passim*, 181

Schröter, Corona Weimar (actress) 87–8, 90, 94, plate 13

Schubert, Gotthilf Heinrich (writer) 179

Schuch, Franz (director) 8, 168

Schulz, Friedrich (critic) 92

Schumann (Weimar court painter) 88

Schwerin 6

Scott, Walter 114

Seidler, August Gottfried (Weimar courtier) 88

Semper, Gottfried (architect) 119

Seven Years' War 8, 11

Seyler, Abel (actor and director) 22, 57, 161, 162, 163, 169, 170, 171

Seyler, Mme (Mannheim actress) 22, 23

Shakespeare, William 3, 12, 14, 16, 23, 38, 56, 58, 69, 83, 87, 108, 114, 119–21, 141, 156–7, 175; *Hamlet* 15, 59, 121, 159, 169, 170, 171, 174, 176, 182; *Henry IV* 174; *Julius Caesar* 59, 77, 177; *King John* 174; *King Lear* 39, 40, 59, 121, 169, 171, 175, 182; *Macbeth* 51, 59, 121, 170, 176, 184; *Measure for Measure* 170; *The Merchant of Venice* 59; *A Midsummer Night's Dream* 59, 121, plate 19; *Othello* 15, 59, 62, 169, 170, 178; *Richard II* 171; *Richard III* 51, 168, 171; *Romeo and Juliet* 17, 168, 180, 186; *The Tempest* 119

Shaw, Bernard 141

Sheridan, Richard Brinsley 16; *School for Scandal* 170, 171

Sichardt, Gisela (critic) 88

Siddons, Sarah 171

Singspiele 57, 69

Smith, Adam 126

Sonnefels, Josef von (writer): *Programme of a National Theatre* 168

sound effects 108, 133

Spain xiii

Staël, Mme de (Staël-Holstein, Anne Louise Germaine de) 55, 57

stage-directions 104–5, 141, 152–3, 154–5

stage-sets 2–4, 26–30, 38–45, plates 2–3, 19–20; *see also* décor

Stanislavsky (Alekseev), Konstantin 31, 37, 74, 77, 118, 149, 152

Stein, Charlotte von (Weimar courtier) 87

Stein, Heinrich Friedrich Reichsfreiherr von (Prussian statesman) 178, 179

Stein, Peter (director) 157, 160

Stoppard, Tom 115

Strasbourg 2, 5, 168

Sturm und Drang (Storm and Stress) 14, 16, 37, 38, 53, 132, 141, 142, 158

Sturz, Helferich Peter

(playwright) 16
Stuttgart 128, 171; Court Theatre
112, 179, 181, 182
subsidies 1, 112, 159
Sulzer, Johann Peter (writer) 168

Talma, François Joseph 173, 179
Terence: *The Brothers* 176
theatre-buildings 1, 26, 62–7, 112,
plates 7–10, figures 1–2, 4–6
Thomson, James 16
Thouret, Nikolaus Friedrich
(architect) 63, 67, plate 7
Tieck, Dorothea (writer) 56
Tieck, Ludwig (writer and
director) 3, 116–22 *passim*,
126–7, 141, 143, 169, 181–4
passim, plate 19; *Puss in Boots*
156
Tilsit, Treaty of 178
Tirol 179
Toscani (Mannheim actor) 23
Toscani, Anna (Mannheim
actress) 22
Trinkle (Mannheim actor) 23

unities 2, 6, 12
Unzelmann, Friederike
(Friederike Bethmann) (actress)
128, 176
Unzelmann, Karl Wolfgang
(actor) 75

Vega, Lope de 159
Versailles 19, 62; Treaty of 171
Vienna 2, 5, 9, 15, 16, 55, 124,
171, 179, 181; Burgtheater 92,
126–7, 168–73 *passim*, 175, 176,
180–4 *passim*; Theatre an de
Wien 184; Theater in der
Josephstadt 184; Theater in der
Leopoldstadt 182, 183
Vincenzio, Lorenzo (Weimar
scene-painter) 174
Vohs, Friederike (Weimar actress)
93–4, 176, plate 13
Voigt-Ludecus, Amalie (critic) 90
Voltaire (François-Marie Arouet)
16, 170; *Semiramis* 20; *Tancred*
176

Voss, Johann Heinrich (writer):
Othello adaptation 178

Wagner, Heinrich Leopold
(playwright): *The Child
Murderess* 170; *Evchen
Humbrecht* 170; *Remorse After the
Deed* 169
Wagner, Richard (composer) 128
Wahr (director) 169, 170
Wallenstein, Christiane
(Mannheim actress) 22
wandering players xiii, 1–4, 16,
17
Weber, Carl Maria von
(composer): *Der Freischütz* 181
Weimar 56–7, 173, figure 3;
Amateur Theatre 58, 87–92,
170, 171, 172; Court Theatre
xiii, xiv, 7, 15, 16, 18, 19, 20,
23, 35, 36, 37, 47, 53–98 *passim*,
112, 158, 159, 168–83 *passim*,
figures 4–6, plates 4–5, 7–8,
11–18
Weichberger, Alexander (critic)
67
Weisse, Christian Felix
(playwright) 16; *Richard III*
adaptation 168; *Romeo and Juliet*
adaptation 168, 186
Werner, Zacharias (playwright):
Martin Luther 178; *The Twenty-
fourth of February* 80
Wieland, Christoph Martin
(writer) 90, 91, 168, 171
Wiener Schlussakte 181
William III, King of Prussia 175
Wolff, Anna Amalie (Weimar
actress) 94–8, 174, 178, plate 16
Wolff, Pius Alexander (Weimar
actor) 77, 96–8, 113, 176–9
passim, plate 18
Wothe, Karl (director) 18–19
Württemberg, Duke of 21

Zadek, Peter (director) 160
Zelter, Friedrich (critic) 96
Zuccarini, Franz Anton
(Mannheim actor) 23
Zurich 184